Mary Francis Cusack

Life Inside the Church of Rome

Mary Francis Cusack

Life Inside the Church of Rome

ISBN/EAN: 9783744777094

Printed in Europe, USA, Canada, Australia, Japan

Cover: Foto ©Lupo / pixelio.de

More available books at **www.hansebooks.com**

LIFE INSIDE THE CHURCH OF ROME.

BY

M. FRANCIS CLARE CUSACK,
"THE NUN OF KENMARE."

TORONTO:
WILLIAM BRIGGS, WESLEY BUILDINGS,
29 TO 33 RICHMOND STREET WEST.

Entered according to the Act of the Parliament of Canada, in the year one thousand eight hundred and ninety, by WILLIAM BRIGGS, Toronto, in the office of the Minister of Agriculture, at Ottawa.

PREFACE.

THIS book will be characterised by plain speaking, and contain a record of plain facts. I hesitated long and thought much before I began this work, because I knew how great its importance would be, and I did not forget that I shall have to answer to God for what I have written. I know that all the treachery and deceit of which I have been made the subject is the common, ordinary practice of the Church of Rome; and if my sufferings have been great, and if the treatment which I have received has been cruel, it has simply been because I was at the mercy of a power which knows no mercy, and which makes persecution a dogma of her Church.

As I shall have occasion to mention my autobiography several times in the course of this work, I may at once refer the reader to the end of this volume for particulars of its contents. It may be well to state here that any one who reads Roman Catholic lives of Roman Catholic canonized saints, will find in them ample evidence of the persecuting spirit of the Roman Catholic Church. Every one of those "saints" whom the Roman Church now honours so highly, was in his or her lifetime made the subject of the bitterest opposition, and the victim of the most cruel persecution. Rome hated her own saints while they were living, but canonised them when they were dead.

Rome need not boast of the good works which have been done in her Church, because they have been accomplished, for the most part, not because of the help of the Church, but in spite of its opposition.

Would to God that the eyes of all mankind could be opened to see Rome as she is! It has the power in many countries to trample on and crush the weak, because it flatters and bribes the strong to act as its ally in evil, until the strong also become weak; and then they, too, learn what are the tender mercies of this professedly Christian Church.

Rome, or rather the Pope, sits in the temple of God, showing himself to be God, for he claims the very authority of God to add to the commands of God at his pleasure. I shall show that Rome is a Church which has always tolerated, if it has not encouraged, immorality; and I shall show this from facts which cannot be disputed. I beg of my dear Roman Catholic friends to read patiently before they condemn. It is a man's own loss if he lives in wilful ignorance. Truth remains; facts are there all the time, whether we believe or disbelieve them. It is no wonder that Rome is afraid of history, of education, and of truth. If Rome was not afraid of truth, why should she persecute those who declare it? *Magna est veritas et prevalabit*—"Great is truth and it shall prevail." If a man is denied all knowledge of facts, if he must not read the history of past ages in which he will find the history of the Popes, how can he know that they were too often the most corrupt and immoral men, even in an age when corruption was common? What advantage is it to him to be ignorant of facts? How does he know that the Roman (so called) Catholic Church is a system which depends on ignorance for its perpetuation, and for its existence? In order to be a "good Catholic" you must be an ignorant man. You must not know that Popes committed incest, that they committed unnatural crimes. You must believe that they were saints, all good and holy men, with perhaps, when the evil cannot altogether be denied, a few exceptions; for it will be admitted that "a few Popes" were not as good as they should have been. You must not know that they committed the most fearful crimes to advance their illegitimate children : and that they even had their mistresses in the very Vatican palace, where you go to kneel with such reverence, and from whence you take your orders not only as to your religious belief, but as to your political conduct.

I do not ask you to take my word for these things, but I do ask you to read later, in this book, the facts of history as told even by Roman Catholic historians. I ask you to consider facts, and I shall give you the opportunity of ascertaining that these facts are well founded, by placing before you the sources from which they are derived.

If the facts which I shall bring forward shock you, amaze you, startle you, the question is not whether they are very dreadful, but whether they are true. Some of these awful disclosures were made by a Roman Catholic bishop still living and ministering in the Roman Catholic Church. Your reason is a gift which God has given you, and for the use of which He will most certainly hold you accountable. Do you not know the parable of the talents? Do you not know that God condemned the man who hid the one talent which God had given him, and cast him into outer darkness because he had not used it?

Where and when has God told you that you are not to use the talent of reason, which He Himself has given you? If that talent was withdrawn from you, what would you be? If you had not reason, you would be no better than the beasts of the field, and a man who refuses to use his reason will be classed hereafter as a beast, as one unworthy of this sublime and best of God's gifts. No wonder the Roman Catholic is forbidden, except with a special license, to read the Bible. If he did he would become too wise, he would become wise unto salvation. Now and then the Church of Rome makes a great show of permitting or advising the Roman Catholic to read "parts" of the Bible, as Cardinal Gibbons has done lately. But if he may read parts to his advantage, why not read all? Is it not all God's word? Where does God say read "parts" of the Bible? No; He says, "search the Scriptures;" not a part of them, but all of them, so that you may know what God wishes you to believe. And what man shall dare forbid you to do what God Himself has told you to do? Why, the inspired Apostle Paul says that even if an angel from heaven should preach another Gospel than that which he preached, let him be accursed. Hence the Church of Rome actually curses herself when she preaches to you that you may not "search the Scriptures," since it is the very command of God in the Bible that you should do so.

Few Protestants have the least idea how entirely ignorant even the best educated Roman Catholics are of the Bible. I was often surprised to find that very few of the sisters knew anything of the Scriptures. They knew nothing of them, in fact, except the short extracts from the New Testament to be found in the Prayer Books they are allowed to use.

It is wise to keep people in ignorance when you desire to deceive them.

I have been often asked how it was that I remained so many years in the Roman Church, when I ought to have known that it was a corrupt Church. The question is a fair one, and it has direct reference to what I am now saying. It was because I was kept in ignorance. I had read history as most people read it, in a general way. I was well informed as to the history of England, of Ireland, of Scotland, of ancient Rome, of Greece, of Eastern, and of pagan nations; but I had not read the history of Rome under the Popes. Possibly it was thought, if the subject was considered at all, that the study was an unfit one for a young girl. Here, then, is another example of the danger of ignorance. If, in my early years, I thought at all about the Popes, it was to suppose that they were much like other princes, and that their personal history was a matter of little importance. So ignorant are Roman Catholics of the true history of their own Church, that it comes to them as an overwhelming shock when they first hear that many of the Popes were bad men. They are indignant with their informant; they will not believe him; all of which shows how wise the teachers of their Church are in keeping them in ignorance. And their indignation is equally great when they are shown the plain teaching of the Scripture from their own Douay Bible, which, notwithstanding all the corrections of its translation the Roman Church has given it in this nineteenth century, is so plainly Protestant.

Surely it is time for people of intelligence to ask themselves what kind of religion is this which depends for its existence on the ignorance of its followers? Why is it, if this religion is Divine, that it fears the light of history, of the Bible, or even of every-day facts? If the Church is so sure of her infallibility, why does she take so many, and even such violent means to prevent her claims from being fairly questioned or canvassed?

I was long in the Roman Church before I knew anything of the evil lives of priests or Popes, and, I may add, of the priests and the Popes of the present day.

Some years since I wrote a life of Pius IX., who, I then believed, was a persecuted saint. I believed this because I was told so, and because I had no means whatever of knowing the contrary. See again the great importance of keeping people in ignorance. No books are allowed to be read, no papers are allowed to be seen, above all in convents or colleges, where the young are educated (?), which will give the least idea of the facts of daily life, if those facts are supposed to be in any way adverse to the Roman claims. And this is religion. The priests of Greece and ancient Rome have been the models of the priests of to-day in this and other respects. Keep the people ignorant, and they will believe. What! will they believe truth? No; for they must at all hazards be prevented from knowing it. Again, we ask, if the teaching of the Roman Church is so true, and so Divine, why is it that the priests are so afraid lest the people should know anything to its disadvantage?

What a strange religion! It boasts of its Divine origin, yet strives to conceal all damaging facts, in order that it may retain its hold upon the people. It boasts that it was founded by Christ Himself, and yet it will not allow the plain commands of Christ to be obeyed. It "teaches for doctrines the commandments of men," a thing expressly forbidden in the Bible.

But to return to my own case. I believed that Pius IX. was a persecuted saint until I learned later, that his own people, who certainly ought to have known him best, could not support his tyranny and oppressions, which may have been foreign to his own nature, but which he was obliged to carry out in submission to the Jesuits who ruled his court, and ruined his life.

Later in this work I shall tell of my experience in Rome, and show that the old proverb is but too true, —" The nearer to Rome the farther from God." If Rome is not pure, rather we should say if Rome is corrupt, what can the Church under the rule of Rome be? I learned, even before I went to Rome, that Pius IX. had for his dearest friend and guide, a man whose immoralities were so well known in Rome, that even after his death no one was surprised when one of his illegitimate children went to law with the Papal authorities for a share of his immense property. How could a man be a saint if his chosen friend was one who violated not only the law of God, but what is of far more importance to the Roman Catholic, the laws of his Church, which requires, nominally at least, purity in its ministers? And we may well ask, if, in this so-called enlightened nineteenth century, Cardinals can retain their paramours and concubines unreproved, what may not have been done by the Cardinals of past ages?

We live in startling times, in which the prophecies of Scripture are being rapidly fulfilled. For ourselves and for our children it behoves us to "know the signs of the times," and to study them carefully. If we fail to do this, we are without excuse, and we must take the consequences of our indifference or our folly. I shall show in this book that Rome is the true "mystery of iniquity," from facts within my own personal knowledge, and which cannot be controverted. I shall even use Roman Catholic authorities to prove this; for there is a vast and almost unknown field of information on such subjects which, as far as possible, has been sternly repressed by Romanists, but which exists all the same. In this field may be found statements of facts of the most startling character, which have been published (despite the Inquisition), and clearly prove the utter corruption of the Roman Church, not only in centuries past, but even in the present day. These damnatory facts are vouched for—not by Protestants, but by Roman Catholic (so called) saints; so that Rome has approved these condemnations of herself, and, therefore, out of her own lips she is judged and condemned.

What a terrible, what an amazing fact this is, and how seriously it should be considered by Protestants, especially by those who are so liberal to the enemy which would, and is bound, according to her most solemn teaching, to burn them at the stake, if she only had the power. Who is there who would sign his own death warrant, and hand it to his enemy for execution? Surely such an one would be either a fool or a lunatic; and yet men who help Rome to obtain the political power for which she clamours incessantly, are committing this very folly.

The prophecies must be fulfilled. They are a part of the inspired word of God, and in view of this undeniable fact, it is amazing how those who profess to love and believe in the Scriptures should be blinded to its plain predictions. It is this indifference which gives Rome its power,—indifference which cloaks itself under the name of a false charity, and which is a crime against God and man. How can the true Christian be indifferent to the interests of the Kingdom of God? How can he be indifferent to the true interests of his fellow-men, for whom Jesus died? Oh, fatal folly! oh, fatal blindness! which can for one moment approve, even by silent toleration, that which God Himself has condemned.

I think that there will be evidence of a satisfactory character found in this book, that there is at present a great stir in the Roman Catholic Church. Romanism is practically dead in France and Italy; and except for its political power it would have been dead long since in Spain. In Ireland the power of the Pope is shaken as it has never been before, by the conduct of the present Pope, his political interference, and his many political vacillations, which have not increased the respect of the Irish people for his decisions. As it is of importance that proof of this should be on record, and available at any moment, I have gone into the subject fully. In England the directly spiritual—but not the political—power of Rome is decreasing, and would soon be a dead letter if Protestants were true to their principles, and stood up with courage for the right of every man to a free Bible, and to liberty of conscience.

In America and in Canada the political power of the Pope is daily increasing, and I believe it will increase until it becomes so strong, with the usual result of being more and more intolerant, that at last the mass of the people will rise, and once for all claim freedom. At present the outlook is deplorable. Secret societies are permitted to do their evil work of assassination and demoralisation, because they are principally manned by Roman Catholics and Irish, and the politician finds their help necessary, and therefore buys it, though at the expense of principle. Roman Catholics of the upper class are received in society, and courted because of their enormous wealth and political influence. The wealth of the American and Canadian bishops, priests, and sisters, gives them the power which wealth will always give. Proof of all this will be found, on evidence which cannot be disputed, in the present work. The demoralisation and degradation of the lower class of Roman Catholics will also be described. Lamentable and indisputable facts will be given to prove all that is advanced on these subjects. I shall feel, great as my sufferings have been at the hands of men who profess to be holy, and demand the veneration, if not the worship of their followers, that it has not been in vain if I have stirred up Protestants, and thinking men of all denominations, to realise the evil and to promptly seek a remedy.

In concluding this Preface it may be well to say something of the painful experiences which I have had, since I wrote my autobiography, of the treachery and deceitfulness practised in the Roman Church. For myself it matters little, but it matters a great deal for others. What has been done to me may be done in a future time, and with far greater severity, to others. My case, if people would only consider it, is simply a carrying out of the practices of persecution, which never have ceased, and never will cease, as long as Rome has power to persecute. It is amazing that men should be found who are willing to place the rod of persecution in the hands of those who have never failed to use it. Rome sometimes finds it convenient to say she does not persecute; and there are liberal Protestants, who are so indifferent to the peace and happiness of the next generation, that they care little for the certain results which must follow their present liberality to Rome. If they think that Rome does not persecute now, what have they to say to my case, and to that of Dr. McGlynn? The matter is too serious to pass it over lightly.

In the case of Dr. McGlynn, it may be said that the Church had a right to excommunicate him, as he had disobeyed the Church. Granted that this is so, but the question arises, Why does Rome excommunicate at all, when she declares that she no longer upholds persecution or penalty? All that, she tells those who will believe her, belongs to a past age. But if Rome excommunicates, will she not carry out the consequence of excommunication? If she excommunicates Dr. McGlynn would she not, if she could, take the next step, and hand him over to the civil power for execution? for the execution of the excommunicated person is the duty of the State when the State is under the control of the Pope. The torture and the execution of every excommunicated person is a duty of the Roman Church; and it is a duty in which it never fails when there is the least chance of success. But let it be remembered that every insult and indignity possible was shown to Dr. McGlynn by this so-called Christian Church. His persecutors were devoid of even one thought of mercy, or of justice. How any one could study the facts connected with his case, and read of the gratuitous insults to which he was subject, and yet believe that Rome has changed from, or abandoned her policy of persecution, is incomprehensible.

It may be the duty of a judge to pass sentence,

and of the executioner to inflict the sentence; but there never was a criminal executed in New York who was treated with the open insult and exultation over his fate, which was shown to this blameless priest. I have given some details on this subject in the present work, to which I ask attention.

As regards my own case, the very law of the land has been set at defiance in order to heap injuries on me; and so strong is the power of Rome, that I have appealed in vain for protection. I warn the public that what has been done to me is a mere trifle to what will be done later when Rome has all the political power she is seeking for. When we are not touched personally, we are very often indifferent to what happens to others; but the consequences of giving power to those who know neither justice nor mercy, will make themselves felt in the end.

I only wish the reader could have had personal knowledge of the difference between the way in which I acted towards the sisters, and the way in which the sisters were compelled to act towards me. I say the way in which they were compelled to act, because I can prove from their letters to me that they would have acted very differently if they had been left to their own sense of justice and affection. I took every care that nothing should be done which would cause them, I will not say any loss, but even the least inconvenience. It should be remembered that I was the founder of the Order; and I may truly say that it was my personal influence which made it a success, so far as a success could be made in the face of the opposition of priests and bishops, who were too ignorant to realise how much the work was needed for working-girls, and who had so little respect for the Pope himself as to pay not even the slightest attention to his approbation.

For years I had a very large correspondence all over, I might say, the world, especially in Amercia, England, and Ireland. Many comparatively poor persons had contributed to the work which I had begun, and I was anxious to show them that I had not given it up from any caprice, or without grave cause. I wrote to the sisters to send me the book in which I had kept the addresses of all my correspondents, but it was refused; and the sister who refused to send to it me, said that she had consulted the priest, as of course she was bound to do, and that it would be against her conscience to give it to me. The Kenmare sisters had done the very same thing, without even this excuse. They refused to send me my address book; and when at last I compelled them to give me a list of the names in it, they only sent a few. Their object was to prevent me from telling any of my numerous correspondents that I had left Kenmare, as they knew well that very little money would be sent there when it was known that I had left. Their conduct was specially reprehensible, because there was not even the excuse of religious motives. Their motive was simply selfish. What made their conduct inexcusable was that the name of Kenmare would never have been well known beyond the county Kerry if it had not happened that the large circulation of my writings had brought it into notice everywhere. My name brought, and still brings, large sums of money to the Kenmare sisters, which they enjoy, but without one word of even the commonest thanks to the one who procured it for them. On the contrary, they have left nothing undone to calumniate and injure me; and this is religion according to Rome. Thank God it is not religion according to the Gospel.

I need not say that the Kenmare sisters and the priests and bishops, whose treacherous conduct, I have proved from their own letters, was the cause of the failure of my efforts to do what even the Pope had authorised me to do, were in great fear that the truth about their treatment of me should be publicly known. Rome ever dreads the light; and this is one of the greatest proofs that her deeds are evil. If these bishops had done nothing wrong they would not have been afraid of my having the addresses of those persons to whom I had been writing for so many years. But this is not all. I notified to the postmaster of Jersey city, where my letters were to be sent after I left the sisters, but not one was sent. I know that a number of letters were addressed to me at the convent, but not one did I receive. From this it will be seen that the post-office in the United States is not free from the control of the Papacy; for it is the Pope who governs when such injustice can be accomplished at the demand of sisters or priests.

I recently received a letter from a gentleman who lives in Pittsburg, to say that he had written to me a letter addressed to the convent, but as he had not received a reply, he suspected that I had not received it. He was quite a stranger, but he wanted to tell me how truly and sincerely he sympathised with me in my efforts to work for the poor, and in the trials which I had undergone in the Roman Catholic Church. I told him that I had not received his letter nor any others addressed to me since I left the sisters, and he at once wrote to them, and threatened them with public exposure if his letter was not sent back to him at once. By return mail they sent him the letter, dirty, torn, and of course opened. Would to God that Protestants realised from these things that Rome will do all the injustice which she dares; and that it is only want of power, and not want of inclination, which restrains her. Even the law of the land will not protect me from such injustices, for I never even received a reply from the postmaster at Washington, when I appealed to him. Most of the public officials in the United States, no matter what their private religious opinions may be, feel it safest to have Rome on their side, and they act accordingly. Perhaps their children will not arise and call them blessed when they have to feel the power of that Rome rule which their parents have helped to establish.

Again I ask, if the bishops and others who persecuted me, as I have said and proved in my book, were not afraid that the truth would be known, why did they take so many and such dishonest precautions to prevent me from stating my case? I considered that the public had a right to know the facts; and most assuredly, especially after I had left the Roman Catholic Church, no one in it had a right to prevent me from justifiying my action; but I know that hundreds of those whom I wished to have communicated with will never know the truth, and I am sure that hundreds are longing for a letter from me. It would of course have been impossible for me to remember so many names and addresses. If this book should fall into the hands of any of those who were my old and constant correspondents, they will now know the cause of my silence. But we may well ask if we are living in a free country, or in the nineteenth century; when a person can be deprived of the means of communicating with her friends by the priests of Rome, and when the subjects of the Pope can thus interfere with private correspondence and the acts of public officials.

I observe that some Irish Member of Parliament is making a great noise because he says that a letter addressed to him from Washington was tampered with. But no one will trouble himself when the Roman Catholics take possession of my private correspondence.

I have had to bear yet another injustice. Not only

are my letters kept from me, but I am also deprived of all means of support, and obliged at my advanced age to earn my own living, notwithstanding all the property which I have left in the Church of Rome. If I starved it would matter little to those who are now living in comfort, on an income which should have been mine. I know so well how Rome hardens the heart and destroys all natural affection, and I may truly say all Christian charity, that I believe it would be a subject of rejoicing, even to those whom I have benefited so much, if I had to endure all possible privations. Such is the teaching of Rome. Burn, but if you cannot burn the heretic, inflict all the sufferings possible. And yet Rome claims to be a Christian religion!

I may add that those who wish for special information can always reach me by letter, by addressing their communications to the publisher of this work, who will take care that they shall all be forwarded to me promptly.

M. F. CUSACK

("*The Nun of Kenmare*").

CONTENTS.

CHAPTER I.
THE CELIBACY OF THE CLERGY . . . . PAGE 1

CHAPTER II.
THE MORAL EFFECTS OF THE CELIBACY OF THE CLERGY OF THE PAST AND IN THE PRESENT 34

CHAPTER III.
THE CELIBACY OF THE CLERGY IN THE MIDDLE AGES . . 51

CHAPTER IV.
THE OUTSIDE TEACHING AND THE INSIDE PRACTICE OF THE CHURCH OF ROME 63

CHAPTER V.
IMPORTANCE OF UNDERSTANDING THE ROMAN CATHOLIC DOCTRINE OF INFALLIBILITY CLEARLY 77

CHAPTER VI.
THE FALLIBILITY OF INFALLIBILITY 102

CHAPTER VII.
THE HISTORICAL FRAUDS OF THE ROMAN CATHOLIC CHURCH 116

CHAPTER VIII.

HOW THE POPE WAS MADE INFALLIBLE IN THE NINETEENTH CENTURY 146

CHAPTER IX.

THE TEACHING OF THE BIBLE AND THE TEACHING OF THE CHURCH 183

CHAPTER X.

CONVENT LIFE 211

CHAPTER XI.

"BY THEIR FRUITS YE SHALL KNOW THEM" . . 248

CHAPTER XII.

SOME ROMAN DIFFICULTIES WHICH PROTESTANTS SHOULD CONSIDER 279

CHAPTER XIII.

PROTESTANT SUPPORT OF ROMAN CATHOLIC FAILURES . 301

CHAPTER XIV.

THE EFFECTS OF ROMAN CATHOLIC TEACHING—ROMAN CATHOLIC UNIVERSITIES AND HIGHER EDUCATION . . 323

CHAPTER XV.

THE CONFESSIONAL AND THE LIVES OF THE POPES . . 366

CHAPTER XVI.

ROMAN CATHOLIC LITERATURE AND ROMAN CATHOLIC HIGHER EDUCATION 387

APPENDIX 399

CHAPTER I.

THE CELIBACY OF THE CLERGY.

"A bishop must be blameless, the husband of one wife."—1 Tim. iii. 2.

I HAVE been convinced for many years that the celibacy of the Roman Catholic clergy is the source of nearly all the moral evil in the Roman Church. If this unchristian observance was abolished, the moral tone of the whole Church of Rome would at once be raised and purified. The enforced celibacy of the Roman priesthood has been, and is at present, the fruitful source of much crime.

It has been fraught with the greatest moral danger to Rome, while the doctrine of the infallibility of the Church has proved the greatest spiritual danger. The enforced celibacy of the priesthood would long since have been abolished if it was not found to be necessary for the support of the Church, no matter what the moral evil which it causes. The laity would long since have risen up against it, and have forbidden it, if the Roman Catholic Church had not kept them in such ignorance of Scripture and of history. Where shall we find a Roman Catholic, no matter how well educated, who is conversant with the teaching of Scripture on this subject? Where shall we find a Roman Catholic who knows anything of the history of celibacy in the Roman Church?

As for Scripture, the fact that St. Peter was a

married man, and that our Divine Lord had so special an interest in his family as to have made the healing of his mother-in-law one of His recorded miracles, should be in itself sufficient for every Christian. We have in this an evidence which cannot be disputed, that vows of celibacy are not of Divine institution for the Christian priesthood; and Rome acts wisely in keeping, as far as possible, the Bible from her followers, lest they should ascertain for themselves even the one fact, that he who they claim to be the first infallible head of their Church was a married man.

It is quite true that St. Paul speaks of the celibate state as a higher state; but it should be well noted that he draws a marked line in this matter. He says truly, that for those to whom God has given the call to virginity, the life of virgin love and devotion to God is the higher; but he makes, almost prophetically, the plain statement, that he had "no commandment of the Lord" (1 Cor. vii. 25) on this subject; and in fact so plain is all Scripture teaching on this point, that the Roman Church in enforcing celibacy on her priesthood has been obliged to fall back on her infallibility as her only justification for requiring this vow from her priests. The other texts of Scripture which deal with this subject are so plain, and so well known to Protestants, that it would not be necessary to call attention to them here, if it were not that this work is intended, amongst other objects, to be a handy manual of explanation for controversial purposes; and it may be well for even Protestants to have at hand all the help possible on any point of discussion with Rome. It is also most important that children should be carefully instructed on such subjects, and armed for future trials. We are apt to read Scripture mechanically, or even when studying it to pass over the significance of certain texts; and we do not realise all their value in disputed subjects, as I know now myself to my grievous cost.

In considering St. Paul's recommendation of celibacy it should be remembered that he is speaking to the whole Church, and that there is not even the remotest hint that he is speaking only to priests. If, therefore, his recommendation has any present value, it is of equal importance to all Christian people. I knew personally a Roman Catholic bishop, the late Dr. McCarthy of Kerry, who told me himself that he thought St. Paul's recommendation was intended to be of universal application, and that no one should marry. This opinion, like many others more or less sensible, he took care not to express in public, as it is dangerous for the clergy of the Roman Church to ventilate any opinion, no matter how well considered, on that subject. Such is the miserable want of charity in that Church, that there are always men on the watch to take hold of anything which may serve to disgrace or discredit a " brother," especially if that brother is a person of any prominence, when jealousy finds an easy way to gratify itself. I shall return to this point later, when entering on some recent developments of dispute in the Roman Church; and I have given evidence in my autobiography* of the way in which the good works in which I was engaged were frustrated by the petty jealousy of ecclesiastics.

The good bishop was once asked what was to become of the world if, by common consent, all men and women remained celibate? He smiled, and replied that he did

---

* "The Nun of Kenmare." An Autobiography. With Portrait. Crown 8vo, cloth, 7s. 6d. London: Hodder & Stoughton.

not think it would be much loss to the world if it came to an end. But there was a reason for St. Paul's recommendation of celibacy which does not exist at present. The early Christians, and the apostles, were looking for a speedy termination of this life, by the second coming of their Lord. To them this world mattered so little, and the world to come mattered so much. To us, absorbed as we are in the things of time, all is different, and we are more inclined to ask, "Where are the signs of His coming?" than to expect it. To us it seems as if all things go on as they ever have done, and as if there had been no changes since the fathers fell asleep. To the Christians of St. Paul's day, wrongly interpreting, as we know they did, certain of our Lord's words, it seemed as if at any moment the things of time might pass into the things of eternity. They did not ask, "Where is the promise of His coming?" for at every moment they expected that coming. Why, then, should they not sit loose to the things of time and sense? Why should they sow when they did not expect to reap? Why should they concern themselves, or embarrass themselves with wives or children, when they daily and hourly expected the opening of the gates of the City where there is neither marrying nor giving in marriage?

But to the hapless Roman Catholic of the present day, who is kept in wilful and deliberate ignorance of the Scriptures, the real meaning of St. Paul's advice on the subject of marriage is unknown. He knows only just so much of the letter as may "kill," but he knows nothing of the spirit which quickens. St. Paul clearly bases his advice, or rather his suggestion, on the subject of marriage, on the ground of the shortness of time,—alluding evidently to the popular hope and expectation of the immediate coming of the Lord. "The time is short;" and doubtless this sense of the nearness of the second coming of the Lord was of no little help to the early Christian, surrounded as he was with temptations and persecutions. We should remember, too, that the expectation of martyrdom was hourly before the mind of the Christian of St. Paul's time as an ever-present hope, and that it was a hope constantly realised. The man or the woman who was freed from worldly ties, however blessed they might be under other circumstances, was much more likely to suffer generously than one who was bound by ties of flesh and blood. But as we have said, how can the poor Roman Catholic of to-day know this? He is only allowed to know that St. Paul recommended virginity in the strongest terms, he is not allowed to know the circumstances; nor indeed, if he came to know them, would it avail him, for he is bound to interpret the Bible only as the Church allows. Nor may he know that in the very next chapter St. Paul claims for himself the right to marry, as St. Peter had done, if he pleases. The words are well worth noting. He says, "Have we not power to lead about a sister, a wife, as well as other apostles, and as the brethren of the Lord, and Cephas?" (1 Cor. ix. 5). Here we find the very fact of St. Peter having a wife brought forward, not as a reproach, but as a fact, and one which could be used as an argument why "other Apostles" might do the same thing.

But this argument would scarcely be needed if the facts of history were better known. The Roman Church had made its claims to supremacy for several centuries before any attempt was made to enforce the celibacy of the clergy. And the history of the lives of the clergy after this enactment was put in force is at once the best proof of its miserable results, and that the Roman Church, of all others, has the least claim to be called "holy."

I shall give from Roman Catholic authorities only some of the statements on this subject made in synods and councils of the Roman Church.

There is no doubt that the canon of the Roman Church which bound its priests to celibacy was a masterpiece of human diplomacy. If it was a Divine necessity it would have been proclaimed as such by the Founder of Christianity. Admitting even that it was a counsel of perfection, that it was a higher degree in the Christian life to be a virgin than to marry, it is perfectly clear from the very words of Christ, and from the teaching of St. Paul, that it was not a counsel intended for all. We have St. Paul's distinct statement, that the Apostles, like St. Peter, had a right to have a wife if they so desired; and let it be noted that a right which is merely a toleration, or to which any penalty or discredit is attached, is not a right in the sense evidently intended here.

An unmarried clergy might be a support to the Church in a time of persecution. A married clergy, for whom special counsel is given in the Gospel, is the normal condition of the Church, and intended to be an example and a strength to the Church in times of peace. Where is the priest who dares to preach on the words of St. Paul to Timothy, in which he so expressly states the duties of the Christian priesthood as regards their wives? How any Church calling itself Christian could forbid the marriage of its clergy, with the Scriptures and especially the instructions of St. Paul in regard to the family life of the ministers of the Gospel, is a mystery of the perversity of human nature, and like all attempts to be wiser than God, it has ended in disastrous failure. The bishop, says St. Paul, "must be blameless, the husband of one wife." What word could be plainer? And then the plain practical inference is drawn to make the edification to be derived from marriage yet more clear. "For if a man know not how to rule his own house, how shall he take care of the Church of God?" (1 Tim. iii. 5). Words could not express more clearly or more wisely the duty of a Christian minister, and we shall see presently how this enforced and unchristian law of celibacy has acted, just as the Scriptures imply it would act. The priest of the Church of Rome, not having a household of his own to rule, has "not known how to rule the Church of God." Instead of becoming the father of his people, he is the tyrant of his people. It was not long before I left the Church of Rome that a priest high in the Roman Church in New York said to me, "The bishops tyrannise over us, and we in turn tyrannise over the people." He spoke these words in all sober truth, and in sad earnestness. And those who know anything of the inside life of the Roman Church at the present day, know but too well the truth of these words, while the past history of the Roman Church is simply one long cry for power at the expense of Gospel truth.

Let us look at the position of the unmarried priest. He is a man with all the God-given passions of a man. The first instinct of man is to propagate his species. To this end God has given him the desire to do so, a gift of infinite love, the results of which are of the highest benefit to the human race. This was God's precept in the Jewish dispensation, approved in the Christian dispensation, and sanctified in it to a degree unknown before Apostolic days. The priest, being a man, has these God-given instincts. He desires to propagate his species, but he is told that to do this by marriage is to commit a deadly sin. How awful is his case! God has given him certain instincts, lawful, Divine, because God-given, and man says, "Thou shalt not profit by them. I, the human head of the Church, forbid you to do what God, the Founder of the Church, has permitted you to do." For, let it be well noted, even the Roman Church has not ventured to say that this forbidding to marry is a Divine command. No, it is a command only of the "Church," which claims a right, and—oh, the pity of it!—is allowed power, through the folly and sin of man, to do exactly what God has forbidden to be done.

Again, is it not St. Paul himself who has said, "The Spirit speaketh expressly that in the latter times some shall depart from the faith" (1 Tim. iv. 1)? and has he not said that one of the signs of this departure from the faith is "forbidding to marry" (verse 3)? and is there any Christian Church to which this accusation applies except to the Church of Rome?

The man, then, who is for ever at war with his God-given nature, and with the instincts which his God has given him, is not fit to be a leader of men; and this is, above all, what a priest should be, and what God intended him to be. If he keeps his vow of enforced celibacy he is for ever in the misery of fear, lest he should be tempted to break it. His very vow, far from helping him, is a most terrible hindrance to him. The teaching of the Roman Church that his vow will protect him in temptation is a fallacy, as all history, even history according to Roman Catholic historians, goes to prove. How can a vow help, when it is a vow to do what God has said shall not be done? He makes a vow which pledges him not to have the very opportunity of doing just the very thing which an inspired Apostle declares a minister of the Gospel should do. How can he fulfil the Scripture precept of "ruling" his family well, as the first step towards ruling well the Church of God, when he has no family to rule? How can he have "faithful children," when the only children he may have are the fruit of his own unfaithfulness to a most solemn vow? No wonder that the priest, in his despair and his loneliness, takes refuge in drink, and tries to forget his misery in dissipation and sin.

The fatal and diabolical policy of his Church deprives him of all Divinely sanctioned privileges, and drives him to the indulgence of unholy gratification, binding him by unnatural vows to an unnatural life. One of two things must happen; either he keeps his vow, or he breaks it. If he keeps it, his life is one long misery of fear and self-repression. Far be it from me to say that all priests break their vow of chastity; and it may be said that there are some men, as there are certainly many women, who are not desirous of married life. To such, remaining by choice, or a providential necessity, in a state of virginity, the grace of God is an all-sufficient protection against sin. But such cases are the exception and not the rule; and there can be no possible comparison between the case of such persons and the case of a minister of the Christian dispensation who takes a vow that he will not marry, when the Bible, the source of Christianity, and of instruction for Christian people, has given express directions not that priests should remain unmarried, but how they can fulfil the end for which God instituted marriage, to the edification of the Church to which they have been called to minister.

He would be a bold man who would deny that priests are intemperate as a class. It is true that there are honourable exceptions; but the Church of Rome looks with toleration on the sin of intemperance, hence its half-hearted efforts in the cause of temperance.

There has probably never been a more urgent advocate of temperance than Cardinal Manning, and to myself he said, on one occasion, when I was deploring the intemperate habits of Irish priests, "I need temperance for my priests more than for my people;" nor did I take this to mean a reflection on the priests of his own diocese more than others. It was a statement of an incontrovertible fact, that intemperance is the besetting sin of the priest everywhere. It is curious how this evil is condoned by Roman Catholics. If a word is said to imply that a priest does not keep his vow of chastity, no matter how flagrant the case of his fall may be, the Roman Catholic is excited to the wildest anger. It seems a little matter whether he knows the accusation to be true or not. It is the accusation and not the doing of the evil which angers him. And this is because the vow of the priest to remain celibate is one of the great sources of power in the Roman Church; and the Roman Catholic from childhood has been taught to consider this vow so sacred, that he looks upon a breach of it as the greatest scandal which can befall a priest. It is a source of power in more ways than is generally supposed. Hence it is that when a priest leaves the Church of Rome, every effort is made to disgrace him in the eyes of Roman Catholics, by saying that he wants to break his vow and get married. The persistence with which false charges are continued, despite all proof to the contrary, is one and not the least serious evidence that this Church needs falsehood and slander for its support. No amount of profligacy which a priest could commit in the "Church" would shock a Roman Catholic so much, or at all, in comparison with an honest following of God's law, and the Apostle's advice, to become the husband of one wife.

It needs a personal and intimate knowledge of Roman Catholics to understand this strange perversion of right and wrong, which has been instilled into them from childhood. I cannot easily forget the horror of a well-educated Roman Catholic to whom I was speaking of a priest who had left the Roman Church, as so many have done of late years, and who had married some years afterwards. It could not be said of him that he had left the Roman Church to marry, though of course the falsehood of a charge against one who leaves Rome never hinders a Roman Catholic from making it.

It was many years after he had done so that he took a wife; but when I pointed out to her that he had only followed the example of St. Peter, whom Roman Catholics claim as the head of their Church, though they are so very unwilling to imitate his example, her astonishment was unlimited, and her perplexity was so great, that I trust it may lead her to inquire in how many other things Roman Catholics have failed to follow the example and the precepts of the great Apostle for whom they profess so much honour. Claiming his headship as they do, they might at least do him the respect to follow his example.

The confessional, as practised in the Roman Church,

is a cesspool of iniquity for the temptation of the priest. It is all very well, and true, to say that the laity may escape danger, but most certainly the priest cannot do so. He is obliged, by the most sacred obligations of his office, to probe to the bottom of every evil thought as well as to the end of every act. Those who have not been guilty of gross sins may think the priest has only to hear a few of the little faults of which they have been guilty.

In this case it may be said, as in the case of the celibacy of the clergy, that if it was of Divine ordinance, God would protect the priest from the evil; but no fair-minded man who has read, I will not say the Bible, but the " Fathers," of whom the Roman Church boasts so much, can assert that they ever inculcated or practised confession as it is practised to-day in the Church of Rome. I do not myself think that there is so much harm done at present to the young in the confessional as some would suppose. Of course there are priests so evil-minded as to ask young women questions on subjects on which they are, and should be, absolutely ignorant. I know that an English convert priest, since dead in the odour of sanctity, gave a young girl her first knowledge of evil in the confessional; but from what she told me, I think that he did not know the fearful harm he was doing. But he should have known it; and I know that it was long years before that lady recovered from the shock which she received. It must be remembered that all this, and even worse, far from being made a reproach to a priest by his Church, would be considered a matter of duty. A priest is like a man who is always handling inflammable materials. He knows theoretically that he may be blown up some day, and that he may, by the least want of caution, cause fearful injury to others. Using explosive material has led to practical indifference to danger, and too often he pays the penalty, or makes others pay it. So it is in the confessional. A priest may not be personally evil or inclined to evil, but he is handling inflammable material all the time, and the result in the spiritual life is even more likely to be fatal than in the temporal.

I must confess for myself that the wonder to me is not that there are so many priests who drown their misery in drink, but that any escape. Hour after hour, for long weary hours, they are seated in the confessional listening to tales either of the most contemptible petty squabbles and scruples, or to sins of the blackest hue. Hour after hour they have to give the same mechanical absolution, and the same stereotyped advice. Hour after hour they have to sit in a constrained position, often productive of terrible disease, and to inhale the breath of the drunken, the dissolute, and the diseased. Often, too, these hours have to be spent fasting altogether from food, as in many places the priest has to "hear" his penitents before saying mass, and of course while he is fasting. With an unnaturally weakened body, there must be an unnaturally weakened mind. Where, then, is the wonder if there is a fall? Where is the wonder that the Roman Church is sickened with the bodies of the slain, who have made shipwreck in this stream of pollution? Wearied, worn in body and mind, the priest goes to his cheerless home, if home it can be called; and what comfort does he find there? Often he has a long office to say before he retires for the night, which must be said still fasting, as at the late hour when he leaves the confessional there is no one to give him a meal, and often the obligation of a fast day would forbid its being taken. What more natural than that he should drink to obtain a temporary relief from his terrible burden, and that at last drink should become a habit? What wonder if, craving human sympathy, and having none that is lawful for him to seek, he should have recourse to that which is unlawful. The housekeeper, the niece, is at hand, with the natural compassion of woman, and with the added reverence of a Romanist for the "priest." A little familiarity, a little affectionate sympathy, and the end is not far to seek; and when the priest falls, he falls, like Lucifer, never to rise again.

Sometimes, too often, it is the schoolmistress who is the victim, and I speak of what I know. It was my infinitely sad lot to have been asked by an English bishop, and by an English cardinal, to take charge of a mission where the priest had ruined four of his schoolmistresses, one after the other. His last victim had a child whom she could not support, and so her pitiful story came out. The priest was sent, not into banishment, as would have been done if he had committed any sin "against the Church," or offended his bishop. As he had only sinned against God, he was simply removed from one diocese to another, where he retained his rank and his honours. If such things are done in the green tree, what has been done in the dry? If such deeds as these are done, and even condoned in England to-day, what will be done in England when the Church has the power to shield evildoers? And I have reason to know that this is not an uncommon case. I have heard the sad tale of many girls, teachers, who are under the absolute control of the priest, who have been led on step by step to evil, and no hand was stretched out to save them, because none dared to interfere with the priest who led them to ruin. I have heard their weary story of shame and sin, and how they were consoled and silenced in the confessional; for with the infatuation of Roman Catholic teaching they would, even in their misery, seek absolution from the very authors of their shame. Could the horrors of Pagan rites afford more terrible instances of depravity? And all this is happening in the England, and in the America, of to-day, and all must be hidden at the peril of the ruined woman, because the sinner is "a priest," and because the "Church" teaches, by example and custom, that it is a far greater sin to accuse a priest of sin, than to sin with a priest.

I know that it will be said indignantly by Roman Catholics that the Church does not sanction these evils, but what use denials, when facts are all the other way? No one can possibly be intimate with Roman Catholics in private life without knowing how they fear and silence the least word of scandal where a priest is concerned. A Church which finds it necessary to hide or deny evil which is well known to exist, must rest on a very insecure foundation. And it is a curious circumstance, that while Roman Catholics will talk quite freely about priests who are guilty of intemperance, and seem to think it a matter of very little consequence, they will shrink with horror from connecting the name of a priest with immorality. Yet the one sin is most assuredly the parent of the other.

I might fill a volume if I related the many instances which I have known of priests who drank to excess, *and still remained honoured members of the Church.* More than one bishop and priest are at present in lunatic asylums in the United States, who have been the victims of this crime, and of still greater crime. I do not ask that my word shall be taken for these statements. It is not so long since the whole world was made aware of the moral condition of one diocese in America by the highest possible authority in the diocese, the bishop himself.

The St. Louis *Republican* of June 20th, 1887, printed a letter from Bishop Hogan, of the Roman Catholic diocese of St. Joseph, Mo., which was brought out in court, and was never intended for publication; but it reveals a sad state of affairs. In June, 1887, the Bishop had placed a German priest over an Irish congregation. The Irish people were indignant at this proceeding; and, as we shall show later, from Roman Catholic sources, there is no small fear on the part of certain American ecclesiastics lest there should be an open rupture between the German and Irish element in the Roman Catholic Church in the United States, where the Church is far from being in the condition of religious harmony which the rulers of the Papacy would like the world to suppose. At last a gentleman interfered in the interests of peace, and the bishop was obliged, or at least thought it wise, to justify himself.

His defence was that the priests of his diocese were such a drunken lot that he was compelled to supply the parish as he did. He then gives a list *by name* of twenty-two priests who were received into his diocese from 1869 to 1876, but whom he was compelled to dismiss on account of immorality and drunkenness. Some of them are described as "constantly drunk;" one is "now going around from city to city a drunken wreck." The Bishop wrote :—

"The constant shameful public and sacrilegious drunkenness of the three last-mentioned priests who were by my side at the cathedral determined me to put them and their kind out of my jurisdiction. H——, after repeated drunkenness, went on a spree for a week in my house; while in my house broke out at night, got into a house of disreputable women in his drunkenness, and was thrown out into the street, picked up drunk, recognised, and taken into a house and made sober, and put into a carriage and taken back to my house. That evening G —— and K—— were told by me to prepare for the proper celebration of the Feast of the Patronage of St. Joseph for Easter Sunday. On Saturday night they stayed up all night drinking, carousing, and shouting. K —— fell down, blackened, and almost broke his face in falling. Of course the two sacrilegious priests said Mass the next day; and K—— went into the pulpit and preached with his blackened and bruised face to the people of the cathedral. This was on the Feast of the Patron of the Diocese and of the Universal Church. It was time for me to begin a reformation."

From personal knowledge of several dioceses I must add that this state of things is far from uncommon. In the western states of America the conditions of life are freer, and priests are more careless in their public conduct. I can only say that the very same condition of things, I have reason to believe, exists in other places, but hidden from public view.

Since my arrival in America priests have often come to beg from me while they were in a state of intoxication, saying, that they came because it was well known I never refused a priest anything. This was true until I found out how my kindness was imposed upon. A priest who had treated both myself and the sisters most shamefully in England, was sent with a high character to America by his bishop, who wanted to get rid of him, and he also came to beg from me. I know that there are priests who are living by their wits in every part of the world, the wretched victims of drink and immorality, diseased beyond description, and supported by the poorest of the people, who have a superstitious respect for a priest, no matter how degraded.

And the above is the condition of a large and important diocese in the United States, where we hear, *ad nauseam*, that the Roman Catholic Church is making rapid advances. Certainly if building immense Churches, and not paying for them, notwithstanding the millions of money yearly wrung from the poor, is a sign of advancement, it is advancing. Certainly if building and establishing Roman Catholic convent schools, which are principally filled by Protestant children, is a sign of advancement, the Church is advancing. In one sisters' school in Toronto, Canada, there are sixty Protestant pupils against forty Roman Catholics, and it is much the same everywhere.

There are Roman Catholics who will not trust their children to convent teaching, but Protestants supply the deficiency. In Roman Catholic nations the Roman Catholic Church is deprived of all temporal power. In Protestant countries it rides triumphant. No wonder that the Pope boasts that he rules America, and that an American bishop boasts that if the people of America are not yet all Catholics, they are Papists in their love of the Pope, and in obedience to his orders.

If Bishop Hogan had not spoken out about the condition of his diocese it might have been pointed out as a model diocese, where sin was unknown. Who can suppose for a moment that these priests, abandoned as they were to intemperance, were not also abandoned to immorality? Would to God that the Roman Catholic laity, and especially men,—for it is their duty to act and protect the weaker sex,—inquired for themselves as to the real moral condition of the Roman Catholic priesthood. I have met many Roman Catholic men, both before and since I left the Church of Rome, who quite frankly avowed that the priests of their Church were, as a class, drunkards. It certainly seems amazing that they cannot see the inevitable consequences. Even according to the very lax teaching of the Roman Church drunkenness is a sin, though it is only venial when men do not drink to the unconsciousness of complete intoxication. What, then, even according to Roman Catholic theology, is the condition of a priest who drinks habitually? Is he not already fallen? Will he make nice distinction about crime, or think it more sinful to break one commandment than another? Will he be in a state of mind to resist and avoid evil, and above all an evil which needs all the grace or the resolution which he possesses, even when he is in what his Church would consider a state of grace? And does not the priest know well how safely he may sin? The laity are so terrorised into silence, that it is but very rarely they dare say one word, no matter how flagrant his offence may be.

As I have said, I was asked to take sisters to a parish in England, where it was well and publicly known that the priest lived in sin with his schoolmistress for many years. As the evil was too notorious to be concealed, the people at last lost all faith in religion, and left the Church, so that scarcely more than five or six families remained in communion with it. To get them back was the one object of the bishop of the diocese, who seemed to me to concern himself very little about the character of the priest, so that the Church did not suffer numerically from his sin. I made it a condition of going to this place that the priest should leave before I brought sisters there. And here I have a right to say, that if Protestants choose to listen to the petty sneers that priests have to say about me it is their own loss. It was but yesterday that a Protestant gentleman said to me, "Oh, the priests say that you always wanted your own way when you were a sister, and that when you could not get it you left the Church." I am sorry for Protestants who can be so easily deceived. The charge, in one sense, is true. No priest can say with truth that I ever did any one act while I was in the Roman Catholic Church contrary to the orders, or even the known wishes of those who were then my superiors. If I had done this, Protestants may be very sure that the world would have heard of it again and again.

But there were some points on which I was firm, and as they happened to be points on which no objection could be raised, for very shame, the bishops concerned did not oppose me, though it is convenient now to make it appear as if I was always in opposition to their wishes. Certainly I objected to go to this place or to bring young sisters there until the priest was removed. I knew that the bishop considered me a little fastidious, and I know my action in this and many other matters did not improve my position in the Church, and was the cause of much of the unmanly persecution which I endured. Still my action in these matters could not by any possibility be construed as being that of one who wished to place herself in opposition to her ecclesiastical superiors. But long experience has shown me how very easy it is to deceive Protestants, and how slow they often are, to their own loss, to realise the truth as to the deliberate deceit and treachery which is practised in the Church of Rome. If they only knew how much amusement is given to Roman Catholics when they accept their version of affairs, it would not help to increase their respect for that Church, or even for their own wisdom in such ready belief.

I was perfectly within my rights, and within the line of duty as a good Catholic, in refusing to take this mission until the priest was removed. But, as I have said, my action in this and similar matters was not one which was likely to make me very acceptable to ecclesiastical authority, and of course in all such cases I was the person to be blamed. In this case I must give the bishop in question the due credit of not having made any opposition to my wishes. But I was desired by him, as the case was an important one, to listen to all that I could hear when I went on the mission. In fact, the bishop did not expect much thanks from Rome for his interference. It is the policy of Rome to prevent the only thing which passes as "scandal" in that Church, the exposure of the fault of a priest, as much as possible. The fault, if it can be hidden, is not considered a scandal. I had indeed a difficult position. This priest was a person of great influence in the town which was the scene of his disgrace Protestants only laughed, but there was one Catholic family where the matter was taken seriously. The last of his victims had been engaged to a young man of good position, and whose friends were old residents of the town. I believe he sincerely and truly loved the erring girl. It may be well believed that his indignation knew no bounds. If he had been a "good Catholic" he might have married her, and saved the Church. But great as his love had been, he was not a Catholic of the type which will shield the priest at his own expense. He spoke out plainly, refused to have anything to do with the girl, and threatened summary chastisement even on the priest. His courage, however, fell short of actually inflicting it. To strike a priest, no matter what the aggravation, is a crime too terrible for a Roman Catholic even to contemplate.

Public opinion was well roused, as the young man did not see that he was bound to keep silence on a subject on which every one was but too well informed. I had to listen to a flood of recrimination and scandal when at last I arrived. I did my best as peacemaker, and tried to bring the people back to the almost deserted church. I had also orders from the bishop, who was in deadly fear as to the view which Rome might take in regard to his interference with so influential an ecclesiastic, to ascertain all the particulars and gain all the proof I could of the criminality of the priest. The deserted church was built by a convert who had left it free of all debt, a marvel for a Roman Catholic church; for notwithstanding its enormous wealth, there are few churches which are free from debt,—a curious commentary on the great boast which is made of reverence for the altar.

The young man never returned to the Roman Church. He and his parents joined some body of Protestants, which, I do not remember. The rest of the congregation stayed at home. I was told by "good Catholics" that this priest said Mass during his every-day career of evil, and left his paramour in his room when he descended to offer up the sacrifice, which, according to the teaching of the Church, is of so sublime a character, that angels might fear to approach it.

These good people did not know that the Roman Church before now has sanctioned the profligacy of her ministers, and that, as I shall show in the history of celibacy in the Roman Church, every sin against chastity which a priest can commit is provided for by a regular scale of indulgence. But this history of my experience, miserable as it is, does not end here. I was staying with some of the sisters waiting until —— should be removed to another diocese, where he was received with all the honours due to his position in the Church, and naturally I was anxious as to who would be appointed to take his place. That also was soon provided for. I was introduced to a priest who was certainly more kind and considerate in his manner than the generality of priests are to sisters. I hoped we had found one who would give us some peace after our long experience of, I must say, brutality and unchristian conduct. I expressed to the sisters my satisfaction.

Unhappily, it did not last long. We were in the act of preparing for our departure when Canon —— rushed into my room, and asked me if I knew the kind of priest the bishop was sending to take the place of the priest who had been so quietly removed. I was amazed at his excitement, little knowing the cause.

"Why," he said, "this man is not long out of gaol. He was arrested in the streets, and locked up there for being drunk and disorderly;" and he added significantly, "he has a housekeeper." I only wish that those persons, whether Protestants or Roman Catholics, who are anxious to criticise my conduct while in the Church of Rome, had been placed in my position for one hour.

What to do I knew not. It seemed as if I was destined to suffer from priests, and then to be blamed as if I had been the cause of the trouble. I knew priests so well by this time, that I had not a doubt that the object of this communication was to get me into trouble with the bishop, who would certainly have been very angry if I had complained of his arrangements. I felt that the bishop had acted very badly to me, to say the least, in not having put me on my guard as to the person to whom he was sending me; but I knew too well that the very priests who were trying to make me have a disagreement with the bishop would be the very first to blame me and not him. I say again it is simply impossible for any one who has not some such experience as mine to have even the least idea of the wickedness and misery of the inner lives of priests and sisters; and I can well understand how those who have not had such an experience may be slow to believe that such things can be.

My distress and despair can be well imagined by any Christian heart. I had left Knock, hunted out, as I have told in my autobiography, by the injustice of priests, and people acting under the permission and under the control of priests. I had come to England hoping, or rather feeling sure, that here at least there would be some spiritual good, some true religion. I soon found, what a wider experience has since confirmed, that the Roman Catholic Church is everywhere the same. How can it be otherwise when it never admits the necessity for reform, and when there never was a Church wherein reform was so sorely needed, as its indisputable history proves too well.

A few moments' reflection made me consider what could be Canon ——'s object in this sudden communication. I was well aware that he knew, for at least a week previous, that this priest to whom he gave such a bad character, was to take the place of the gentle and honourable exiled "canon." "Why, I asked myself, "did he not speak before? Why did he give such solemn injunctions 'not to tell the bishop' that he had spoken to me? Why, if he was so zealous for our welfare, did he not speak to the bishop himself?" All these thoughts flashed through my mind with unhappy rapidity, and still I did not see my way to act. I saw at once that if I said a word of objection, the bishop would be sure to ask who was my informant; and I never could bring myself to adopt the Roman Catholic custom of betraying others, after the most solemn promises of secrecy. In fact, a great deal of my trouble in the Roman Church arose from my having different ideas of truth and honour from those who were opposed to me.

An honest man is a poor match for a rogue, even when he suspects the rogue; and it was very long before I learned to suspect priests. I thought also that it was very unmanly of Canon —— to come and tell me all this under a pledge of secrecy, and not to go himself to the bishop, and speak to him on the subject. But I knew that it was always a dangerous thing for a priest to make any representation to a bishop, no matter how grave the case might be. I can only say that I went to —— only to find that the canon was right. The good-natured priest had been in gaol for public disturbance and drunkenness a short time previous, and as priests are always well posted on each other's affairs, I found the whole story was true, even to the existence of a "housekeeper." The priest was Irish, and had been all over the world; but as the bishop said afterwards, and as many American bishops have said, if a bishop is too particular, what is he to do for priests? He must take them as they come.

The result was what might have been expected. I was at last obliged to write to the bishop, and tell him that the whole town knew of the previous character of the priest, who had been sent to minister to a people who already had almost lost faith in God and man, in consequence of the scandalous conduct of his predecessor, and that the "housekeeper" was evidently an institution, as she had lived with him for years. I heard, to her credit, that she tried all she could to keep him from drink. But—alas for me!—here was another flagrant instance of "my inability to agree with my ecclesiastical superiors." Very little was thought of the discreditable conduct of the priest. I had seen him intoxicated on the altar, but admit cheerfully that he was one of the very few priests I ever met who had a kind word for me, except when I had plenty of money to give them. If I had consulted my own peace of mind I should have let things go just as they were; but unfortunately I thought that such men ought not to be allowed to administer the Sacraments. He also was "honourably removed" to a country place, where it was supposed his delinquencies would be less noticed, especially if he kept out of debt; and for all I know he may be there still.

Before I pass to other instances of the same unhappy kind, I may say that the priest sent to take his place was a youth just come from college, whose ignorance was such as might be expected from the way in which he had been advanced beyond his station, and the small amount of brains which he had to balance his advancement. He was sober as far as I knew, but the secret life of a priest gives them so many opportunities for intemperance, that it is difficult to know who abstains and who exceeds. I was also informed by the same "canon" who had warned me about his predecessor, that he had been a servant in the bishop's house in ———, and that the bishop had taken a fancy to him, as he had shown considerable aptitude for ceremonies. Some bishops will make any sacrifice to promote such men, as these things attract Protestants to their churches, and make converts of people who have not intellect enough to discern the difference between show and reality.

This boy, for he was little else, thought he could add to his dignity by treating me with contempt, which at least was a proof that he was not a gentleman even by education, as he might have been, if he was not such by birth. I soon found that there was little difference among the priests. Our new "pastor" left nothing undone to annoy the sisters; and I could occupy pages with their letters of complaints, all but too well founded, written to me after my arrival in America. For petty annoyances and petty persecution, as a general rule, priests are unequalled. What else can be expected when the life they lead is considered? This boy's father was Irish, and had been a common soldier; yet he was so ashamed of his nationality that he made the most ridiculous attempts to hide it, as well as to conceal the humble origin of his father.

There was another priest who lived in the neighbourhood to whom I showed many kindnesses. He repaid me by giving me all the annoyance in his power. At length he got so deeply in debt, and the bishop had so many complaints of him, that he was shipped off to America, the refuge of priests who cannot be got rid of at home. I heard that the bishop gave him the highest testimonials. I know that he had the coolness to come to me in Jersey city, and to ask me to pay his expenses to Canada. I refused even to see him; and no doubt he has said all he can against me in consequence. I must admit, however, that I was amused at the coolness with which he came to me for money, after the way in which he had treated me and the sisters in England. But priests are so much in the habit of having their sins overlooked, that probably he considered he paid me an honour in asking my help. God help those to whose spiritual necessities he has gone to minister!

I could give many more instances of the profligacy and tyrannical character of priests; but I will only mention two other cases in which evil was actually going on before my very eyes, and I did not see it. One of these was the case of the officious canon who was so anxious to warn me against the bishop's favourites. I did many kindnesses for him, but the influence of his housekeeper was against me. This woman went by the name of the "canoness." A great deal has been said by Roman Catholics about the wives of Protestant clergymen interfering in the affairs of their husbands' parishes; but it would need another Anthony Trollope to describe the feats of the "canoness" in this line. Whenever the canon was absent the "canoness" took his place, and did everything but say Mass. The curates rebelled again and

again against her tyrannical rule. She dictated the
hour of rising and rest; and if they did not please her
by telling her all the affairs of the parish, spiritual and
temporal, she had a handy way of punishing them by
cutting off the food supplies. As for her interference
with the sisters, her attempts in this direction were
ludicrous, and would have been mischievous, if they
had not kept her, in some degree, in her place. At last
the young priests rose in rebellion. The sisters wrote
to me that the bishop, worn out with ceaseless complaints of the "canoness'" interference, gave the
canon his choice between parting with the "canoness"
or dividing his parish, so that he would not need a
curate. The canon kept the "canoness," and submitted, with as good a grace as he could, to the loss
of the greater part of his parish.

If only one-half of the affairs of this sort, which are
of daily occurrence in the "Holy" Roman Catholic
Church, were known to the world at large, what a
revolution there would be. But such things are kept
secret. Sisters know a great deal of the inside life of
priests, but they find it best to be silent; and it can
easily be seen that they could do no good by speaking.
The Church alone can reform the Church, and that is
the last thing which she can or will do, embarrassed as she is by her own infallibility. To her
may well be applied the reproach made to the Church
of the Laodiceans, "Because thou sayest, I am rich,
and increased with goods, and have need of nothing,
and knowest not that thou art wretched, and miserable,
and poor, and blind, and naked: I counsel thee to buy
of me gold tried in the fire, that thou mayest be rich;
and white raiment, that thou mayest be clothed, and
that the shame of thy nakedness do not appear; and

anoint thine eyes with eyesalve, that thou mayest see" (Rev. iii. 17, 18).

When I had but just entered the Roman Church, I was equally shocked and surprised by the way in which a young French lady spoke of the Jesuit who was the parish priest of the mission to which we were then attached. She talked of certain familiarities which she resented, and of a very pretty girl who was a great deal at the priest's house, helping the priest's housekeeper, and who I believed, on that account, to be above all suspicion. The girl was certainly very like the priest, who was a very good-looking man. The remarks of the French governess were not taken in good part by the ladies whose ears they reached. For myself I was too shocked, at what I supposed to be French lightness, to believe one word the young lady said; and the matter ended in her being dismissed from her situation as a gossip and a detractor. At that time I supposed that the French were a devoted Catholic people, and wondered much at a French lady criticising the character of a priest, and above all of a Jesuit. I soon dismissed the subject from my mind. It was pleasanter to believe that the girl was accusing the priest falsely, than to suppose that he had done wrong; for like all converts, I believed that priests were immaculate, and that it was a sin even to suppose them otherwise. It took a long experience to undeceive me; and that fact has made me understand how so many Roman Catholics have formed an ideal of a priest quite different from the reality, and how they will shut their eyes to anything which threatens to break the charm.

On the day of my reception into Newry convent, a young priest, who I learned long years after was a confirmed drunkard, acted very strangely. So high was my reverence for a priest, that it never even entered my head that he was not sober on the solemn occasion. Even when I heard his sister lamenting, as she did loudly and periodically, the misery of a priest who had fallen from grace, I never suspected that her own brother was the source of her trouble, and I fear that the disgrace of the family was a great deal more felt by her than the sin against God.

And what has been gained to the world, or to the Church, by enforcing this law of celibacy? It is one of those burdens grievous to be borne, which has most certainly caused more sin than sanctity. We know, on indisputable historical authority, that the result in the ages when Rome had all the power which she craved, was that the Church which would not allow or bless the honest wedlock of the priests was driven to permit concubinage. Could there be possibly a more terrible charge against any Christian body? Surely one would think that the results of this "infallible" interference with the laws of nature, and with the express direction of Scripture, as to the manner of life by which God's priests should be distinguished, would have been sufficient to condemn Rome for ever.

Rome is ever craving for power to enforce all her demands. It would be well if those who are anxious to increase her power would ask what has she done when she has had all the power she craved?

What was the state of Italy in the Middle Ages? We hear a great deal at the present day of the injustice done to the Pope in depriving him of temporal dominion, but how did the Popes live when they were free to rule as they pleased? Did they benefit humanity? Did they preach the Gospel? Did they even live good moral lives? Did they reform their clergy? Rather, we may ask, were their priests good men, who lived for their God and for His poor? Alas! all history proves that they were a curse rather than a blessing.

And what of the effects produced by the celibacy of the clergy at the present day? What is its effect on the Church at large? It is just what might be expected. An unmarried clergy must inevitably be a selfish clergy. It is supposed that celibacy lifts a man to heaven, and detaches him from the things of earth. Can any one who knows the clergy of the Romish Church say that their vow has had this effect? Is it not well known that they are grasping, avaricious, oppressive to the poor, whose cries do not reach the ear of the world, but nevertheless do reach the ear of God? Is it not well known that they often leave large sums of money to relatives, all of which has been obtained from God's poor, who, worshipping the ideal of the priest, know little of the reality. Even with all the precautions which Rome uses, and with all the secrecy which she can command, she is not able to hide altogether, as she could have hidden in earlier ages, the demoralised condition of so many of her priests. It is true that very little comes before the public, for the press is under a control which compels silence, but facts are told in private which one day will be remembered, and told in public. It is true that this careful guarding of the press has left the so-called upper class in utter ignorance of the true state of affairs, and consequently they give all the weight of their influence to uphold a system which they would denounce unsparingly if they knew it as it is. They see the priest on the altar and in society, where he is on his guard, and they do not know him as he is elsewhere. They see his zeal for the Church, but they do not know that he has had his hours of agony, and of deep and bitter despair, which he has drowned in drink, or driven away as best he could in active work for the Church which has been the cause of all his misery, but from which he sees no escape.

CHAPTER II.

THE MORAL EFFECTS OF THE CELIBACY OF THE CLERGY IN THE PAST AND IN THE PRESENT.

"After my departure shall grievous wolves enter in among you, not sparing the flock. Also of your own selves shall men arise, speaking perverse things."—Acts xx. 29, 30.

IT must never be forgotten that the Church of Rome makes her holiness a special ground on which she claims a divinely given authority. She claims not only to be "holy," but to be "the" holy Catholic Church. And people are so apt to take her, as they so often take others, at her own valuation. Rome says she is "holy," and the world, too lazy, or too ignorant to test her claims, acquiesces, and is duly impressed.

Perhaps there was never a greater fraud practised on the credulity of mankind than this. Probably of all Christian Churches there is not one Church which has so little to show of the fruits of the Spirit as Rome; and yet she is believed by millions to be the one Church which has an extraordinary record of good works. If only Roman Catholics were allowed to read history, and if only Protestants would read its pages (and they can read them), what a revelation they would find of the supposed sanctity of Rome. We shall return to this subject later. Here we are chiefly concerned with evidence on one point only viz., that Rome is very far from being a holy Church. The chief ground for this claim of pre-eminent holiness is, that her celibate priesthood are, of all those who minister at God's altars, the most perfect in their conduct, and the most self-sacrificing in their lives. And at the first glance it looks as if this claim was well founded. Here we have men who certainly make a vow which deprives them of all the comforts of family life. Here we have men who are, to all appearance, leading a life of superhuman self-sacrifice. And from time to time events occur which appear to verify this claim of Rome to a self-sacrificing priesthood. We need not go beyond the current news of the day for an example, and a fair one, of the way in which Rome establishes and perpetuates her claim to an exceptionally holy priesthood.

Who has not heard of Father Damien, the priest who has so nobly sacrificed his life in the sacred cause of humanity? The admiring Protestant gives his sacrifice the meed of praise it deserves; but the admiring Protestant does not stop to think, or does not know, that the noble deed which Father Damien has done is being done every day in the year, and was done long before he ever thought of following the example of the Protestant ladies who first devoted themselves to the leper. For many years there has been an institution for lepers outside the walls of Jerusalem, attended by German Protestant deaconesses, who have called no special attention to their work, but have gone on the even tenor of their way, year after year, being infected by the horrible disease, and dying by inches in its loathsome tortures. We do not say this as any depreciation of Father Damien's work. But the "capital" (there is no other word for it) which Roman Catholic papers acquire out of such things makes it incumbent on

Protestants, or rather I should say on all who value truth, to make the truth known. Let us give·honour to Father Damien; but all the honours do not belong to him. And yet Roman Catholic papers, and to my knowledge one under the special patronage of Archbishop Corrigan, edited by the late dynamiter, F—— breaks into wild cries of childish anger because a New York paper ventured to allude to this fact.

The New York paper will no doubt be more careful in the future how it offends Roman Catholic sensibilities, by stating any fact which, however true, seems to lessen the glory of a priest. The simple stating of this fact about these German deaconesses is called by this (late) dynamite advocate "a mean fling at the dead hero." It is ever thus that the Church of Rome supports her claim of exceptional holiness by false pretences. It is a crime, to be punished with the most severe penalties, if one word is said either in public or in private of the fault of a priest, or of the oppressive conduct of a bishop. New York society was ringing with suppressed laughter at the "ten dollars or ten days," joke, made on the way in which Archbishop Corrigan punished an unfortunate priest who had dared to say one word of fact as to the way in which Dr. McGlynn was treated by the orders of his ecclesiastical superior. But the laughter had to be low, for even Protestants could be made to feel the weight of episcopal displeasure, if the echo of their mirth reached the archiepiscopal ear.

And in the case of any priest whose name can be brought forward in the cause of science or humanity, all the glory must be given to the "Church" as the source of his inspiration. It matters little that the deed or the discovery for which he is honoured is common to many others. Even the least hint that the glory does not belong exclusively to Rome is treated as an injustice to that much-belauded Church A hundred deaconesses who may have sacrificed their lives in the cause of the leper are as a mere nothing in comparison with the one priest who has only followed their example. And, as I have said, the world takes the Church at her own valuation. I do not deny that the unnatural life of a priest is a true martyrdom; but there are many men, and many missionaries amongst Protestant denominations, who live quite as hard a life, as far as privation of the comforts of life is concerned, and there have been many Protestant ministers who have sacrificed their lives in time of pestilence as freely as any priest of the Roman Church.

It is so also in the case of sisters. I do not deny that the life of a sister is often one of great privation, but there are many sisters who live far more comfortably in the convents than they ever lived in their own homes. This, however, does not, to my mind, detract from the reality of their suffering, for they surrender their liberty, which makes all else of little value to them.

But the Church of Rome is ever making "capital," especially for the benefit of Protestants, out of the self-sacrificing lives of the sisters, while there are many women who live quite as great a life of self-sacrifice who never saw the interior of a convent. The secrecy and romance of the life of a nun prepares Protestants to give unlimited credit to any claim that may be made for the admiration of sisters; and, as in the case of Father Damien, they do not stop to think how many self-sacrificing lives are spent in their own denominations. There are many ministers' wives who not only bring up their little ones in the love and fear of their Creator, but who spend, and are spent, day after day in the service of the poor; and yet there is never a demand for praise of their self-sacrifice. It is time that all this claim to exceptional sanctity, in the Church of Rome, on the ground of the exclusive practice of good works, should be disproved and silenced for ever.

I know not whether to think it a providence, or to call it a peculiar coincidence, but I have had occasion to see a friend, the wife of a Methodist minister, between writing the last sentence and that on which I am now engaged. I had not been speaking to her on any matter connected with the Roman Church, but our conversation led accidentally to the subject of the indifference of sisters to the poor. She then told me of a case within her own personal knowledge. She had a servant, an orphan girl, who had been educated by sisters. When they found out that the poor girl was in a miserable state of health, the sisters would neither take her back, nor send her where she could have care and rest. One morning the girl was unable to rise, and my friend saw that she was dying. At the request of the girl she sent for the priest and the sisters. She begged the sisters to remain with her, or to send some one to remain with her until she died; but they said the superior would not allow them to do so. Mrs. H—— was very willing to do all she could for the girl; but she had a baby of her own to care for, besides all the additional work which the girl's illness threw on her. The sisters were perfectly indifferent. The girl died, and they would not even watch by her remains, or send any one to do so. Next day an undertaker was sent by some poor friend of this friendless girl, and she was buried from the Methodist minister's house; for the sisters would not even allow the coffin to be brought to their convent, or concern themselves in any way about their former pupil. Not even a candle was sent to burn by her lonely coffin; and Roman Catholics will know from this what indifference was shown. How different, said my friend, would their conduct have been if the girl had not been utterly destitute.

It was because I saw so many evidences of heartlessness on the part of sisters to the poor, and neglect of their most sacred duties to orphans, that I was anxious to found an order of sisters whose exclusive work should be for the poor. With a few honourable exceptions, the sisters who commenced by working for the poor have ended by caring for the rich. Certainly the rich can, and do repay them well in this world; but I shall return to this subject later.

What could be more sublime than the Roman Catholic ideal of a celibate clergy and an unmarried sisterhood, whose lives are devoted wholly to God and to the saving of souls? Even the human ambitions of churchmen may be made to look holy when it is claimed that their desire is the advancement of the Church, and the glory of God. How little is it known that the glory of God too often proves an excuse for the glorification of man, and that schemes for the advancement of the Church are too often invented for the glorification of the individual. One thing is certain; if the celibacy of the clergy is not a Divine institution it is impossible for it to benefit the world. It would need all the grace that God could bestow to enable a man to live the life of a celibate with his human instincts and desires quickened to a degree far beyond what is ordinary. One might say that the very virtue of a celibate priest actually invites temptation, and incites to crime. But our present purpose is to consider the result of this vow. Has this celibacy of the clergy proved a blessing to the Roman Church and to humanity? I can show that far from being a blessing it has proved a curse. I have already given some specimens of how men live who are vowed to celibacy. The fact that all breaches of this vow can be so easily concealed is one of the greatest dangers to the tempted priest. The superstitious terror which Rome inculcates, and which is so much used to prevent a word being said of any ill deed of a priest, is at once their temporal protection and their spiritual ruin.

Fear of exposure is one of the greatest preventives of crime, whether that fear is a dread of public opinion or of penal consequences. From this fear the priest is absolutely free. The bishop is the only person with whom the priest has to account. The bishop does not know everything, and the bishop is also human, and knows the history of his Church well, and that there is nothing new (in clerical incontinency) under the sun. I have seen a "canon" of the Church, who stood well with his bishop and his brethren, sitting with the grown-up child of his housekeeper in his lap, and the child embracing him as a child would embrace a father. Who shall say whether simple affection, or something very different, prompted the caresses he lavished on her, or whether what was done by a child— I should say rather by a girl of twelve—would not continue to be done by the woman? No priest with a real respect for the vows of his office would have allowed these familiarities. But how few priests have such a respect. I might multiply instances of this kind. I might quote from letters which I have seen from a penitent to a priest, in which there were allusions to such familiarities as these passing between them as an ordinary affair; but I have no wish to write on these subjects beyond what is of absolute necessity.

The great question is how did this rule of celibacy work when Rome had unlimited freedom in the Middle Ages? I think the world at large would be surprised if they knew what has been the result of the Church's free permission to her priests to have concubines, and of her stern prohibition of lawful marriage. Human nature is the same in all ages of the world and of the Church. History repeats itself. The question to be asked is, How do certain rules work under all conditions, and not how do they work under exceptional conditions? It is amazing that people cannot see for themselves that Rome has failed as a Christian religion. Take it on this one point of clerical celibacy, and what has been the result? He would be a bold man who denied, in the face of every-day facts, that the Roman Catholic clergy, as a class, are given to intemperance. That they are given to immorality is not so well known, because that sin is easier of concealment. Still there is quite enough evidence before the world to show that there is good ground for believing that, if hidden matters were revealed, a great deal of wickedness would see the light for the first time.

A priest at present on the mission, as it is called,— that is, a priest who is pastor of a large and influentia parish, but whose relations with his ecclesiastical superiors are rather strained, and would probably snap if it were not that he is immensely wealthy, independently of his ecclesiastical income,—told me that his archbishop employed a private detective for some time to watch him, as he was anxious to prove that he was in the habit of going to certain houses, so that he might have him in his power. A lady told me that the priests of a religious order, supposed by a credulous public to be so full of the odour of sanctity that they can work miracles, were in the habit of taking her husband at night to places where she would rather they had taken some one else's husband. She had no reason for disliking these priests, nor had she ever had any disagreement with any of them. The matter was only mentioned to me as an unpleasant fact. Nor did this in the least weaken her faith in the Church, so strange is the infatuation of Romanists where their priests are concerned. And yet we have the authority of Scripture for judging a tree by its fruits.

There are few persons of any intelligence who do not know the deplorable state of the Roman Church in Mexico, where for years it had full sway, until the people rose up at last against the iniquities practised, and screened in the name of religion. It is now some years since I saw a letter written to a lady in Ireland by her brother, who had gone to Mexico as a superintendent of some mines. He had married a Protestant, and had taken her with him. He told his sister that he had no hope of his wife's conversion now, as she had seen too much of the evil lives of the priests there, who lived in shameless concubinage, and kept their women and children openly in their houses. And Rome, tied by her infallibility, to which she must hold at any cost, tolerates all this; and by tolerating it proves that she prefers sin to virtue.

It is well known in Rome that it was the lives of the priests which first turned the people against the Church. A whole nation does not turn against the Church without cause, above all when the nation is as conservative and superstitious as the Italians. Surely it should strike thinking minds that so superstitious a nation must have had some great cause for uch a stupendous change. It was not the caprice of an hour which made the Italians infidels and free thinkers. They saw, at first with grief, at last with contempt, that those who professed to be priests of the "Holy" Catholic Church were leading lives the very reverse of holy; and losing their faith in the Church as incapable of producing good fruit, these Italians soon lost their faith in God, of whom they knew so little. The knife of persecution has no doubt been of service in Rome, and greater care is taken in morals. But there is still ample room for reform. How striking a commentary on the boasted holiness of the Roman Church it is that the fewer the priests in any country the purer are their lives.

A circumstance with which I became personally acquainted while in Rome, showed me that opportunity only was wanted to enable priests to live the guilty and sinful lives which every ecclesiastical history, written *by members of their own Church*, admits to have been the normal condition of the Roman Catholic Church in past ages. A young lady was visiting Rome with her brother in the early part of the year 1884. I was at that time in Rome, and I was asked to go and see her. She was in very delicate health, and at that period was confined to her bed. She was apparently alone in the world, having no relative except a young brother to whom she was guardian, and who appeared to have every confidence in her, and the tenderest affection for her. She was also a person of great wealth.

Miss D—— was attended with unremitting care by two priests, who seemed to be rivals in their devotion. Both were well known in Rome, and were superiors of religious orders. I easily accounted for their attention to this lady, on account of her wealth and her devotion to the Church. So closely did they watch her, that they never left her apartments. If one was absent for a few hours the other remained on guard. As her state of health was not so dangerous as to require such close watching, it seemed strange to me that they should have guarded her so closely. She had also the paid services of a sister belonging to a nursing order of sisters. I could not help thinking that the young and very pretty sister who had the care of the invalid day and night, would have been better employed working for the poor, and a great deal safer.

The poor sister, when she could get a moment free, which was seldom indeed, used to come to my rooms, which were close by, and throw herself on the bed utterly worn out. I thought that her superior would have a good deal to answer for, as certainly she was cruelly overworked, and in a most dangerous position. It was pitiful to see the broken-down look on her face, and to note her depression and utter prostration, and all this was done for a lady who could well afford to have the best of nurses in Rome at her service. I failed to see where the charity came in, or what one who professed to devote her life to the work of a spouse of Christ, could have to do with the service of the rich. In fact, this poor sister worked harder than any servant. Though she did not complain, I could see that she felt the indifference of her superior to her sufferings. In fact, this superior was too full of her imaginary revelations and of plans to trick the bishop, whom she had left in England, to concern herself about so trivial a matter as the health of a sister. Some one, I do not know who, suggested that I should see Miss D——, and a day was appointed for me to call on her.

She was in bed, and certainly looked very ill, but I saw in a moment that there was a great deal more the matter than mere bodily suffering. The poor lady seemed very pleased to see me, and begged me most earnestly to come again soon. I did not ask for her confidence as, though I saw she was ready to give it to me, I thought it would be better not to press her at the time. Even yet, I was not prepared for all the duplicity and deceit which a priest will practise to gain an end. In a day or two, I asked the sister when she thought Miss D—— would like to see me again. She put me off with some excuse, which did not arouse my unsuspicious nature.

These excuses were repeated whenever I asked the same question, till at last even my suspicions were aroused, and I thought that her superior did not like me to get intimate with Miss D——, as of course all were looking to benefit by her money, "for the greater glory of God and the Church." I soon discovered that these suspicions were well founded. I was determined to see the matter through, as I did not think it likely that Miss D—— had changed her mind about wishing to see me. At last the sister told me plainly that the two priests were very angry indeed when they found that she had allowed me to see Miss D——, and that they had given her the most positive orders, which it is needless to say she dared not disobey, that I was never to be allowed to see her again. Such is the tyranny of priests, and such their power. Even in her own house this poor dying lady was not allowed to be mistress.

The young brother, who was greatly to be pitied, was treated with indifferent contempt by all parties. He was very gentle and unassuming, full of Irish veneration for priests, and too innocent in his own life to suspect evil. I knew too well that it would be worse than useless to make any effort to see Miss D—— again, or to try and help her in any way. It need not be said that the priests offered her all the "consolations of religion." Mass was said in her room every day, special blessings were obtained from, and special indulgences asked, and granted by the Pope. At last came a grand climax. The priests, anxious to outdo themselves in their efforts to win her affections and her money, proposed that she should be carried on a litter to the Pope himself, and obtain his blessing personally. So with all possible pomp and circumstances poor Miss D—— was carried to the Vatican, guarded zealously, or jealously, by the priests.

But a few days passed when Rome was startled with a cry of horror. It was discovered that Miss D—— had given birth to an illegitimate child, and murdered it. An intolerable stench in her rooms betrayed the guilty secret. How the affair escaped the knowledge of the sister no one can tell. Miss D—— had arranged to be conveyed to a villa outside the walls of Rome, from whence she expected to be able to make her escape to some distant place. But the priests, fearful of losing their prey if she went too far from them, urged the delay till it was too late. The unhappy woman, without a single friend, committed the crime in the room where Mass was said day after day. At last the people of the house discovered the ghastly secret, and the police were called in. I heard that the superior of the nursing sisters used some very plain language about the folly of the priests in keeping me from Miss D——, as probably if they had allowed me to see her she would have told me her state; and as she knew that I had an extensive experience in dealing with painful cases, she might have asked my advice, and I could have had her quietly removed to a country place before the child of shame was born. But the priests were too eager to secure their prize; and they knew well that a priest can soon reinstate himself, no matter what he does, if he has not committed any sin against the "Church." Sin against the law of God is a matter of comparatively little moment. As for the public, one sensation soon effaces the memory of another.

I heard that the Pope was exceedingly angry when the affair came to his ears, as well he might be. These self-same priests had made a great deal of capital out of their zeal for religion in obtaining the favour of an extraordinary audience for Miss D——. Protestants were duly impressed with the great care which the Church has for the souls of her suffering children, and were not likely to notice specially that this care is most lavishly bestowed on the children who have most money. Even some few Catholics were shocked at the undeniable fact that the priests said Mass daily in Miss D——'s room, and of course heard her confession, and knew all the particulars of her state.

Her young brother was truly to be pitied. He had revered his sister almost as a saint; and as I have said, he was a young man of sensitive mind, and I believe of truly good life. I heard that he remained for hours without eating or moving from the one spot, where he had sunk down in an agony of shame. As for the priests, they took the matter coolly. They were expelled from Rome for a time in deference to public opinion. The police guarded Miss D—— in her house until her death, which took place in a few days after the discovery of her ruin. I never could ascertain what became of her great wealth, or of her poor brother. I heard that he left Rome the day of her funeral and went to England.

The *Popolo Romano* and other Italian papers had full details of the whole affair, with portraits of the actors. It scarcely increased the love of the people for the Roman Church or the respect of the public for priests. But there are, and always will be, a certain class of people so infatuated with a system, no matter what its evils may be, that nothing will lessen their confidence in it. And no doubt there were Catholics who sympathised with the priests when they were obliged to leave Rome, even in "honourable" exile. To a thoughtful mind it was a marked evidence of how Rome works. Here was a young lady of education and good family, availing herself of all the sacraments of the Church, receiving the highest favour which the Pope could confer on her, and living in sin all the time. It is this faith that the Church can save the soul, no matter what the life of the sinner may be, that has been the ruin of thousands. It may be said that the Roman Catholic Church does not teach this doctrine. Certainly it does not teach it in plain words. But it teaches it practically; and it is by its works it should be judged in this world, and by its works it will most assuredly be judged in the next.

It might be supposed that these two priests would have been disgraced for ever. But such is far from being the case. I can scarcely say how shocked I was when I heard a short time since that one of them was in New York, received, of course, with all honour by the ecclesiastical authorities there. Such honour and such reception was denied to me, though I had the good fortune to have the Pope's recommendation, which nevertheless I was told was of no use. The more fortunate priest had come to beg for a new Church in Rome. Once more I could not but admire the skill and craft of the priesthood. There are numerous churches in Rome, as every traveller well knows, and one of them would hold nearly all the church-goers of that city. But what matter? To build a new church, whether wanted or not, is considered so meritorious a work, that it will cover any number of sins. Thus it was that the mediæval baron used to wipe away the stain of a life of crime, by donating to the Church, when he had no more use for them, the lands which he had plundered from some one weaker than himself. The priest wanted to get back to Rome. It is a pleasanter place than exile, and has much to interest the resident. Besides, he wanted to wipe out the recollection of his adventure, and to win back the Pope's favour. But it was necessary, before he could build the Church, to get the money to build it. The plan which he hit on was certainly a masterpiece of diplomacy.

It is what is called in England "bringing coals to Newcastle" to build a church in Rome. Of course the Papal authorities would be pleased; but, as I have said, they would not supply the money. Who was to do it? The priest was not at a loss. The Irish are always ready to be plundered, and an appeal to their piety or patriotism never fails. There was not a church in all Rome dedicated to St. Patrick. This was easily represented as a great injustice to the Irish nation. With the hundreds of churches there, somehow St. Patrick was overlooked. It was quite too shocking. It did not occur to the ever-credulous Irish that they were asked to give themselves a present; but what matter?

The priest got back to Rome. It did not matter that the church might never be built. The plan to do it, and the money to do it, was all that was necessary. It did not matter that there was already a church in Rome where there was an Irish community, and where for many centuries the feast of St. Patrick was kept with all pomp and solemnity, and that the long-established custom of calling this the "Irish Church" made it unlikely that a new church would attract its worshippers, few as they were.

The priest wanted to get back to Rome and to the favour of the Pope, and he accomplished his object.

CHAPTER III.

THE CELIBACY OF THE CLERGY IN THE MIDDLE AGES.

"Full well ye reject the commandment of God, that ye may keep your own tradition."—MARK vii. 9.

THERE is no question whatever that the priests of the Catholic Church, in the first ages of the Church's history, were allowed to marry. There was no law, human or Divine, against the marriage of the clergy. We have shown what cannot be disputed, that the Holy Scripture, in its express teaching, approves, and we might almost say expects, the marriage of the clergy. Why should such particular instructions be given as to how the minister was to bring up and rule his family, if it was unlawful to have a family, or even if it was more perfect for him to remain a celibate? The question seems one of common sense. We now proceed to show from Roman Catholic sources the origin of the unscriptural command to abstain from marriage, and the fatal result of being wiser than the God who made us.

The arguments made by Roman Catholic theologians to defend the enforced celibacy of the clergy are amusing. They may satisfy the ignorant, but they will never convince those Romanists and Protestants who have the facts of history before their eyes, as written by Papal historians and theologians. I shall refer the reader to three indisputable Roman Catholic authorities on this subject. I will first mention St. Augustine, who was one of the early Fathers. I may remark in passing that it was very necessary for the Roman Catholic Church to put some portions of St. Augustine's works on the Index of expurgated books, for there are so many anti-Roman Catholic statements in the writings of this great author, that he might have proved a dangerous antagonist. As regards St. Augustine, I need do no more than to mention his name. With regard to other authorities, though they are all well known to the learned, those who have not had special opportunities of study may not be familiar with their names or writings; and as I am anxious to make this book available as an authority to all, I give some information as to the others from whose works I quote.

Gratian belonged to the learned Order of Benedictines, and lived in the twelfth century. He occupied twenty-four years in compiling an abridgment of the canon law of the Roman Church, and this is known as "Gratian's Decretals." He freely admitted that the clergy were allowed to marry in the early Church, and indeed no one can deny this. Thomas Aquinas, a canonised saint, whose name need only be mentioned, so well is he known as the great theologian of Rome, admits, as freely, that celibacy was not a law of the early Church; and in this connection he uses a curious argument well worth noting. He says (*Summa* II. ii.) that the early Christians were so much holier than their (Roman Catholic) descendants, that it was not necessary to enforce a law of celibacy on the clergy. This is a curious and valuable admission. It is an evidence that, in the opinion of this great divine, who certainly ought to have known the social and moral state of his Church well, it had sorely degenerated. The fact was simply that the Roman Catholic clergy lived, in his day, such grossly immoral lives, under a law of enforced celibacy, that they had corrupted the Church, and as a necessary consequence demoralised the world. There is indeed an overwhelming consensus of Roman Catholic evidence to prove that clerical celibacy was simply a rule of the Roman Church, and that it was not a rule of the Gospel. In 1564 Pope Pius IV., in an encyclical letter to the German princes, explains the enforced celibacy of the clergy as a necessity of the age.

An evidence which is important from two points of view may be quoted here. The Bishop of Portus denounced Pope Calixtus for admitting men to the priesthood who had married twice. This shows that the abject submission to Rome of the bishops of modern times was then unknown, and it shows also that there was nothing against the marriage of priests. So common was the marriage of the clergy, or rather so little was it against the rule or custom of the Church, that in A.D. 414 we find Pope Innocent I. complaining that many bishops were married to widows. The fact was that the early Christians were undoubtedly influenced by Pagan ideas in more respects than would have been supposed possible. When the Jesuits went to evangelise India, they were surprised to find so close a resemblance between the rites and ceremonies of the Pagans, whom they had come to convert, and their own. They were at a loss to understand this, and were divided in opinion as to whether the devil, who is generally fathered with the inexplicable, had parodied the Christian religion, or whether it was the traditions of a pre-existing knowledge of the Catholic faith.

It is remarkable that while marriage was respected and encouraged both amongst priests and people in the Jewish Church, it was forbidden in many countries to those who were dedicated to the service of false gods. As far as the "Fathers" of the Church are concerned, they differed with each other, and even with themselves, so constantly, that their testimony on disputed points is really of little value. It may be remarked here, in this connection, that Pope Leo the Great, who is the first Pope whose writings have been preserved, excommunicated every one who received the sacrament in one kind only. The Manichæan heresy was then rife; and one of the tenets of this half-Pagan sect was that the cup should be given only to the priesthood.

It would require a volume, or rather several volumes, to give a full history of the introduction of sacerdotal celibacy into the Roman Church; but we are more concerned with the results of this observance than with the origin of it. There are a multitude of records of local synods, and enactments of pastorals and of local councils, all tending in the same direction, and all having the same object. This was unquestionably to make the Church more powerful, by making the clergy a distinct class, by detaching them from all secular (personal) interests, and by concentrating their energies, as well as their interests, on the one grand object. The one question for us, and for all believers in the Gospel of Christ, is, not how this regulation worked for the increased power of the Church, but how far it tended to the increased holiness of its members?

As I purpose in another chapter to give some account of the lives of the Popes, who according to the Roman Catholic Church have held the most awful and responsible power which God ever gave to man, I shall say but little of them at present. Popes, emperors, princes, and some few prelates tried again and again, to stem the torrent of corruption, which was ever growing in the Roman Church, as the inevitable outcome of the effort to enforce celibacy. In the fifteenth century the Rector of the University of Paris, who was also the private secretary of Pope Benedict XIII., declared that the vices of the clergy were so universal, that there was little faith left in the virtue of any ecclesiastic. In the same century Gerson recommended an organised system of concubinage, as preferable to the gross immoralities of the "celibate" clergy. The very fact that such a proposition should be seriously made, is in itself an evidence of the evil which is inevitable, when man tries to be wiser than God in regulating human affairs.

Nor were the priests alone guilty. Gerson, whose authority cannot be questioned, since he is one of the shining lights of the Church of Rome, says that the nuns in the fourteenth century were as guilty as the priests and friars. He says the nunneries of his time were "houses of prostitution, the monasteries were only used for purposes of trade and amusement, while the priests, at best, were keepers of concubines." His writings are well known, and their authenticity has never been questioned, while his position, for many years, as the Chancellor of the University of Paris, gave him ample opportunity for acquiring correct information. He took a leading part in the Council of Constance, and lived and died in full communion with the Roman Church. Nicolas de Clemanges, already mentioned as the secretary of Pope Benedict XIII., says, "that to take the veil was simply to become a public prostitute."

The plea of modern bishops, that it is better to have intemperate priests than not to have any, which is acted on every day in the present century by bishops, who dare not inflict too heavy a censure on priests who are guilty of drunkenness, had its counterpart in this age, when it was declared openly by the Chancellor of the University of Paris, that it was better to tolerate incontinent priests than to have none. Theodric à Niem, who wrote a history of the Council of Constance, declared, merely as a matter of fact, and without making it a reproach, that some bishops carried their concubines with them when they went to make their pastoral visitations; and indeed many bishops made a considerable income by demanding large fees from their clergy for the permission to keep concubines.

The state of the Church was such at the time of the Council of Constance, that the three honest men who gave themselves to the work of reform were well nigh in despair. These were the men already mentioned. After the Council had sat for two years, Clemanges declared that as the members of this " general" Council themselves " considered reform the greatest evil which could befall them," they were not very likely to make any effort in that direction. The contemporary accounts of this Council, and be it remembered that all these writers were Roman Catholics, inform us that crowds of people flocked to this meeting of the heads of the Roman Catholic Church. The number of " courtesans " ran well up into thousands, and the jugglers and play-actors were nearly as numerous.

Every effort was made to purify the Church by the few reformers. Even the Papal privileges were sharply assailed. It had been made a law of the Church that the children of priests should not be allowed ecclesiastical preferment; but infallible Popes were constantly giving (for a consideration, of course) exemptions from this rule. It was now sought, but uselessly, to cut off this papal prerogative. The ecclesiastics of Italy and Germany were equally immoral, and equally unwilling to reform. Cardinal Branda, who was sent by Pope Martin V. to preach a crusade against the Hussites, has left his testimony on record. He says concubinage, simony, gambling, drinking, and fighting were the occupations of the priests of the "holy" Roman Church. In 1428 the bishops of Angiers declared that licentiousness had become so habitual amongst the clergy that it was no longer considered a sin. The Archdeacon of Paris says, that he attributes to enforced celibacy and the great wealth of the Church, all the crimes which had made the clergy so odious in the sight of the laity.

This miserable condition of the "holy" Roman Catholic Church was universal. How little Roman Catholics, who live in the fond delusion that their Church has been always holy, know of its real history. To try to enlighten them seems almost a hopeless task, so deeply are they imbued with the false teaching of those whose very existence depends on concealment of evil. The same causes which worked the ruin of the Church of Rome in those countries where she was able to sin unreproved, are always at work, and sooner or later, every country where Rome gains unrestrained power will know the truth when it is too late.

From time to time some earnest souls spoke out, and denounced the wickedness of ecclesiastics in high places. Martyrdom was the usual reward of their fearlessness. Rome does not tolerate reformers. A Church which can burn or destroy any one who dares to reprove the evil in it is safe for a time. But the hour of retribution will surely come. In the year

1414, Henry V. had a series of articles prepared with a view to the reformation of the Church in England. This monarch preceded the Reformers in the work of trying to reclaim what was past redemption. In these articles the undisguised profligacy of the priests is fully described, and deplored. So terrible was the evil, and so injurious to public morals, that public chastisement was proposed to be inflicted on those priests who persisted in open fornication, the pecuniary fine, which had been the only penalty hitherto adopted, not being of the least avail to check the ever-growing evil.

But of what use were all efforts at reform, when the court of Rome made merchandise of souls? Even when she denounced the evil she "reserved" special cases, which would bring her increased wealth; and thereby she sanctioned the continuance of sin in her own priesthood, and what was, if possible, still worse, she made sin a matter of trade.

The following facts are taken from one of the most important books which has ever been published on the Roman controversy. The title of the work is, "An Historical Sketch of Sacerdotal Celibacy." One great value of this work is that its author, Mr. Lea, shuns polemics. There is not one word of controversy, or of anything approaching to it, in the whole work from end to end. It is simply an historical *resumé* of facts bearing on the question of the celibacy of the clergy.

In the second place, the work has been compiled from authentic documents, which, though they are scarce, are nevertheless known to scholars, and are accessible in such libraries as make a speciality of rare works. In every case the reference is given to the authority from which each statement is taken. Roman Catholics have not even attempted to answer this book. In fact, silence in regard to it is their best policy, as all the statements are taken from Roman Catholic sources, and many of them from the published decrees of episcopal synods in all ages of the Church. How any honest man could read this book, and still call the Roman Church "holy," is past comprehension.

But it need scarcely be said that books like this, written for the student, are not easily accessible to the general public, the price and other causes limiting the circulation; and it must be borne in mind that if a priest discovered that any Romanist had been studying Mr. Lea's book he would certainly give him a severe penance, and strictly forbid him to read another word of the volume. The truth about the Roman Church, whether historical or social, is the last thing which the Church can afford to have known. There is a curious little tract, printed in Cologne in 1505, with the approbation of the faculty, which is directed against concubinage in general, but particularly against that of the priests. Its laborious accumulation of authorities to prove that licentiousness is a sin is abundant evidence of the existing demoralisation, while the practices which it combats of guilty ecclesiastics who were in the habit of granting absolution to each other, shows how easily the safeguards with which the Church had sought to surround her ministers were eluded.

The degradation of the priesthood, indeed, can easily be measured when, in the little town of Hof, in Vogtland, three priests could be found defiling the sacredness of Ash Wednesday by fiercely fighting over a courtesan in a house of ill-fame, or when

Leo. X., in a feeble effort at reform, was obliged to argue that systematic licentiousness was not rendered excusable because its prevalence amounted to a custom, or because it was openly tolerated by those whose duty it was to repress the evil. In fact, a clause in the Concordat with Francis I. in 1516, renewing and enhancing the former punishments for public concubinage, would almost justify the presumption that the principal result of the rule of celibacy was to afford to the officials a regular revenue derived from the sale of licenses to sin. The old abuse, which rises before us in every age from the time of Damiani to Hildebrand, and which, since John XXII. had framed the tariff of absolutions for crime, now well known as the "Taxes of the Apostolic Penitentiary," had the authority of the papacy itself to justify it. In this curious document we find that a concubinary priest could procure absolution for less than a ducat, "in spite of all provincial and synodal constitutions;" while half a ducat was sufficient to absolve for incest committed with a mother or a sister.

That no concealment was thought necessary, and that sensual indulgence was not deemed derogatory in any way to the character of a Christian prelate, may be reasonably deduced from the panegyric of Gerard of Nimeguen on Philip of Burgundy, grand-uncle of Charles V., a learned and accomplished man, who filled the important see of Utrecht from 1517 to 1524. Gerard alludes to the amorous propensities and promiscuous intrigues of his patron without reserve; and as his book was dedicated to the Archduchess Margaret, sister of Charles V., it is evident that he did not feel his remarks to be defamatory. The good prelate, too, no doubt represented the convictions of a large portion of his class, when he was wont to smile at those who urged the propriety of celibacy, and to declare his belief in the impossibility of chastity among men who, like the clergy, "were pampered with high living and tempted by indolence." Those who professed to keep their vows inviolate he denounced as hypocrites of the worst description; and he deemed them far worse than their brethren, who sought to avoid unnecessary scandal by keeping their concubines at home.

Even this reticence, however, was considered unnecessary by a large portion of the clergy. In 1512, the Bishop of Ratisbon issued a series of canons, in which, after quoting the Basilian regulations, he adds that many of his ecclesiastics maintain their concubines so openly that it would appear as though they saw neither sin nor scandal in such conduct, and that their evil example was the efficient cause of corrupting the faithful. In Switzerland the same abuses were quite as prevalent, if we may believe a memorial presented in 1533 by the citizens of Lausanne, complaining of the conduct of their clergy. They rebuked the incontinence of the priests, whose numerous children were accustomed to earn a living by beggary in the streets; but the canons were the subject of their especial objurgation. The dean of the chapter had defied an excommunication launched at him for buying a house near the church in which to keep his mistress; others of the canons had taken to themselves the wives of citizens and refused to give them up; but the quaintest grievance of which they had been guilty was the injury which their competition inflicted on the public brothel of the town. What was the condition of clerical morality in Italy may be gathered from the stories of Bishop Bandello, who, as a Dominican and a prelate, may fairly be deemed to represent the tone of the thinking and educated classes of society. The cynical levity with which he relates scandalous tales about monks and priests, shows that in the public mind sacerdotal immorality was regarded almost as a matter of course.

CHAPTER IV.

THE OUTSIDE TEACHING AND THE INSIDE PRACTICE OF THE CHURCH OF ROME.

"In vain do they worship Me, teaching for doctrines the commandments of men."—MARK vii. 7.

IT can scarcely be a matter of surprise that the members of a Church which at least discourages the study of history, and which forbids the unrestrained reading of the Bible, should be in ignorance of the true history of the Church to which they belong. But this ignorance is by no means confined to members of this Church, which has so much reason to dread the light of truth. There are very few persons who make a careful and exhaustive study of any subject, unless compelled to do so by special circumstances; and to the vast multitude, books, which would give the information necessary to form an unbiassed opinion, are not easily accessible, even if the general public had the leisure to peruse them. But this need not be a hindrance to the most accurate knowledge of the past history of this strange world of ours. Compendiums of history or of general information may be had, and are within reach of the purse and the leisure of all; nor is it by any means difficult for the ordinary reader to judge as to the veracity of the compiler. A general honesty or dishonesty of purpose makes itself apparent at the first glance to an intelligent mind. Prejudice defeats itself by its very manifestation. After reading a few pages of any work of importance the reader would do well to ask himself, Is this writer worthy of my confidence? There are certain names which are a guarantee for honour and honesty, and there are men on whose statements we may rely with every confidence. But there is one plain and obvious test of accuracy.

If a well-known Protestant writer quotes from recognised authorities, we may be sure that a respect for his own reputation will make his quotations accurate, and therefore reliable. We have used the word Protestant, not without consideration. Unhappily, Roman Catholic writers, as we shall prove later, are on many points absolutely unreliable, and persist in historical misquotations, and in the use of authorities long since discarded as forgeries, even by some of their own writers. We have, then, in the works of reliable authors, a ready means of obtaining correct knowledge of any subject of which they treat; and we may enjoy, at their expense of brain and labour, what we could not otherwise obtain for ourselves.

I am very well aware that Roman Catholics will deny that their Church discourages the study of history, and forbids the indiscriminate reading of the Bible. But I shall prove, from their own ecclesiastical enactments, that such is the case.

It is dishonest, and unworthy of a man of common intellect to contradict, or try to explain away, the plain statements of the heads of his Church. If a Roman Catholic denies or tries to explain away the doctrines of his Church he is simply a Protestant, and he does this either because he is ashamed of these doctrines, or because he is ignorant of them. There are, in fact, more Protestants in this sense of the word in the Roman Church than is generally supposed. The truth is, that some of the doctrines and practices of the Church of Rome are so monstrous, that when Roman Catholics of intelligence are brought face to face with them, and their necessary consequences, they are aghast with shame and amazement, and have no resource but denial of their own creed. For example, the Roman Catholic Church teaches plainly and undeniably in her catechisms that all Protestants, except in cases of "invincible ignorance," will be damned, no matter how good their lives may be. A Romanist brought face to face with this monstrous doctrine is heartily ashamed of it, and denies it. A priest who is faced with it by a Protestant inquirer or controversialist tries to minimise it. But of what use? The fact remains the same.

The doctrinal teaching of the catechism cannot be altered, even to deceive Protestants or anxious inquirers. The decrees of the Church and the decisions of Councils remain. But there are so many people in the world who are too lazy to investigate for themselves, and who take their information at second hand, with little inquiry as to the source from which it has come, that they are easily deceived. The Romanist will tell his Protestant friend that he has "asked the priest," and that the priest has assured him "it is all a mistake;" and the Protestant friend goes to his better enlightened friend, and assures him that "the priest ought to know best, and that he has said that the Roman Church does not teach that all Protestants will be damned." And so the matter ends. The Protestant is thoroughly and deliberately deceived, not having access to Roman Catholic catechisms or theologians which teach this doctrine.

When Galileo was compelled by the infallible Church to swear to what he knew was a lie, he did so, and let us pity him while we blame; but he had, for all that, his "mental reservation," a resource allowed and indeed approved by Jesuit theology, as we shall see presently from their own writings.

Condemned as he was to lie, not only in the name of God, but in the name also of the blessed Virgin, or to bear punishment for telling the truth, he did what thousands have done before and since; he believed in truth, but submitted to brute force.

When Pius IX., or, as he might well be called, Pius the ambitious, got himself proclaimed "infallible," in spite of the "infallible" teachings to the contrary of his infallible predecessors, there were many bishops, and thousands of the laity, who revolted against this new doctrine, which had not been "delivered to the saints," and which clearly came under the Apostolic ban, since St. Paul has declared that if even an angel from heaven should preach any other Gospel to the world, than that which he had preached, he would be accursed. It is indeed marvellous how many curses this Church of Rome, which is the Church of cursing for others, has brought on herself in her, let us hope, unconscious impiety.

When the doctrine of the personal infallibility of the Popes past, present, and to come, was proclaimed as being as obligatory on the belief of all Romanists as the doctrine of the existence of God Himself, there were, as I have said, thousands of men who would have none of it. These men were, by birth and by education, Roman Catholics; they had all the attachment to their creed and to their religion which is the natural consequence of inheriting it as a birthright.

A choice had to be made between accepting a new article of faith, and the abandonment of the Church of Rome. These men could scarcely be expected to understand that if they opposed the dogma, it was the Church which had left them, and not they who had left the Church. But that Church, with a wisdom which can scarcely be called Divine, considering the use which is made of it, solved the difficult problem in her usual convenient fashion. Confessors were told not to ask troublesome questions, but to give absolution to all who might ask it, if they did not positively declare their refusal to accept the new creed; and so the difficulty was wisely, if not honestly, tided over for the time.

If Rome had the temporal power for which she so ardently craves, these recalcitrant children of the Church would have had a short shrift and a fiery grave; but it was deemed, above all things, advisable to have an appearance of unanimity in acceptance of this new departure from the faith once delivered to the saints. It matters little to Rome whether this unanimity is secured by force or fraud, so that it is obtained. The eyes of Europe were on the Vatican Council at that moment to note every difficulty. The ubiquitous and inquisitive nineteenth century reporter was abroad in the land. An open declaration of revolt or objection was, above all things, to be dreaded and avoided; and it was avoided. Future generations will read with great edification of the " marvellous unanimity " of acceptance which greeted this proclamation of the Pope's infallibility ; and this " fact " will be appealed to as another note of the Church's unity, and as another proof of its Divine character, and, above all, of the wisdom of the Pontiff, and his special enlightenment by the Holy Ghost, in proclaiming this new departure in faith.

The young men who will be educated in Roman Catholic colleges, and young women educated by Roman Catholic sisters in coming years, will not be allowed to read any history of the times which has not been carefully expurgated of those facts which refute Papal Infallibility; and so the lie will continue to be believed, and will be handed down to posterity, in the name and for the honour of the God of Eternal Truth.

Silence as to the existence of known evil has always been, and always will be, the price of peace in the Roman Church. It is not unjust to that Church to say this, because it is true; and it can never be unjust to make the truth known in such cases, for eternal justice demands it. Why should evil be condoned and concealed? Do we not become participators in evil when we conceal the evildoer from the just punishment of his crime? What government on the face of the earth would demand from its subjects that evildoers should be protected in their crime by silence? What government would condemn the exposer of evil, and let the doer go free? And yet this is done every day, and has been done for centuries by the Church of Rome. A careful study of history will prove that this, sad as it is, is an indisputable historical fact. A little knowledge of the inside life of the Roman Church will prove it to be an every-day occurrence. My own history proves it. If I had been silent as to the commission of evil, I might still be an honoured member of the Church of Rome, but I should be this at the cost of self-respect and conscience.

I have seen a priest drunk at the altar; I have seen a priest who had been guilty of the ruin of four of his school-teachers removed to another diocese, but only to be welcomed there, and never the worse thought of for his sin, or the scandal he gave, public as it was. But if one dared to speak of it publicly, that indeed was a crime too terrible for forgiveness.

My experience of the Church of Rome is, that the only sin for which there is no forgiveness is to condemn evil, and the only fault for which there is no pardon is to try to work for the good of the poor and suffering, unless this work is done in a way which will bring temporal advantage to ecclesiastics. Has not Dr. McGlynn boldly and publicly stated that the priest who puts the largest sum of money in the bishop's Prayer Book when he comes to the priest's house, is the best beloved of those men who profess to be the only true followers of Him who had not where to lay His head?

I have seen a priest in Kenmare lay himself full length on a convent lounge, and put his head in the lap of a sister who was sitting on it, and who dared not condemn the outrage, because of the position which the priest held. She could only express her unutterable disgust and loathing of his drunken familiarities by her expression of contempt and hatred, and by not paying the very least attention to him as he lay there. I do not say that such scenes are common in convents, but I know such things are not altogether uncommon, though I have said many times in public, and say again, that as far as my experience goes, sisters are moral, and few priests would dare to approach them for immoral purposes.

The irresponsible power of the bishop over the priest, and the irresponsible power of the superior of the convent over the sisters, is the source of fearful evil. The sister to whom this outrage was offered, for

I can only call it an outrage, had already felt the weight of the tyrannical rule of an evil-tempered and cruel superior; and she knew well that if she said one word of the conduct of a favourite, her position, which was already harder than she could bear, would have been made intolerable. It is certainly very convenient for the doers of evil to feel sure that their deeds of darkness will be concealed; and we may add that this compulsory system of concealment, though it may for a time appear to be a strength to the Church, becomes eventually the cause of its decay.

There is another source of temporary strength as well as of eventual weakness in the Roman Church, and this is found in a servile press, which dares not even mention the shortcomings of priests, unless they are so extremely notorious as to compel attention; and even then the subject is dropped with an alacrity which should at least arouse the suspicions of those who are not aware of the motive for this suppression. If the Roman Church herself denounced and punished the sin of her priests or of her subjects, there would not be so much cause for blame. But this is far from being the case. Evil is weighed not by its real sinfulness, but by its effects on the "Church." Have we not daily examples of this? Does not the whole world know that the present Duke of Aosta obtained the Pope's permission to commit incest for the sum of $50,000? This was at the time a matter of public notoriety; but I doubt if there was one newspaper in the United States of America which would have dared to publish a criticism on this Papal permission to sin, such is the power of the Church to protect evil. Public opinion, which is in all governments the great safeguard of liberty, and the great protection of good government, is non-existent wherever the Church of Rome has power.

The cesspool of evil must not be stirred; the festering sore must not be probed; and the inevitable result is rottenness and corruption. In fact, the idea that a priest cannot sin was at one time so firmly believed in Ireland, the only country in the civilised world which held far into this century to papal superstitions, that no matter what a priest did he was exempt from criticism. No matter how sinful the deed might be, it was supposed that the fact that the sinner was a priest excused it; and the crime of accusing a priest of a sin, no matter how plain the evidence might be, was made to appear so terrible that he would be a brave man indeed who would peril his eternal interest by even a passing remark, and it may be added, that his temporal interests would not fail to suffer also.

Instead of sin being considered more sinful if the defilement was in the sanctuary, it was held practically to be just the reverse. There are certainly some things in which Rome keeps to her proud boast of never changing. Burdened with the incubus of her infallibility, she must perish sooner than save herself by reform; and for all practical purposes she has perished in every European country where she once reigned as a queen, save only in unhappy Ireland. Yet even in Ireland there are symptoms that her power is not what it was, and even there she must temporise to rule. It was the proud boast of Pius IX. that America was the only country where he could be a king, and the boast unhappily is but too well founded. But America will find out, though it may be through loss of her liberties, what Rome, and Italy, and France have discovered long since —that Rome and freedom cannot exist in the same state. The reins of ecclesiastical government are held loosely at present in the United States, and the whip of persecution is hidden away under the flatteries of a priesthood trained to diplomacy; but the time for tightening the reins will come, and the time for using the whip will follow. Let it be said once more, Rome cannot change. Her very existence is bound up in her infallibility. When the Romish hierarchy has anything to gain by flattery and diplomacy, when she cannot persecute because she cannot command the secular power to do her bidding as she did in the days when she burned Joan of Arc at the stake, for the love of God, and burned Bruno at the stake, in Rome, to show her appreciation of intellectual freedom, then she speaks softly to the confiding heretic. She throws the dust of her flatteries in his eyes, until she can place the fetters of her power on his hands. And she finds fools who will listen to her, some for love of that political power which she claims a right to exercise, by right of the position she claims of supreme ruler of all the affairs of human life. The greedy politician accepts the help, which, appreciating his greed, she offers so graciously. Why should he not use her for his purpose? Why, indeed? But in his infatuated blindness he fails to see that she is using him for her purposes, until she can crush him at her pleasure. Men who care for neither politics nor science, but who are impressed by power and position, are the easy prey of this powerful Church. They are freely applauded for their "liberality" by a Church which will deprive them of liberty the very hour in which she has attained, through false liberality, the power to crush all liberty except that of those who submit abjectly to her ruling in all matters temporal and spiritual. The struggle between the human race and the power of Rome has never ceased since she took on herself to proclaim to a subservient world that her rights were quite as much temporal as spiritual, the words of her Divine Master, of Him whom she claims to be her Master, notwithstanding. She claims a power which Christ Himself has expressly declared that His Church should not exercise. In all the plenitude of her rule in the Middle Ages, when Popes made and unmade kings and emperors, in all the poverty of her decadence, when even her own subjects would have none of her rule, the Popes continued the same cry, "My kingdom must be of this world." Our Divine Lord sent forth His disciples without scrip or staff; the Popes cannot maintain the power which they profess to derive from Him without crowns and palaces. How ghastly the contrast between Christ poor and humble, and the Popes crowned and enthroned. If there was no other evidence against the Roman Church but only her failure in following the Master whom she professes to serve, this alone should be sufficient.

And what has been the result of all this demand for earthly power, and pomp, and authority? Let the history of the Popes of Rome tell the miserable tale. It is no wonder that Rome is afraid of history, that Cardinal Manning, a churchman of churchmen, has uttered these memorable words: "An appeal to history is a treason to the Church." What, are we to abandon our very senses, as well as our God-given reason, to the Church? And what does this Church offer us in return? A certainty of salvation, if we can only bring ourselves to believe that her contradictory creed is divinely inspired, that the faith once delivered to the saints may be added to at the convenience and caprice of "infallible" sinners, whose lives were too often a disgrace to our common humanity.

I am about to show that the lives of these infallible Popes, who have taken on themselves to remodel the Gospel, to abridge the commandments, to retain or to hold the soul from bliss or woe, have been so scandalous, that the much-decried Henry VIII. was a very model of virtue in comparison. But even as the earth moved in its divinely appointed course despite the opposition of ignorant Cardinals and jealous Popes, so also the facts of history remain to confound the pride of a Church which claims to sit as the queen of virtue, and desires that all shall call her holy despite her utter corruption, and her persistence in denying it. Of her truly it may be said, "Thou sayest I am rich, and increased with goods, and have need of nothing, and knowest not that thou art wretched, and miserable, and poor, and blind, and naked." In vain have the very saints of the Church of Rome, who have been saints not because they belonged to her, but because they abhorred her iniquities, called on her to repent. In vain did a Francis reproach the Church with her love of riches, or a Catherine of Siena cry out against the corruption of her priests and Popes. All has been in vain, and will be so until she has fulfilled the measure of her crimes, and ended the term of the Divine patience towards her iniquities.

I am very well aware that these words of truth and soberness will not be acceptable to those whose evil deeds are denounced, nor to those who desire peace at the cost of principle. Such people are the curse of humanity. Under the cloak of charity they are guilty of the most serious breach of charity. Those who support the evildoer, whether by silence when speech is a duty, or by assent which lies perilously near consent, are alike guilty.

It needs some moral courage to stand for the right when all the powers of evil are prepared to make us suffer for it. Why should Rome be so afraid of facts? Why should she be so afraid of knowledge? Why, if her cause is so sure and so Divine, should she be so afraid of the least criticism, or the least independent inquiry? It is a noteworthy fact that Roman Catholics are the only religious body who get angry when the tenets of their Church are made the subject of discussion. Other religious denominations can discuss their respective creeds without excitement or acrimony. But one word of disapproval sets the Romanist in a flame of anger and excitement, and leaves no hope of calm and judicial investigation.

And the same anger and excitement may be observed in the discussion of any scandal which may arise. The members of other Churches will quietly discuss the circumstances of any discreditable conduct on the part of a minister of their creed. But their creed does not depend for its acceptance on the personal infallibility of any individual. It is not so in the Roman Church. If the most trifling event is commented upon in which a priest or bishop has acted, even unwisely, though the action may not have been criminal, the person who dares even to allude to the matter is at once denounced as an enemy of the Church. It would be amusing, if it were not sad, to observe the conduct of Roman ecclesiastics in regard to those who leave their Church. They may be pardoned for condemning them to eternal perdition, as their creed teaches them to do this; but where is the tender charity of Christ towards those whom they believe to be in error? Where is the desire to reclaim the fallen? Where is the hand of the Shepherd stretched out to recall the wandering sheep? Where, I may rather ask, is the Christianity? There is no convert who has left the Roman Church who has not been the victim of the most outrageous reviling, and often of the most carefully elaborated calumnies. Where does Christianity come in when such is the regular practice of Rome? What claim has a Church to be called the "Holy" Church when it acts as if it could not exist without the support of lying and defamation?

CHAPTER V.

IMPORTANCE OF UNDERSTANDING THE ROMAN CATHOLIC DOCTRINE OF INFALLIBILITY CLEARLY.

"Behold, I lay in Zion a chief corner stone, elect, precious: and he that believeth on Him shall not be confounded."—1 PETER ii. 6.

CHRIST is the chief corner stone of the Christian Church. The dogma of the infallibility of the Church of Rome is its sole support. Deprived of this doctrine the whole fabric falls to the ground. If Rome is not infallible she descends at once to the level of the sects above which she exalts herself, and which do not profess to be infallible in the sense in which Rome claims infallibility. Nothing is ever gained for the cause of truth by mistaking or misrepresenting the case of an adversary. Rome does this without hesitation, as when she teaches that Protestants are infidels, and have no religion; and that she does teach this I shall give proof from her own mouth.

But in order to understand the subject thoroughly, and to realise its immense controversial importance, we must ask what Rome means by her claim of infallibility, and how she exercises this claim. We shall give the very words of the Roman catechism as taught by the authorities of the Roman Church; and she cannot certainly refuse to accept her own authorised teaching.

We find in a Catechism of Christian Doctrine (note

the exact expression), published with the special approbation of Cardinal Gibbons, and approved January 3rd, 1888, that the following definition of the Pope's infallibility is given :—

"Q. What power had St. Peter as supreme head of the Church?

"A. Peter had the power to govern the whole Church of Christ, the pastors, and the faithful, make laws for them, and enforce these laws.

"Q. What special gift did Christ ask of His heavenly Father for St. Peter, as the teacher of His whole Church?

"A. Christ asked of His heavenly Father to bestow upon St. Peter the special gift of teaching infallibly His whole doctrine. 'I have prayed for thee,' said our Divine Saviour to St. Peter, 'that thy faith fail not; and thou, being once converted, confirm thy brethren' (Luke xxii. 32)."

Now for a sample of special pleading this is certainly unique. Everything is taken for granted; nothing is proved; the word "confirm" is used instead of the word "strengthen," another evidence of how Rome, when she appeals to Scripture, changes its meaning to serve her purpose. But even as the text is quoted by Rome, there is not one word in it to support the monstrous assertion that "Christ asked for Peter the special gift of teaching infallibly His whole doctrine." There is not even anything approaching such an expression; but Roman Catholic children who are taught this Catechism are not allowed to reason or discuss the matter. Their duty begins and ends with learning the words of the Catechism, and also, let it be well noted, of believing that whatever interpretation is put on the words of Scripture, must be accepted as the true interpretation. Rome says that in these words Christ asked His heavenly Father to bestow the gift of infallible teaching on St. Peter, the words not bearing the least proof of this notwithstanding.

But there is yet more. It remained to be proved that the successors of St. Peter were infallible also. But this could not be difficult to an infallible Church. No attempt is made to find Scripture for this doctrine. A Council, which was not held until 1438, is fathered with the responsibility; so that, according to this catechism, it took the Church fourteen hundred years to find out that the successors of St. Peter were infallible.

Here is the question and answer.

"Q. Who is the lawful successor of St. Peter?

"A. The lawful successor of St. Peter is the Pope or Bishop of Rome." (*Council of Florence*, 1438.)

Such an important matter having been thus proved past all question to the hapless and ignorant learner, the next statement is easy,- shall we say the next step in deceit?—and in the most cruel of all deceit, the deceit of the young is accomplished.

"Q. What power has the Pope as the lawful successor of St. Peter?

"A. As lawful successor of St. Peter, the Pope has the same gift and power of infallibility that St. Peter had from Christ."

The cool assurance is amusing of thus "proving" a doctrine on the authority of a text which does not even allude to the subject of St. Peter's infallibility, and then asserting, without a shadow of proof, that the

Pope is also infallible. And all this is taught to children who have not, and who are deliberately prevented from ever having, any proof that it is mere assertion. Let it even be supposed that Christ did pray that St. Peter might be personally infallible, where is there one word, or even one inference, that his successors were to be so? What an awful account these men will have to give at the last great day for the way in which they have deceived the ignorant; and above all for the blasphemy with which they have invented words for Christ which He never said, and then used them for the destruction of the world. What a stupendous fabric of deceit has been thus built up, and what untold misery has been the result.

If, notwithstanding the prayer and presence of Christ Himself, Peter denied his Master with oaths and curses, how can the successors of St. Peter, even if he had successors, hope to be more secure?

It is certainly a matter of no small moment for the Protestants of the whole Christian world to know what is taught, by the express authority of the Church, to the young, who will have the fate of empires and states in their control in a few short years. Now on the page which contains the episcopal and Papal approbation for these Catechisms (for this is one of a series prepared for use in parochial schools), a long list is given of Roman dignitaries who have expressed their great admiration of this system of Christian doctrine, and last, but not least, in the estimation of pious Roman Catholics, and in importance to us, is the approbation of Rome itself of the use of this catechism, *pro scholis parochialibus* (for parochial schools).

Before proceeding further I desire to call attention to the title "Christian doctrine," and to show how very misleading Rome can be—perhaps I might say how very deceptive,—and wilfully so. A Protestant minister, who was so liberal of God's truth as to take the part of the Roman Church on the school question, wrote a letter to the Boston press, in which he said that all the Roman Catholics wished to teach their children was "Christian doctrine;" and he was shocked that there should be any opposition to such a good work. He, for his part, approved this truly religious teaching.

All this was very well, if he and his Roman clients had meant the same thing by the same words. But to him "Christian doctrine" meant the religion of the Bible, to them it meant the religion of the Pope. He believed in the religion of Christ, and in the Bible as the source from which it should be obtained. They believed that the Pope, and the Pope alone, had a right to define what was Christian doctrine and what was not.

Now there are two points to be observed in connection with this claim to infallibility, laying aside for a moment the curious fact that it is an entirely new doctrine of the Roman Church. First, it should be noted that the Catechism appeals to Scripture to prove that St. Peter was appointed the visible head and chief pastor of the Church by Christ Himself. It is added, further, that St. Peter had "power to govern, to teach, and to make laws, and that Christ obtained for St. Peter the special gift of infallible teaching when He prayed for him" (Luke xxii. 32).

Of course the necessary sequel is that the Pope is the successor of St. Peter, and as such has the same power. But how very remarkable it is that the Pope's infallibility was not discovered until the year of grace 1870. Previous to that time it was taught in Roman Catholic actechisms and books of theology, that the doctrine of the Pope was infallible, was no article of the Roman Catholic faith Such are the inconsistencies of the Roman Church.

In the Rev. Stephen Keenan's "Controversal Catechism" (which was taught to Roman Catholic children, and to all who needed instruction), in all editions printed before the Vatican Council, there was the following question and answer:—

"Q. Must not Catholics believe the Pope himself to be infallible?

"A. This is a Protestant invention, it is no article of the Catholic faith; no decision of his can bind on pain of heresy, unless it be received and enforced by the teaching body, that is, by the Bishops of the Church."

In all editions printed since the Vatican Council this question and answer is omitted, and without a word of explanation. This Catechism had the approbation of the late Archbishop Hughes of New York, and was in general use. And yet Romanists will tell those whom they can deceive that the teaching of the Roman Catholic Church never changes. Here certainly is a change, and a stupendous one, when what was once condemned as "a Protestant invention" is now the received doctrine of the Church of Rome, and one moreover which Roman Catholics are obliged to believe under pain of sin, as much as the doctrine of the Trinity.

To-day we are told that the temporal power of the Pope is a doctrine which Roman Catholics ought to accept. "The Pope," says the author of this approved Catechism, "is a temporal prince, but not by Divine right." How long will it be before this doctrine will be made an article of faith, and added to the long string of "faiths" which were certainly not delivered to the saints?

We have said that nothing is gained to truth by misrepresentation of error. We leave such misrepresentations to those who find it necessary to make them; and as there is one point on which Protestants are sometimes in error as to Roman Catholic belief, I will explain it here. Although the Roman Church has made it an article of faith, as obligatory on her people as a belief in the Blessed Trinity, that the Pope is infallible, she does not teach that he is "impeccable;" in other words, a Pope may be a very wicked man,— and how wicked some Popes were no one knows better than Romanist theologians,—and yet he may be infallible in his teaching. For instance, Pius IX. might have been as wicked as his friend and adviser Cardinal Antonelli, whose moral character will not bear investigation, and yet he might have all the same the power infallibly to declare what the Church should believe. Romanists are very triumphant when they find any mistake made on this point by Protestant controversialists; and it is very important for the great cause of truth that there should be no mistakes on these subjects.

Our Divine Lord distinctly told St. Peter, after the very interview in which the Popes of Rome claim that He conferred infallibility on him and his successors, that he was "Satan," and that he savoured not of the things of God, but of the things of men. Certainly if the Popes of Rome claim the honours of Peter, they should also claim the reproof of Peter; and how well they have followed him in "savouring of the things of men" all history can tell. How many of them have been an offence to Christ, no matter how the Church may try to conceal their festering sores of worldliness and vice? St. Paul, far from yielding deference to St. Peter as the head of the Church, declares that he was himself the one to whom the Gospel of the uncircumcision was committed, and that the Gospel of the circumcision was given to Peter. This remarkable statement, which is left on record in the Holy Scriptures, and which cannot therefore be disputed, has not received the attention which it deserves. St. Paul's testimony is one which cannot be disputed; and here the statement is made in the plainest language, that by the Divine appointment he, and not St. Peter, was the person chosen by God to preach the Gospel to the Gentiles, while St. Peter's mission was to the Jews; and we find, on the indisputable evidence of the Bible, that St. Paul founded the Church of Rome, while there is no reliable historical evidence to show that St. Peter ever spent a day in that city. St. Paul, in his Epistle to the Romans, reminds them of his claim on them as the founder of their Church; for as he says, he "never built on another man's foundation." (St. Paul's Epistle to the Romans xv. 20.) It is noteworthy also, that while St. Paul took charge of the spiritual instruction of the Roman Church, St. Peter, following his divinely inspired vocation, devoted himself to the Jews, as we find in the Acts of the Apostles. If St. Peter had been endowed with the powers which Romanists now claim for the Pope, it is strange that he never claimed this authority, and that, far from its having been known to the other Apostles, they actually disputed points of discipline with him, in a way which would have made a modern Pope shower down excommunications, and call down upon them the vengeance of his infallible condemnation.

In the Epistle to the Galatians St. Paul says "they all saw," that is, the whole Church saw, "that the gospel of the uncircumcision was committed to me, as the gospel of the circumcision was to Peter." True, the whole Christian Church saw this, as well as the Apostles and their disciples; and no one else saw any other plan of Church government, until the ambition of the bishops of Rome to follow St. Peter in his fall, led them to "savour of the things which be of men." Would to God that they had followed St. Peter in his repentance for his fall. Would to God also that an apostle could be found in the present day who would imitate St. Paul in his stern rebuke of St. Peter, and tell these imitators of Peter's worldly vacillations that they should cease their "dissimulations," and begin to "walk according to the truth of the gospel." (Gal. ii. 11-14.) If St. Peter had been made head of the Church, as the Pope claims to be, how could St. Paul have dared to say that he was to be "withstood," or to accuse him of not "walking according to the truth of the gospel"? What would the Popes of to-day say if such a charge were made against them by a brother bishop? His excommunication would be only a matter of time. These infallible "Peters" would have sent St. Paul to the stake, if he had reproved them in those ages when the Popes had that temporal power which gave them the liberty to persecute as they pleased. The question in dispute was no mere matter of opinion; it was a vital question, and it was most certainly related to a matter of faith. But if there is not one word in Scripture to show that the Apostles submitted to Peter,—and they certainly must have known it, if he was the head of the infant Church,—and if there is a great deal to show that his alleged supremacy was not recognised, where is there even one word to prove that he was to have an infallible successor? Even if Peter was the rock on which the Church was to be built, and if Christ was not the rock,—for certainly there could not be two foundations, and if Peter was the rock, Christ was not,—even if all this is admitted, where, we ask, is the proof that Peter was to be followed by a series of infallible successors?

All this is most important at the present day. If Protestants who are in constant contact with Roman Catholics do not understand the Roman question from all points of view, how can they convince their opponents, or save themselves from falling into the snares of Rome? It is well worth expending time and careful consideration on all these subjects, for the time has come when the Christian needs to be armed at all points. We ask again, for the question is of the greatest importance, where is there one text in Scripture which proves that St. Peter's successors were to be endowed with the gift of infallibility? The texts of Scripture which Romanists bring forward to prove that the Popes are not merely the successors of Peter, but are also his infallible successors, are as absurd and as misleading as their quotations from history.

First, they quote the words of our Divine Lord to St. Peter: "I have prayed for thee that thy faith fail not, and thou, being converted, strengthen thy brethren." Surely no one with common sense can take this text to mean, either, that St. Peter should be able to declare infallibly what was to be believed as of faith, much less can it be made to mean that St. Peter's successors, if he had any, should be also infallible. Rome, with her usual policy of accommodation, has, as I have already stated, mistranslated the text by using the word "confirm" instead of "strengthen," because the word "confirm" implies authority, whereas the word "strengthen" is not so helpful to their case. But allowing Rome all the advantage of her mistranslations, where does the authority come in declaring St. Peter infallible, or declaring that he should have infallible successors? In fact, if Christ at this time and by these words made St. Peter infallible, he very soon gave painful evidence of his fallibility. For it was not many hours after ere he had denied his Lord. What a tremendous failure for a newly-appointed infallible teacher!

The calm way in which Romanists announce the fictions of their own invention, as if they were well-known and indisputable facts, would be amusing if the subject was not so serious. Texts of Scripture must be interpreted according to the opinion of the Church, and it is made a grievous sin to interpret them in any other way. How easy is it, then, to establish any theory? Statements are made as to the opinions of the Fathers, given with all the assurance of an infallible Church, which are either garbled extracts or deliberate forgeries, and the hapless victims of priestly fraud are not allowed, under pain of sin, to question, nor dare they follow the Apostle's advice to "prove all things." What would be said to a teacher of science or history who should forbid his disciples to read any books except those which he had written, or to inquire into the truth of, or investigate any theory which he had not previously approved? And yet this is just what the Church of Rome requires. The result of this teaching is very convenient for the infallible teacher. When no inquiries are made there can be no disputes. When there are no discussions there is a dead level of calm, which is declared to be an evidence of unity, and so the farce goes on.

I think it would be difficult for Protestants to believe the gross ignorance of even fairly educated Romanists as to the doctrines of their Church. They believe, but they certainly have not an intelligent belief; and can this be called belief? It is true indeed that once infallibility is accepted, there is no further need for thought. We might as well at once shut ourselves up in lunatic asylums, or cease to think at all on the subject of religion. Of what use is it to think, when we are forbidden to reason under pain of the loss of all that is most dear to us? We ask, and ask in vain, for one word of Scripture which says in plain language that St. Peter was to have an infallible successor. To say that the promise of our Lord to be with His Church to the end of time, was a promise that St. Peter's alleged successors should be at liberty to infallibly change, or proclaim, any doctrine which they pleased, is almost too absurd for common sense. It certainly requires an infallible Church to make out such a meaning to require us to believe that our Lord's prayer for St. Peter that his faith might not fail was a promise of personal infallibility. The very fact of our Lord's having prayed that his faith might not fail, is sufficient proof that there was fear of failure. But when the Roman controversialist is driven to a corner with Scripture texts, he has prompt recourse to the wide and fertile pasture of the Fathers. And here his skill in denying what opposes his theory, and in proving and arranging what suits it, is in its full glory.

Now it is self-evident that if the Scriptures have not taught the doctrine of the personal and particular infallibility of St. Peter's successors, no amount of quotations from the Fathers can be of the least value. But as these quotations are being continually brought forward, it is as well, for the good of those who are anxious to meet Romanists on grounds of solid information, to have the facts before them.

In the first place, it may be well to note that the Fathers were divided on almost every subject under discussion. It is clear to the impartial student of history, that if they had believed the Popes to have been the infallible successors of St. Peter, they would have appealed to him, and his judgment on this point would have been accepted as final. It was not till long centuries after the death of St. Peter that the claim was put forward by the Church of Rome of being the only true representative of St. Peter. First, it assumed, without one particle of evidence, that St. Peter spent five-and-twenty years in Rome. Now, so far from this assertion being true, it is so evidently false, that it could only have been made by a Church which requires its followers to believe whatever it says, without any time being lost in proving the point. In fact, the Church acts on the simple plan of first declaring herself infallible, and then saying you must accept her decisions because she is infallible.

It is very important for Protestants to know just what are the arguments, if they can be dignified by that name, which are used by Romanists in stating their beliefs to the people. A book was published in England called "Catholic Belief," which deals in this style of assertion without proof. Another book has been published in this country (America), written by Cardinal Gibbons, which is just in the same style. The circulation of both of these books has been very large, partly because they are issued in a popular form, but chiefly because the names attached to them have insured an immense sale. The priest who could be reported to "his Eminence" as having sold hundreds of his books is sure of a warm place in the episcopal remembrance. In "Catholic Belief" we are told quite calmly, as a simple matter of fact,—so much a matter of fact that it is not worth proving,—that "St. Peter became Pope on the ascension of Jesus Christ, and Bishop of Rome in 42, where he died martyr in the year 67."

One scarcely knows whether to describe this as ignorance or cool impudence. But note well the cleverness of the trick. No Roman Catholic will dare to question this statement, nor will he have any opportunity to examine for himself as to the veracity of the writer. He must swallow the whole story without inquiry, and without question. To question a book approved by the infallible Church would, indeed, be too grievous a sin! And so day after day and year after year the miserable delusion goes on. Mark the use of the familiar word "Pope." Think well of the impression on the young. Those whom the child has been taught to revere, and almost to worship as gods, tell him in his earliest and most impressionable years that St. Peter was "Pope of Rome." Could there be a surer way to make him believe that there always was a Pope?

I have alluded to the gross ignorance of Romanists as to their own religion. Why should they trouble themselves to understand it, when it is not necessary for them to do anything but to believe what they are told to believe? I was conversing one day with a well-educated intelligent lady, who had held a good position as a teacher in a national school in Ireland, or, as it would be called in America, a parochial school. I was telling her of the immense change in the doctrine of the Church which had been made since I entered it, and that I did not see why I, or any other rational being, should be called on to change their belief because the Pope chose to make new articles of faith at his pleasure. I found, to my amazement, that this teacher, who had for years taught the Roman Catholic Catechism, was not aware that what is now the most fundamental doctrine of the Roman Church was added to her faith within living memory, and she would scarcely believe me until I gave her Roman Catholic evidence of the fact.

When I entered the Church of Rome I was told that it was a "Protestant calumny" on the Roman creed to say the Pope was infallible; that infallibility could not reside in a person, but that it resided in the collective voice of the Church. I remember the shock that it was to me, to find that a Church which I had believed could not change its creed, had added to it in a matter of such immense importance. What a stupendous change of belief! What a strange mystery that even St. Peter had not taught the personal infallibility of his successors, and that it should be reserved to a very fallible Pope in the nineteenth century, whose chief favourite was a man of notoriously immoral character, to discover a doctrine of which all his predecessors were ignorant.

It is but a short time since I met a gentleman, a former pupil of a so-called Catholic College in Canada, who calmly told me that the Pope was the "*Paraclete*" whom Christ had promised to His Church. I had found many absurd beliefs among educated as well as amongst ignorant Romanists, but this exceeded all. I asked him did he not know that the Paraclete was the word used in the Roman Catholic version of the Bible for the Holy Ghost? But it was useless. He admitted that Christ had promised to send the Holy Spirit to His disciples, but he was still very sure that He had also promised to send the "Paraclete," which was the Pope. I begged of him to read a Roman Catholic Bible, and see for himself that he was wrong, and that Jesus Christ had never promised to send the Pope, but it was little use; he seemed greatly startled and surprised, but as far as I know that was the end of it.

Nor can I easily forget the surprise of a well-educated Roman Catholic girl to whom, by accident, I made some remark about St. Peter's wife. Her amazement was most amusing, and the shock to her faith in the teaching of the Church was considerable. She had quite sense enough to see that if St. Peter had a wife, and if our Lord showed His approval of it by curing his wife's mother when she was ill of a fever, it could not be such a wicked thing for priests, or even for Popes, to marry.

When the famous Robert College was established in Constantinople the Bible question loomed up as the great difficulty. If men would only pause to think, and then to realise how absurd it is that the very book which is the source of information on the subject of our faith should be denied to us, as it is by Rome, there would certainly be a change in public opinion. We have to face the great fact that the Bible has been given for our information and guidance by the Founder of our religion, and yet one-half of the so-called Christian world considers the free study of this book a danger to religion. It is certainly dangerous to those who do not wish to have the religion which it teaches known to all men. But how it can be dangerous in any other light is a proposition so absurd that it refutes itself.

What right has any human being to come between the creature and the Creator? What authority has any Church to say "You shall not" when God has said "You shall"? He has said to all His creatures, "Search the Scriptures;" and how dare any creature say, "Thou shalt not search them, except in so far as I permit you"? Yet this is what Rome does.

It is very important in reasoning with Roman Catholics to realise their complete ignorance of the Scriptures, and consequently of Gospel truth. If we desire to enlighten them we must do so by a careful consideration of their prejudices, and a clear comprehension of their ignorance, and of its causes. It is no use to employ an argument which they cannot understand, nor to bring forward statements which they have no means of verifying. Show them in the Douay Bible the plain command of God as to reading the Bible. This command the Roman Church has not dared to change or omit. The work of keeping the people in ignorance can be accomplished quite as easily, and far more safely, by telling them they must obey the Church, and that the Church, in her wisdom, desires them not to read the Bible, except with a special license.

I was not a little amused, on one occasion, at the extreme ignorance of the commonest truths of Christianity, on the part of a Roman Catholic girl, who attacked me in the streets of Toronto, Canada, for my apostasy, as she had been told to call it by the priest, and used the most violent and ignorant language to me. Like the gentleman who firmly believed that the Pope was the Paraclete which Christ had promised to send, she as firmly believed that there were a number of different Bibles which the Protestants had made up, and which had originated in the time of Luther, with whose name all Roman Catholics are familiar, as he is a good stalking horse for all the supposed sins of Protestants, in forsaking the " true " Church.

The following specimen of the kind of teaching which is given to Roman Catholics, not only of the poorer class, but of all classes, will show the source of their deplorable ignorance. The extracts are not taken from a Protestant source, they are from the Roman Catholic Catechism from which I have already quoted; and as I have said, it is not only authorised by Cardinal Gibbons, but it is also highly approved by the Pope; and what is of equal importance, it is the very Catechism which all sisters and monks and priests are obliged to teach to the young.

" Q. Have Protestants any faith in Christ?

" A. They never had.

" Q. Why not?

" A. Because there never lived such a Christ as they imagine and believe in.

" Q. In what kind of a Christ do they believe?

" A. In such a one of whom they can make a liar, with impunity, whose doctrine they can interpret as they please, and who does not care what a man believes, provided he be an honest man before the public.

" Q. Will such a faith in such a Christ save Protestants?

" A. No sensible man will assert such an absurdity.

" Q. What will Christ say to them on the Day of Judgment?

" A. I know you not, because you never knew Me.

" Q. Are Protestants willing to confess their sins to a Catholic bishop or priest, who alone has power from

Christ to forgive sins? 'Whose sins you shall forgive they are forgiven them.'

"A. No; for they generally have an utter aversion to confession, and therefore their sins will not be forgiven throughout all eternity.

"Q. What follows from this?

"A. That they die in their sins, and are damned."

If Protestants, after reading this, and knowing that it is taught in every parochial school, help to support such teaching, they will certainly be responsible for the results. Let it be distinctly and clearly understood that this is the authoritative teaching of the Roman Catholic Church throughout the world, and that it is the proud and true boast of Rome that she never changes her teaching. On such points as these she certainly never changes, though she has changed her "infallible opinions" on other subjects a good many times.

There is another subject on which she never changes, and that is as to her duty to burn and destroy "heretics;" but she does not carry out this part of her creed unless she has sufficient temporal power to do it safely, and she is wisely silent on the subject when she cannot act.

There are no doubt thousands of Protestants in the United States who will give their money and their influence towards the support of the new Roman Catholic University in Washington, where all this doctrine will be taught, but their children, and their children's children will be the sufferers, when Rome has obtained sufficient temporal power in America to establish the Inquisition; and in view of the immense political support given to Romanists by the American people, this is only a question of time.

It is true, indeed, that the revised statutes of the United States declare, "The alien seeking citizenship must take an oath to renounce for ever all allegiance and fidelity to any foreign prince, potentate, state, or sovereignty, in particular that to which he has been subject." But what use is this when we have to deal with a Church which claims the power to absolve the subjects of any government from their oaths of allegiance, and even makes it a meritorious act for them to break their most solemn vows at the bidding of the Pope? Nor is this at all inconsistent with Roman Catholic teaching. Once admit an infallible Church, and your only duty is obedience to all its dictates.

Again, observe how the infallibility of the Church is the corner stone of the whole building. It is little wonder that Rome holds to it as she does. And it may be well noted here that there is no reason why the aspirations of Rome should be limited in the United States, when in Canada the Pope's vicegerent has claimed, and has been given, the next place to the Queen in the Dominion Parliament. It is no wonder that Roman Catholics are proud of their Church, and mistake its temporal success for spiritual gain. The unthinking multitude, impressed like children with the rapid advancement of the temporal power of Rome, and by her splendid shows and ceremonies, look no further, and do not know that the advance of the temporal power of Rome is the first sign of her decay.

There is an account in "Our Day" of how the Rev. Cyrus Hamlin, late President of Robert College, Constantinople, kept the Bible in the college under the usual opposition on the part even of Christians to God's Word, which is worth careful study at the present crisis. He says:—

"In the formation of Robert College in Constantinople, an institution designed for students of from eight to ten nationalities, and from six to eight different forms of religion, the question arose, What place shall the Bible have in the institution? It was said by many, 'It cannot be introduced, because you expect to have Catholics, Armenians of the old Gregorian Church, Greeks of the ancient Greek Church, and persons from all forms of Protestantism and Judaism.' I had to decide the question, and send forth the programme of the college, which I did in seven different languages, stating that the Bible would be read morning and evening, and that prayer would be offered, that there would be worship on the Sabbath, and that the preaching would be on the basis of the Bible ; that the Bible was also to be taught as a text-book to Bible classes on the Sabbath day in the different languages of the students, that is, in English, French, Armenian, Greek, Bulgarian, etc., but that absolute religious freedom would reign throughout the institution ; that when parents should request it that students would be permitted to attend the worship of his Church on their sacred day, that is, the Moslem on Friday, the Jew on Saturday, and the members of the different Christian Churches on their Sunday ; but that all the other students would be required to attend the religious services of the college.

"It was honestly supposed by many that this arrangement was absurd, that non-Protestant parents would not send their children to an institution where the Bible would have such a place. The first year we had but few non-Protestant students ; the second year we had quite a number ; the third year the non-Protestant pupils outnumbered the Protestants ; and ever since the non-Protestant students have outnumbered the Protestants three to one. When a parent, father or mother, requested that a son should be allowed to go to his Church on his sacred day we allowed it, and there was always a number who were thus sent to their Churches. But how long? I never knew a student in that college go five times to his Church. Why? Because the worship was in an unknown tongue to him—in the Roman Church in the Latin; in the Greek Church the ancient Greek; in the Armenian Church the ancient Armenian; and they found that the services in the college were in the language they could understand, and they chose to attend them. Now if we had refused to let them attend their Churches they would have gone, but as we allowed them to go they did not care to go. They did not go after a time.

"In the Bible classes we had no difficulty, because no sectarianism was taught. Nothing was said about Judaism or Islam or any form of Protestantism or Roman Catholicism, or Orientalism of any kind. The Bible was taught, and that was all. There was no trouble about versions. I think we had as many as six or eight versions in the college. We had the King James Version, the Douay Version, the Septuagint, the ancient Armenian Version, and the modern Armenian Version, and the Bulgarian. We cared not what version of the Bible the pupils had; there was no trouble on that point whatever. But our plan had this good effect, that many of the students expressed their wonder that the Protestant Version was so almost exactly like their Version; and many compared the Douay Version with the Protestant, and were surprised to find that in effect the same truths were in both, and wherever there was a difference it led them to inquire into the difference. We never taught them on that point, but left it to their own inquiries.

"This freedom of the Bible and of the pupils commanded the respect of the pupils and of their parents. After some five or six years, perhaps it was in the seventh year, a combination was formed against this plan. The opposition had its origin outside the college. There was a party determined that the Bible should be taken out of Robert College, or that students should be withdrawn; and a real conspiracy was got up against the Bible, and finally the definite ultimatum was given us, 'You take out the Bible, or we shall take out the scholars.' We replied to that, 'The doors of Robert College swing both ways, and as easily one way as another,'—which was the fact materially,—'and any student who wishes to go, is as free to go as any other student is to come.' In point of fact, only seventeen students left. They were students we were very sorry to lose; they were connected with high and influential families, and many of them were ardent hard-working students. They left. But in two weeks, one after another, twelve of them returned, and within three weeks fifteen of the seventeen returned, and the other two called privately at the college to say that they were immensely sorry that they could not come back, but that the pride of their fathers would not allow them to come. Since that time, sir, there has been no demand for taking the Bible out of Robert College. And I have had intelligent men, non-Protestant, but very intelligent Greek merchants, say to me, 'If you should take the Bible out of the college it would ruin it. What we Greeks need is more Bible and less ritualism.'

"This question of the Bible in the schools requires only a little more courage. Stand by the Bible, and the Bible will stand by you. Stand by the Bible in the schools, and the schools will flourish."

"Stand by the Bible, and the Bible will stand by you." Words to be deeply weighed by every one calling himself Christian. Nay, the wonder is that there should be any difficulty on such a subject, and that it should be necessary to urge upon Christians the duty and necessity of reading God's Word, or of helping others to read it. I say fearlessly that I have no doubt that it was my early knowledge of the Bible which saved me from despair in the Church of Rome, and which was eventually the happy cause of my leaving it. Long years of experience of Rome has left no doubt on my mind of the wisdom of the Roman Church in limiting to the utmost the reading of God's Word by her people. It has also convinced me that the one way to enlighten those who are kept in deliberate darkness is to give them the light of the Bible.

And here I can scarcely refrain from the remark that while the Roman Church had not one word to say about the collection of funds to spread what Mr. F—— was pleased to call the "light," but what was openly known to be the lurid light of dynamite and plots of assassination, the same Church would have taken very prompt measures to put down any attempt to collect money for the spread of the light of the Gospel. Would to God that those who have the power would see to these things for themselves before it is too late.

Though the consideration of the share which Rome has in the discontent and outrages which are a disgrace to the Irish people everywhere, as well in America as in Ireland, belongs to a later part of this work, I cannot defer the consideration of the subject altogether.

It is a matter not of opinion, but of fact, that Mr. P——
F—— occupied his time and his talents, and gave the
use of his paper, to the collection of money, regularly
acknowledged in its columns, for this very purpose, that
this continued for many years, and that Archbishop
Corrigan uttered no word of condemnation. On the
contrary, he has now shown his high approval of the
past career of this monster of outrage, by appoint-
ing Mr. F—— to the important position of editor of the
principal Roman Catholic journal in his diocese. But
if Mr. F—— had collected money for spreading the
light of the Gospel of peace, the past history of the
Roman Church would strangely belie itself if he
received any reward.

CHAPTER VI.

THE FALLIBILITY OF INFALLIBILITY.

"Thou hast made us unto our God kings and priests."—Rev. v. 10.

ONE of the great attractions of the Roman Church, to the educated as well as to the uneducated, is the assurance she gives to all men who will believe her that she has always taught the same doctrine. What, Rome to teach one thing to-day, and to teach the opposite to-morrow? Perish the thought. Now it is very easy to defend a case and to prove a statement if those concerned are positively forbidden to hear the other side of the question. We have seen in the last chapter how Rome teaches the young deliberate lies about the Protestant religion, and if she teaches deliberate lies on one subject, why should she hesitate to teach deliberate lies on every subject?

Those persons who have been in France, and above all in Italy or Spain,—for the darkness is darkest in those countries where the light of the Gospel has the least access,—will remember how the poorer classes always speak of Protestants as heathen or Pagan, and this not in a controversial manner, or as any reproach. It is mentioned as a simple fact, about which there can be no doubt. Certainly there is no doubt in the minds of the people. Any one who is not a Roman Catholic is not a Christian, and, like my ignorant accuser in

Toronto, they simply believe what they have been told by their priests, whom they have been taught to look upon as gods, and whom—God help them!—they think could not possibly deceive. And what shall be said of those who knowingly and wilfully "love and make a lie"? There is but one doom for them; it is a doom pronounced by God Himself, and no Pope or priest can turn aside the vials of His wrath.

When children are deliberately taught in these free countries that Protestants "never had any faith in Christ," some are tempted to smile at the absurdity of the charge, while others profess to feel very sure that the Roman Catholic Church does not teach such an absurdity. But the fact remains all the same, whether we believe it or not, and the evidence is before the whole world. Who will believe that Cardinal Gibbons, who appears before the American public as the very incarnation of humility and liberality, has commanded his sisters and his priests to teach that all Protestants die in their sins and are damned, and that "they believe in a Christ whom they can make a liar with impunity"? Such are some of the specimens of Roman Catholic truthfulness and charity in representing the doctrine of Protestants of all denominations. Even the Episcopal Church, some of whose members have such deep sympathy with Rome—unless when Rome interferes with her plans for securing public property,—even this Church is not excluded from this fell condemnation.

But if Rome was as open in her popular statements as she is in her creeds and in her authorised teachings, the world would be alarmed, and the result would be that she would be known as she really is, and this is the very last thing which that Church can afford.

For this reason, from time to time she proclaims her liberality of doctrine, at the expense of her solemn professions of an unchangeable creed.

When Protestants have to listen to liberal sentiments, coming from the lips of Romanists, they would do well to bear in mind the candid warning which was given, on this important subject, by the Roman Catholic *Rambler*, published in England, September, 1851. "Believe us not," said that magazine, "Protestants of England and Ireland, for an instant, when you see us pouring forth our Liberalisms. When you hear a Catholic orator at some public assemblage declaring solemnly that 'this is the most humiliating day of his life, when he is called upon to defend once more the glorious principle of religious freedom' (especially if he says anything about the Emancipation Act, and the 'toleration' it conceded to Catholics)—be not too simple in your credulity. These are brave words, but they mean nothing."

The world at large was lost in admiration at the liberality of Rome when she permitted the circulation of the Bible in France, when M. Lassere issued his household edition of the Scriptures. But the world at large had not long to wait before the reading of it was forbidden, and the unfortunate author was compelled to call in the whole edition, as it was condemned when the circulation became too great, although the work had been previously sanctioned.

Protestants and Roman Catholics can never meet on equal terms in controversy. The average Protestant, accustomed to say what he means, especially on religious subjects,—and what need has he of concealment?—is no match for the Romanist in the art of dissimulation. The Romanist is in the position of a man who is fencing with truth, and who, knowing perfectly well that his arguments are based on equivocation, or on positively false statements, equivocates boldly while his Protestant friend thinks he is telling the pure truth. The other resource is perhaps as pitiable; it is the resource of honest ignorance, and the amount of honest ignorance in the Church of Rome has alone saved it from utter destruction on the part of its own followers. If I reiterate my statements on these, or kindred points, it is because I have long seen the great necessity for doing so. It is so difficult for the ordinary honest Protestant, who is not driven to make out a case for his Church, who knows the evidence for what he believes, and has sifted it for himself, to understand either the duplicity or the ignorance of the Roman Catholic.

When Protestant children are instructed, they are sent to the Word of God to prove all things; with the Roman Catholic child the very reverse is the case. The Roman Catholic child is told what he must believe, and he is told that he must believe it because the Church (represented to him by the priests) says so. There is no explanation, no argument worthy of the name; and it is a terrible thing to say to the impressionable mind of a child that eternal damnation will be the penalty of not accepting implicitly all this unproved teaching. Even should an intelligent child fail to find in the expression "Thou art Peter, and on this rock I will build My Church," a convincing proof that Peter and all his successors were at the same moment pronounced infallible, he dare not say so. Such a thought would be a "sin," to be confessed as a mortal sin, not against God, but against that mysterious entity "the Church," which first faintly points to Scripture as the warrant for its being, and then tells its subjects that they must not accept Scripture except as explained by itself; and that this same Scripture is a dangerous study for the unlearned, including in that category all who are not priests, no matter what their education and intellectual attainments may be. Who does not see in this method of educating the young the source of the superstitious belief of the masses? A child is at the mercy of its teachers. First impressions are all but ineradicable. A child who is taught to believe a certain thing by priests, to whom its parents teach it to look up to with awe as more than mortal, a child who is taught to believe that its hopes of future happiness depend solely on believing without question what it is taught by its priests, is prepared in later life to cling to its early teaching as the shipwrecked mariner clings to the wreck from which he expects salvation.

One who has been taught as a child that it is a sin to question what he is told, and on whom this cruel perversion of truth has been impressed with all the force of a Church which compensates, by appeals to the senses, for what it refuses in appeal to the reason, is safe to remain in ignorance of all that might prove the deception practised on it by its early teachers.

Take, for example, the teaching of the Roman Catechism for children on the question of infallibility. Where in the Bible is there one word to prove that St. Peter's successors were declared by our Divine Lord personally infallible? But this matters little to infallible Rome. If you think the texts are not sufficient proof of this stupendous claim it is your fault. The Church that you are bound to believe says that they prove it, and you have nothing to do but believe against the evidence of your senses. In fact, according to the Church of Rome, your senses have been given you for the sole purpose of believing not their evidence, but the evidence which this Church says you must believe.

When the Roman Church finds the testimony of the Bible against her she turns with wonderful composure to the Fathers. Now if the Fathers had anything like a general agreement on all, or even on any one, of the points in dispute, it would be of some value to her to appeal to their testimony. But the very reverse is the case. There is scarcely a subject of controversy on which the Fathers agree. Disputes on grace, on predestination, on free will, on Church government, and on every theological subject, were as rife in the centuries immediately after the first preaching of the Gospel as at the present day. Disputes were rife even in apostolic times; and Scripture tells us that, at the first Council of Jerusalem, St. Peter was not the infallible decider of these matters, and that at Antioch he was the very one who was decided against. But how can a Roman Catholic know this when he is not allowed to read the Bible which would tell him this plain truth? No Roman Catholic book or catechism will tell him what the Bible tells him, that St. Paul "withstood" St. Peter to the face, because he was to "be blamed." Imagine the fate of a bishop to-day who should follow the example of St. Paul and dare to blame a Pope. It is true he would only be excommunicated at the present day, but he would escape death merely because it would not be possible for the head of his Church to burn him alive.

Moreover, this rebuke of Peter was made in the most public manner possible. It was made, St. Paul himself tells us, "before them all." (Gal. ii. 14.) Before the whole Church assembled at Antioch St. Paul denounced St. Peter. It would seem indeed very plain that the great fault of St. Peter was, at that time, dissimulation, a curious coincidence in view of all the dissimulations of the Church of Rome which claims him as its founder. He said one thing before the Jews, and another thing before the Gentiles. The Church of Rome has followed him in his dissimulations, but, alas! not in his repentance.

St. Paul knew better. Ever bold and brave for truth, what a clean sweep he would have made of the tergiversations of the Roman Church of to-day. Were he in the flesh there would be no mental reservations, or false quotations of Scripture, or of the much-maligned Fathers. And St. Paul it is who says plainly that he, and not St. Peter, was the divinely-appointed Apostle of the Gentiles, while no plainer language could be used than that which he has used in Holy Scripture to prove that the divinely-appointed mission of St. Peter was to the Jews. (Gal. ii. 7, 8.)

The testimony of the Fathers all goes to show that the claim of the Church of Rome to the "Chair of Peter" was a comparatively modern one, and that they were divided in their interpretation of those very texts in regard to which the Church of Rome claims that they were in perfect and harmonious agreement.

The bare-faced tergiversations of Roman controversialists, and the way in which they quote and misquote the Fathers, has been exposed so often that it scarcely needs more than a passing allusion. But the fraud literary or otherwise, is easily concealed from Roman Catholics and from the great mass of mankind. The Roman controversialist starts into the controversy with all the prestige of the infallibility which his Church claims. If he quotes Scripture his readers must take his interpretation of it, no matter how far-fetched or obscure it may be, because it is the dictate of an infallible Church. It is little matter what is the plain meaning of any text of Scripture; it is the meaning which is decided by the Church which is of real account. What would be said of a judge who quoted from law books with this restriction, that his interpretation of the cases was the only one admissible? Certainly he would be ruled out of any court of common sense, or common honesty.

The argument of Rome is: "I say it is so, therefore it is so. You must not, at your peril, inquire further. I do your thinking, and I do it infallibly. What more do you want? Rest, and be thankful."

Let us now look briefly at some of this ready-made thinking. It is important if it is also amusing. Rome has artfully mixed up two different subjects—St. Peter's alleged visit to Rome, and the supposition that he founded the Church at Rome. The whole history of the Bible goes to show that it was St. Paul, and not St. Peter, who was the Apostle of Rome; but what does this matter, when it is necessary for an infallible Church to say it is just the other way?

The French have a proverb difficult to translate in all its freshness. But it may be rendered thus without a misconstruction of the original, "Lie, but lie boldly;" and this, in plain English, is what the Church of Rome does, when the question of her supposed descent from, and consequent authority as, the successor of St. Peter comes in. She begins by teaching children, in her Catechisms and books of instruction, that St. Peter was the first Pope of Rome. This being received, and no dispute or discussion allowed on the subject, and being well drilled into children in their early years as a fact, by those whose word they are so sure must be true, what can they do but believe the lie, for it can be called by no other name? Next, they give these children a list of Popes who, they say, succeeded St. Peter in unbroken succession, and never a word is said to these poor little ones to lead them to inquire whether all this is gospel fact, or Roman fiction. We know they are taught, and are as much obliged in conscience to believe all this fiction, as they are to believe that Jesus is the Son of God.

Thus it is that Rome fastens the chain of her forgeries on the young and innocent, and deprives them at the same time of all means of knowing the truth. How are they to know of the disputes of the Fathers, and of their differences of opinion on the most important points? Even Protestant authorities are quoted, or rather, I should say, deliberately misquoted in books intended for the youthful and ignorant. Surely when it has been shown over and over again that Roman Catholics misquote and falsify history, it should be sufficient to make any honest man refuse them credit. And yet there are Protestants who do not hesitate to send their children to such instructors.

A few samples of these perversions of history, which can easily be verified by any one who has access to a good library, will suffice; for truly if one began to go through all the Roman Catholic falsifications of history and fact, the world would not contain all the books which might be written. We have already mentioned two books which are largely circulated among Roman Catholics, and which are also read by Protestants, many of whom have no means of refuting their statements, and who consequently take them for gospel; and doing so, they are not surprised that the Roman Church makes all the claims she does, when she has such apparently strong authorities to support her. If her quotations and inferences were only true, her case would be indeed as strong as she tries to make it appear.

An assumption of authority goes a long way with a great many people. If a statement is only made often enough, and with sufficient positiveness, it will obtain acceptance with the multitude. Rome knows this, and acts upon it. She states boldly that St. Peter was the "first bishop of Rome," and that he was "Pope." The dishonest use of this word is naturally accepted by Roman Catholics, and often by inquiring Protestants, as quite sufficient proof of the supposed fact that there were always "Popes." The use of words and expressions, which were never heard for long centuries after the times in which they are alleged to have been in common use, is not honest, but it answers the purpose for which it is intended. For skill in what logicians call *suppressio veri*, or the concealing of truth to answer a purpose, Rome is unsurpassable. Here is Pope Pius IX.'s declaration of his own infallibility, adopted by the Vatican Council of 1870 :—

"Wherefore faithfully adhering to the tradition received from the beginning of the Christian Faith, for the glory of God our Saviour, the exaltation of the Catholic religion, and the salvation of the Christian people, We, the Sacred Council, approving, teach and define that it is a dogma divinely revealed; that the Roman Pontiff, when speaking *ex cathedra*—that is, when, discharging the office of Pastor and Teacher of all Christians, by virtue of his supreme authority, he defines a doctrine regarding faith or morals to be held by the Universal Church—he, by the Divine assistance promised to him in blessed Peter, is possessed of that infallibility with which the Divine Redeemer willed the Church should be endowed in defining doctrine regarding Faith or Morals; and that, therefore, such definitions of the Roman Pontiff are irreformable of themselves, and not from the consent of the Church. But if any one—which may God avert—presume to contradict this, our definition, let him be anathema."

Pius IX. was elected Pope on the 16th June, 1846. A few months after his election he issued his first encyclical, *Qui pluribus*, in which the theory of his infallibility was plainly indicated, and the intention to declare it, in the following terms:—

"And hence so plainly appears in how great error they are wandering, who, by an abuse of reason, regard the words of God as if they were a human work. He condemns those who rashly dare to explain the words of God and interpret them at their own discretion, while God Himself has constituted a living authority which may teach the true and legitimate sense of His own heavenly revelation, confirm the same, and put an end to all controversies in matters of faith and morals by an infallible judgment, which living and infallible authority exists in the Church only, which is built by Christ our Lord upon Peter, Head, Prince, and Shepherd of the whole Church, whose faith He promised should never fail; which always has its lawful Popes, deriving their origin without intermission from Peter himself, in whose chair they are seated, and are inheritors and vindicators of his doctrine, dignity, honour, and power. And because where Peter is there is the Church, and Peter speaks by the Roman Pontiff, and always lives in his successors."

Now there is one other point worthy of special note in this connection. If the Pope was "always infallible" as an individual, and if it did not require the "consent of the Church" (see above) to make his decisions infallible, how was it that the consent of the Church was asked to make him infallible? If the Pope was infallible without the Church, why did he find it necessary to ask the Church to make him infallible? The truth is, that the whole business was the greatest farce ever enacted in the sacred name of God.

But it was necessary also to make all the dead and gone Popes "infallible." If some of them knew in the other world the honour which was being paid to them, if people can be amused in the flames of eternal torment, some of them must have laughed in the bitterest derision. Their lives were so vile, and their deeds so evil, that even Roman Catholics cannot apologise for them. But all the same they are all (now) infallible! I know very well that the Roman Church teaches that the evil life of a Pope does not affect his infallibility; and it is not for us to quarrel with the decisions of that Church as far as they are conformed to her own discipline. But there is at least Scripture for the solemn assertion that a bad tree does not bring forth good fruit, and it is difficult for an ordinary mind to see where the good fruit of good doctrine can come from when the tree is as hopelessly rotten as even Romanists are obliged to admit that some of the trees in the line of their Popes have been.

In fact, Roman casuistry is of such a slippery and

8

elastic character, that if a Pope issued a solemn declaration that there was no God, the Roman Catholic casuist would make out that he was still infallible. That some Popes were condemned and found guilty of heresy is simply a matter of history, though it is an historical fact which Romanists do not like to admit.

The Council of Constance, in the fifteenth century, deposed John XXIII. from the Popedom, because it had been proved to them, on the evidence of thirty-seven Roman Catholic witnesses, of whom ten were Bishops, that, "It was public and notorious, that he (John XXIII.) hath been, and is still, an incorrigible sinner, guilty of murder, poisoning, and other great crimes, a declared practitioner in simony, and *an obstinate heretic*. That he had obstinately maintained before persons of honour, that there is no life after this, nor resurrection, and that the soul of man dies with the body like that of beasts." And it was publicly declared, in the eleventh Session of the Council, that John XXIII. was "no better than a devil incarnate."—(Leufant's *History of the Council of Constance*, vol. i., pp. 291, 292.)

The whole system of Popery, and I do not wish to use the word in an offensive sense, is of comparatively recent date. It was not until the year 1564 that it was made an article of faith in the Roman Church, that it was necessary for salvation to be subject to the Pope, though Boniface VIII., who became Pope A.D. 1294, had, in a formal Bull which can be found in the Roman Catholic collection of Bulls, declared that "it is necessary for salvation for every human creature to be subject to the Roman Pontiff." It is true that the Bible says that the only thing "necessary for salvation" is to believe in the Lord Jesus Christ.

But, and God knows we do not say it as an idle jest, if the Bible and the Church differ so much the worse for the Bible, because the "Church" teaches that it alone can tell us what the Bible means, though to ordinary intellect the meaning and interpretation may be as plain as it can be.

CHAPTER VII.

THE HISTORICAL FRAUDS OF THE ROMAN CATHOLIC CHURCH.

"If any man have an ear, let him hear."—REV. xiii. 9.

THE outcome of a system which is established on fraud and ignorance can never be anything but demoralising and deplorable. God is the God of truth and justice; and he is a God who abhors a lie, and has said so in the plainest language in His Word. Happily we may give the Roman Catholic laity the benefit of that invincible ignorance of which the Romanists are sometimes so liberal to us. But the only excuse for the Roman Catholic priesthood is that some of them at least are blinded by the mist of prejudice in which all that concerns their religion is enveloped; and I know well that there are hundreds of priests who have seen long since through these mists, and who know but too well all the frauds, historical and religious, which are necessary to keep up this system.

Yet these unhappy men dare not speak. To say out boldly "these things are not so" is to insure a condemnation which will ruin the speaker for life. So, as one unhappy priest said to me, "Some of us drown our misery in drink, some of us try to forget that there is a God, and many of us are simply infidels."

And this is the outcome of the claim to infallibility, for which there is not one word of evidence in the Bible, and none in the early Fathers of the Church. Oh, what oceans of blood, what oceans of tears have been shed, and will yet be shed, to satisfy the ambition of man. It little matters whether this ambition is for the conquest of worldly kingdoms, or for the capture of souls. It is all the same human ambition; and Rome will yet fill up the measure of her crimes when she proclaims the temporal power of the Church a dogma of faith, and there are signs that the hour for this proclamation is at hand. And yet there are Protestants, to whom both the Bible and history are open books, who do all in their power to forward this race for evil.

I have said that the early Fathers are far from teaching or even approving the supremacy of Peter. Let me give the evidence of a Pope who had sufficient Christianity to denounce the very doctrine which his successors have made an article of faith. Gregory I. was a man of far-reaching views, and what was as important, he was a man of liberal education. He was born in Rome about the year 544, so that whatever evidence he has to give on this subject is the result of several centuries' experience; for even then the bishops of Rome, as might be expected, had taken a very prominent place in the Christian Church. This place and this prominence would have been accorded to them willingly by the whole Christian world if they had not made it subsequently the ground for the most extravagant pretensions, and for the most preposterous claim of infallibility; though it must be said they waited for the enlightened nineteenth century to enforce this claim. Before entering briefly upon the history of

Gregory, and giving evidence of his denunciation of any claim on the part of the Bishop of Rome to supreme rule in the Church, I wish to call attention to a point which has not received the notice it deserves. It is often thought that the Popes of Rome could never have attained the power which they wielded, especially in the Middle Ages, if they had not had Divine assistance. This is as much as to say that success is a sign of the Divine approval. If this were true, how many tyrants could claim a Divine right for their tyranny? The simple fact is that the bishops of Rome came before the world with all the prestige of the rulers of imperial Rome. Rome was great even in its decay, and its decay was slow. When Rome ceased to persecute the Christians she had become in part at least Christian, and her military power, and her widely extended rule, gave a civil and social pre-eminence to the Bishop of Rome. Ambitious churchmen were not slow to take advantage of all this. At first we may hope it was a question of advancing the glory of God; but like all human undertakings, even when begun for God, human motives and desires crept in, and the bishops of Rome soon began to use, for their own exaltation, the undoubted prestige which their civil position gave them as bishops in a city of such eminence. In any country the bishop of the chief town becomes naturally the most prominent bishop.

All this is natural, and there is no reproach to a Church for placing the highest offices in the most important places. It was thus undoubtedly that the claim for episcopal pre-eminence began, the opportunity was given, and human ambition used it. But it would never do for the Bishop of Rome to claim Divine and exclusive authority, without showing some ground for it. We all know how easy it is to find a reason for what we are determined to do. The reason was at hand. The early Fathers, while they differed widely as to the precise interpretation which should be put on the words of Christ to Peter, were almost unanimous in their praise of Peter. There is a very human side to the character of St. Peter, which wins our affection and our respect. If he denied Christ he loved Him; and he made brave attempts to prove his love by a subsequent life of devotion. The words addressed to Him by our Lord seemed capable of several interpretations, and the bishops of Rome were not slow to take the one which was the most favourable to themselves, and to keep the others out of sight. What, indeed, is the use of being all powerful if we cannot secure something for our own advantage thereby? Even if the words addressed by our Lord to Peter made him the head of the Church, they do not convey to any rational mind any idea of succession in this office; yet this is the only point of importance to the Roman Church.

One thing is certain. This Pope Gregory I., of whom we have already spoken, declared emphatically in the sixth century that the Popes of Rome had no claim to be exclusive rulers of the Christian Church; and indeed there was even then a claimant other than the Bishop of Rome for the title of first Christian bishop, just as there was in the time of our Divine Lord a cry amongst the disciples who should be greatest. The Archbishop of Constantinople had claimed the title of Universal Bishop, another evidence that so late as the close of the sixteenth century there was no general acknowledgment of the Papal supremacy. The Bishop of Alexandria thereupon wrote to the Bishop of Rome, who was then Gregory I., and addressed him as Universal Bishop. To this compliment the Pope replied in these noble words, which remain on record to show that there was at least one "infallible" Pope who did not believe in Papal Supremacy :—

"If you give to me more than is due, you rob yourself of what is due to you. I choose to be distinguished by my conduct, and not by titles. Nothing can redound to my honour that redounds to the dishonour of my brethren. I place my honour in maintaining them in theirs. If you call me Universal Pope, you thereby own yourself to be no Pope. Let no such titles therefore be mentioned, or even heard amongst us. Your Holiness says in your letter that I command you. I command you! I know who you are, and who I am. In rank you are my brother, by your conduct my father. I therefore did not command; and beg you will henceforth forbear to use the word; I only pointed out to you what I thought it right you should know."

It should be carefully noted that the word Pope simply means father (*papa*). Every bishop was a "Papa" or "Pope" (father) in those ages, and in Russia every priest to-day is called a "Papa" or "Pope." So much of the prestige of the Roman Church is based on false pretences, which easily deceive the uneducated, that no opportunity should be lost of giving such explanations. It remained for the "papas" or Bishops of Rome to claim for themselves *exclusively* in later ages the title of "Pope." Who would suppose that false quotations would be made, authorities cited which are well known to be worthless, and statements brought forward as true which have been repeatedly proved false, so as to influence those who have no opportunity of knowing whether they are genuine or not? Indeed, the history of the Papal claims is so abstruse, and complicated with so many subjects, that it requires no ordinary research to understand it thoroughly. Let it be once more noted that Roman Catholics are forbidden to make independent research, it being, according to the great (Roman Catholic) authority of Cardinal Manning, " a treason to the Church to appeal to history."

As a matter of fact, it was the emperors who convened all the first General Councils and not the Popes, and my authority for this statement is the well-known Catholic writer Cardinal Baronius (born 1538).

Baronius tells us that the second General Council of Constantinople (A.D. 381) was convened by order of the Emperor Theodosius, and was held against the will of the Bishop of Rome ("*repugnante Damaso celebrata*"). This Council conferred a precedence of honour on the Bishop of Rome, but solely on the ground that Rome was the seat of empire or government. The third General Council, that of Ephesus (A.D. 431), was called by the Emperor, Theodosius the Younger. Leo I. did his utmost to prevent the holding of this Council, but, having no jurisdiction, he failed in his attempt. The fourth General Council, Chalcedon (A.D. 451), was convoked by the Emperor Marcian. Pope Leo did all he could, even with tears, to persuade the Emperor not to call this Council. In this he failed. He then tried to have it held in Italy. In this he also failed. Having failed to prevent the holding of the Council of Chalcedon, he was represented at it by two legates, who attempted to prevent the passing of the famous twenty-eighth Canon, which declared that the Bishop of Constantinople should enjoy equal ecclesiastical privileges with Rome. The legates opposed the passing of this Canon, but without avail, and rather than consent they withdrew. On their return they protested that the bishops had been coerced to sign, which was denied; and the Canon was again put to the vote, and passed unanimously (the legates only dissenting), the bishops declaring that they had given their votes freely. That Canon, passed at a General Council, which was attended by 630 bishops, not only stands unrepealed, but has been confirmed by subsequent Councils. This twenty-eighth Canon is all-important. A literal translation is as follows:—

" Everywhere following the decrees of the Holy Fathers, and acknowledging the Canon (which was lately read) of the 150 bishops most beloved of God, who were assembled under the Emperor Theodosius the Great, of pious memory, in the royal city of Constantinople, new Rome, we also decree and determine the same things concerning the privileges of the same most holy Church of Constantinople, *i.e.*, new Rome. Because the Fathers rightly accorded privileges to the See of ancient Rome, inasmuch as that city was the seat of Empire—moved also by the same consideration, the 150 bishops, beloved of God, accorded equal privileges to the most holy See of new Rome, rightly judging that the city which was honoured by the Empire and the Senate, should both enjoy equal privileges with the elder Royal Rome, and also should, in ecclesiastical affairs, be extolled and magnified in no other manner, being second after her. We also decree that the Metropolitan of the dioceses of Pontus, Asia, and Thrace, as also the Bishops of their dioceses, who are among the barbarians (foreigners), shall be ordained by the aforesaid most holy See of the most holy Church of Constantinople. To each of the Metropolitans also, of the same dioceses, together with the Bishops of the Province, it is allowed to ordain bishops, as it is proclaimed by the sacred canons. But the Metropolitans of these dioceses, as has been said, are to be ordained by the Archbishop of Constantinople, after the proper elections have been made according to custom, and reported to him."

These decisions of General Councils, the acts of which have been written and recorded by the highest Roman Catholic authorities, are of great importance, as they prove that whatever ecclesiastical pre-eminence Rome may have had in the early Church was due solely to the fact that Rome was the "seat of empire."

This is a point of supreme importance in the whole controversy. It is no wonder that Rome claims and desires secular power, for it has been through the secular power, and through that alone, that she obtained her pre-eminence.

The secular power is very willing to help religious authority when it suits her purpose to do so, and she is quite as ready to put down religious authority when it has served her purpose and can no longer be of use. Would to God that the Church had obeyed the precept of leaving to Cæsar the things of Cæsar. It is a strange religion which declares that it must have the power of the sword to enable it to teach the truths of the Gospel.

But the Fathers not only differed with each other, but they also held different opinions at different periods of their lives, just as other people who are equally fallible may do. For example, St. Augustine says :—

"It appears in many passages of Scripture that Peter represented the Church, and particularly in that place where it is said, 'I give to you the keys of the kingdom of heaven. . . . For did Peter receive those keys, and did John and James and the other Apostles not receive them ? . . . What was given to him was given to the Church. Therefore, Peter represented the Church, and the Church was the body of Christ."

In his "Retractations," on the expression "the rock" he writes :—

"I have said in a certain passage respecting the Apostle Peter, that the Church upon him is founded as upon a rock. . . . But I know that I have frequently afterwards so expressed myself, that the phrase 'Upon this rock,' should be understood to be the rock which Peter confessed. For it was not said to him 'Thou art *petra*' but thou art *Petrus*, for the rock was Christ. Let the reader select which of these two opinions he deems the more probable."

This is an amount of "private judgment" that the Church of Rome will not permit. This opinion harmonised with the view taken by Augustine in his great work, "The City of God," where he tells us that he and his Church did not believe in Peter, but in Him in whom Peter believed.

"Ut nos, qui sumus et vocamur Christiani, non

in Petrum credimus, sed in quem credidit Petrus." We do not believe in Peter, but in what Peter believed.

Again in his 270th sermon :—

"He says to them, 'But whom do ye say I am?' and Peter, one for the rest, one for all, says, 'Thou art the Christ, the Son of the living God.' This he said most rightly and truly; and he deservedly merited to receive such an answer: 'Blessed art thou, Simon Barjona, for flesh and blood hath not revealed it to you, but My Father which is in heaven.' 'And I say unto thee,' because thou hast said this to Me, listen; thou hast given me a confession, receive a blessing: therefore, 'And I say unto thee, thou art Peter; because I am *petra*, a rock, thou art *Petrus*, Peter; for *petra*, the rock, is not from *Petrus*, Peter, but *Petrus*, Peter, is from *petra*, the rock; for Christ is not so called from the Christian, but the Christian from Christ. 'And upon this rock I will build My Church,' not upon Peter."

And in his 13th sermon he says :—

"Christ was the Rock, Peter figuratively the Christian people. . . . 'Therefore, He said, 'Thou art Peter,' etc.; that is, I will build My Church on Myself, the Son of the living God. I will build thee on Myself, not Myself on Thee. For men willing to build upon men said, 'I am of Paul, and I of Apollos, and I of Cephas, that is, Peter.' But others, who were unwilling to be built on Peter, but would be built upon the rock, said, 'But I am of Christ.' But the Apostle Paul, when he knew that he was chosen, and Christ contemned, said, 'Is Christ divided? Was Paul crucified for you, or were ye baptised in the name of Paul?' Wherefore, as not in the name of Paul, so not in that of Peter, but on the name of Christ, that Peter may be built upon the rock, not the rock on Peter."

In fact, though St. Augustine was the most voluminous, as well as the most revered Father of the early Church, there is not one hint in his writings from end to end that the Church of Rome had any priority of rule. In his eyes every bishop was equal; and when he wrote his famous work condemning the Donatists he does not say one word of the necessity, nor does he even hint at any necessity, for their obeying the Roman Church.

But will it be credited that the Church of Rome has actually placed some of the works of the Fathers on the index, though she praises them so highly when they agree with her?

The audacity of untruth can go no farther. We proceed to give proof of this. Even St. Augustine has not escaped the "infallible" criticism of Rome, although Maldonatus, a Jesuit writer, has said of him,—

"Augustine is an author of that esteem, that, were his opinions neither proved by Scriptures, nor reason, nor any other author, yet the sole reverence of his person deserves sufficient authority by itself."

Yet there are no writings of the ancient Fathers which have suffered so much as those of Augustine at the hands of Romanists themselves. In the index, the condemned passages, as found in various editions of Augustine's works, cover eleven closely printed folio pages, in double columns, from page 54 to page 64, both inclusive.

In the "Belgian Expurgatory Index" published at Antwerp, 1571, at page 5, we read:—

"We bear with many errors in the old Catholic writers; we extenuate them; we excuse them; and by inventing some devised shift, we oftentimes deny them, and feign some commodious sense for them, when they are objected to in disputations or conflicts with our adversaries."

Having expurgated the writings of Augustine of all supposed heretical teaching, they have taken a bolder step by publishing his works, from which they have excluded everything savouring of "heresy," and repugnant to what they are pleased to call the "Catholic Faith."

David Clement, in his "Bibliothèque Curieuse Historique et Critique," refers to the corrupted edition of Augustine's works, which was printed in Venice in 1570, in the following words:—

"The editor warns us, as an honest man, that he has removed everything which might infect Catholics with heresy, or cause them to turn from the orthodox faith."

The same fact is recorded by Le Clerc in his "Bibliothèque Universelle." Referring to the Venice edition of 1570 he says:—

"They inserted in the title that they had exercised great care to cause to be expunged everything that might possibly infect the souls of the faithful with any evil of heresy, or to draw them from the Catholic and orthodox faith."

We give a very few of the passages or sentences from the writings of St. Augustine which the "infallible"

Church of Rome has condemned in her "Expurgatory Index," published at Madrid in 1667. Their significance will be obvious.

"God alone is to be adored" (p. 56, col. 2).

"Angels cannot be our mediators" (p. 59, col. 2).

"Saints are unwilling to be adored" (p. 57, col. 2).

"Created beings are not to be worshipped nor adored" (p. 61, col. 1).

"There are no mediators between us and God" (p. 60, col. 1).

"The dead have no concern for the living" (p. 59, col. 1).

"No help of mercy can be rendered to the dead" (p. 59, col. 1).

"Saints are to be loved and imitated, but are not to be worshipped" (p. 59, col. 2).

"Saints are to be honoured with imitation, but not with adoration" (*Ibid.*).

"John left a forewarning against the invocation of saints" (*Ibid.*).

"The holy dead, after this life, cannot help" (*Ibid.*).

"It is a sacrilege to build temples to created beings" (p. 59, col. 1).

"It is wicked for Christians to place images of God in Churches" (p. 59, col. 2).

"Mary, even in Christ's passion, doubted concerning Him" (*Ibid.*).

"Mary was mother of Christ's humanity, not of His divinity" (p. 61, col. 1).

"The authority of the Scriptures, and not of Councils, is to be relied on" (p. 61, col. 1).

"Nothing is to be added to Christ's words" (p. 60, col. 1).

"That the legends of saints are apocryphal" (p. 59, col. 2).

"Confession is not necessary to salvation" (p. 61, col. 1).

"God forgives sins before confession passes the lips" (p. 58, col. 1).

"That the Eucharist is not a sacrifice, but a memorial of a sacrifice" (*Ibid.*).

"Christ commended to His disciples a figure of His body and blood" (p. 60, col. 1).

"The sacrament of the Eucharist, although visible, should nevertheless be understood in an invisible and spiritual manner" (p. 60, col. 2).

"Peter never claimed for himself a primacy. *Petrus primatum sibi nunquam vindicavit*" (p. 59, col. 1).*

Surely audacity and outrage on the dead could go no further. Even the opinions of the most distinguished Father of the Church must be made to harmonise with the opinions of modern popery. I remember when I was in England many years since, and when the great movement Romewards began under the auspices of Dr. Pusey and the Tractarians, that he published some works that had been written by Roman Catholics long since dead. In editing these books, Dr. Pusey thought proper to leave out any passages of which he did not approve; and observed that these dead and gone saints would no doubt see things in heaven as he saw them on earth. Only the evident sincerity of Dr. Pusey could have saved him from the charge of intolerable pride, or of insufferable self-conceit. For any mortal

---

* For these facts concerning St. Augustine's writings I acknowledge my indebtedness to Mr. C. H Collette's "St. Augustine" (London: 1883).

Erasmus, one of the most learned priests of the Church of Rome, was condemned because he did not omit the passages which went against Romish claims, and Erasmus himself was also condemned in no measured terms, although he lived and died a faithful son of the Church, and even used his able pen against the Reformers, so little mercy has Rome even for her most faithful and noblest sons if they do not submit abjectly to her least desires.

There is a remarkable statement of Dr. Newman's to which I would call attention in this connection. It was published some time before he left the Protestant Church, and was intended to justify his position against the Church of Rome. Such a statement, coming from a man of his intellectual attainments and power of thought, deserves the most serious consideration. What an indictment it is against the Church of Rome; perhaps a more severe charge never was made against that Church, considering the person who has made it, and the circumstances under which it was made. It does not lessen the force of this indictment that Dr. Newman has since left the Protestant Church, for he has not refuted this statement. On the contrary, he has been obliged to justify his change of opinion by one of the most remarkable arguments which has ever been offered to the human intellect for acceptance; that the Church has power to "develop" new doctrines which may be, and certainly are, in direct opposition to those once delivered to the saints. Any one who can accept this mode of reasoning can believe at pleasure whatever a Church may say or do, no matter how contrary to revealed religion, since this power of "development" is claimed to be of Divine right, or it would be practically worthless.

Dr. Newman, in his Lectures on the *Prophetical Office of the Church*, says :—

"The Fathers are only so far of use in the eyes of Romanists as they prove the Roman doctrines, and in no sense are allowed to interfere with the conclusions which their Church has adopted; they are of authority when they seem to agree with Rome, of none if they differ" (p. 53).

"How useless then is it to contend with Romanists, as if they practically agreed to our foundations, however much they pretend to it. Ours is antiquity, theirs the existing Church" (p. 85).

"According to the avowed or implied conviction of their most eminent divines, there is much actually to censure in the writings of the Fathers, much that is positively hostile to the Roman system" (p. 97).

"As far as it is Catholic and scriptural, it (Romanism) appeals to the Fathers; as far as it is a corruption it finds it necessary to supersede them" (p. 124).

"Enough has been said to show the hopelessness of our prospects in the controversy with Rome. We have her own avowal that the Fathers ought to be followed, and again, that she does not follow them. What more can we require than her witness against herself, which is here supplied us? If such inconsistency is not at once fatal to her claims, which it would seem to be, at least it is a most encouraging omen in our contest with her" (p. 99).

In view of the rapid advance of Romanism in the United States, it is an affair of the deepest consequence to every Christian—as so many Protestants send their children to Roman Catholic institutions for education, and thereby deprive them deliberately of knowing the truths of history as well as the true state of the Roman controversy—it is of supreme importance that such facts should be fully explained to the public. I shall now give two proofs of the way in which the young, and for that part of the matter the old, are deliberately deceived in books of instruction authorised and approved by the Roman Church. In a work published in England by Father Bruno, entitled "Catholic Belief," and which boasts of a circulation of half a million, we find the following statements :—

"In the eleventh year after the Ascension of our Lord, which was the second year of the reign of the Roman Emperor Claudius, St. Peter left the Bishopric of Antioch, which he intrusted to Evodius, and chose for himself Rome. Before, however, going to Rome, he first went to Jerusalem. Then it was that Herod cast him into prison, as related in the Acts of the Apostles (chap. xii.). But being miraculously delivered by an angel from prison a second time, he made his way to Rome."

"St. Peter was the first to preach the Gospel in Rome."

"A Council was held, and after sufficient time had been given to debate, St. Peter, who was then Bishop of Rome, stood up, and referring to a special revelation made to him by God, declared that certain Jewish legalities were not binding on Christians; which decision (?) was immediately confirmed by St. James, Bishop of Jerusalem, and by all the rest. (Acts xv. 8.)"

Now mark the painful and deliberate duplicity of these statements, and remember that every Roman Catholic reading this is bound to believe it, for it is issued with the *imprimatur* of the authorities of the "Church." Remember the immense force and power of early impressions, and that even a Protestant child brought up in a convent school, and trusting with the implicit, and I may say holy, trust of childhood in those who teach her, will accept all this fiction as fact, and in later life will be influenced by it to her eternal injury. How could a child suspect that there would be deliberate deceit on the part of the priest or the sister? And as for the poor sister, she is as ignorant as the child. She has no means of verifying the statements placed in her hands, and which she is ordered to teach. She, too, takes them on the word of the "Church," in which she also has been taught to believe in her youth, and which she would think it treason of the worst kind to doubt. Now let us examine these statements; the time will not be lost.

First let it be noted that a certain statement is made by the highest Roman Catholic authority as a simple fact, and is therefore accepted as a fact by the reader. It is said that "Peter made his way to Rome." Now there is not one single historical proof of this statement, the object of which is to connect Peter with the Church in Rome. The Bible tells us that it was there St. Paul taught for so many years; and as he has mentioned in his Epistles the names of those who preached the Gospel with him there, it is certain that St. Peter was not at Rome when St. Paul wrote, as he never mentions his name. In fact, as the Bible tells us, St. Peter was occupied for the greater part of his life in preaching to the circumcision (the Jews), and we are also told this was the work appointed for him by God Himself (Gal. ii.). But the plainest statements of the Bible are of as little account to Rome as the statements of the Fathers, which, according to Dr. Newman, they use only for their own purposes. What is the use of being infallible if you are obliged to give any proof of what you advance? The great advantage of infallibility is that you are above all arguments.

First, there is no evidence, nor has the Roman Church produced any evidence, to show that St. Peter was Bishop of Rome or, for that part of the matter, that he was bishop anywhere. The apostles had a work of their own to do, quite different from the work of a bishop; and it was their Divine and blessed duty to go round to all the Churches teaching and strengthening them, as we find them doing. As the Church of Rome has no proof whatever of the statement that St. Peter was "Bishop of Rome" for twenty-five years, its theologians are driven to such statements as these—"As it cannot be supposed that St. Peter had no see during the last twenty-five years of his life, if he was not Bishop of Rome, of what other see was he bishop?"

It is on such suppositions and such childish reasoning that Rome builds the fabric of the most stupendous assertions. All this might do very well in a novel, but it is a poor support for a creed. And once again, what shall be said of those who put these "supposes" and "ifs" before the young as undoubted and unquestioned facts? We are not told, either in Scripture or history, neither by God nor man, of what place St. Peter was bishop, or that he was a bishop. We only know that he was an Apostle.

To the true Catholic and Christian Church all this is a matter of very little moment, since that Church has not to maintain a claim of infallibility at the expense of truth.

If St. Peter was bishop anywhere, all authorities,

even Roman Catholic, go to show that it was at Antioch. Indeed, this very writer claims that St. Peter was Bishop of Antioch " for a time." If so, then Antioch was the first see which St. Peter founded, and it should, on Roman Catholic principles, be the head of the Catholic Church. But the city of Antioch had not the temporal power of the city of Rome, nor the same worldly advantages; hence its claims are quietly ignored. How many Roman Catholics are aware of this phase of the controversy? Everything that would cast even the least shade on the face of the claim of Rome is quietly ignored, and the unhappy Romanist is led to believe that there is nothing to be said on the other side.

I shall never forget my own amazement when I learned for the first time that there was a Church, which even the Church of Rome is obliged to admit, has the very same orders as she has, the same priestly power, and valid sacraments also. The Greek Church, with its millions of believers, is as much a "true Church" as the Church of Rome, even according to the authorised teaching of the Church of Rome.

If a priest of the Greek Church enters the Church of Rome he is received as a priest, his orders are acknowledged, and he can say Mass at once, without receiving new orders. I believe it would surprise Romanists not a little if this fact were generally known, as it should be. I believe that the great majority of Romanists would deny this statement with indignation, and yet it is well known to the world at large, and cannot be denied by Romanists, though its significance in the Roman controversy may not be known to Protestants. Furthermore, the priests of the Greek Church are all allowed to marry, and are encouraged to marry. Rome tries to make the world believe that she alone has the claim to sacerdotal power. Yet here is a Church the validity of whose orders and priesthood she dares not even question, yet which differs from her in refusing to admit the unscriptural claim of the Pope to be the head of Christendom.

Certainly Rome does well to keep her people in ignorance. The entrance of light would dispel too much darkness. Let Protestants begin to spread the light. Let them take every opportunity of telling their Roman Catholic friends, quietly and patiently, some of the facts of history, and those plain truths which Rome cannot deny, however seriously they make against her pretensions. And it should be noted here that the reason why Rome is so anxious to prevent intercourse between Protestants and Romanists is, that the truth about her claims would thereby inevitably come out, and Romanists, once convinced that they have been deliberately deceived in one matter, would begin to lose their faith in all. Let Protestants never forget the duty and the privilege which God has bestowed on them. Let them, above all, remember the patience which is necessary with those who have been educated in darkness, and how terrible is the first awakening to the long deception which Rome has practised on her unhappy followers. A word in season, and only a word, will be of more avail than days and weeks of noisy argument. I know a case where a Romanist was led to serious inquiry by the remark that St. Peter had a wife, and by being shown the passage of Scripture which proves this in the Douay Bible, and by calling her attention to the way in which our Lord showed His approval of St. Peter's marriage by healing his wife's mother when she was sick of a fever. The natural conclusion from this was as it should be—Why does the Church of Rome forbid her priests to marry? A command which leads to the commission of the grossest sins.

It seems scarcely necessary to point out any more Roman Catholic deceptions, but the importance of having accurate knowledge on these points is of such moment that I maybe excused by some, and I hope I may be of service to many, if I dwell a little longer on this subject. We may well ask why it was, if St. Peter was twenty-five years in Rome with St. Paul, whom no one disputes was there, that St. Paul, writing from Rome, says, "Only Mark is with me"? Observe in the second quotation which I have given from this mendacious Roman Catholic work, the barefaced statement that St. Peter was Bishop of Rome when the memorable Council was held at Jerusalem. (Acts xv.) This is quietly asserted, though there is not one word of proof given, for the very simple reason that neither Scripture nor history say one word on this subject. If the passage is noted carefully it will be seen into what ridiculous inconsistencies Rome is driven. Let us admit that "St. Peter was then Bishop of Rome," and what do we find? Not that he was asked to settle the matter in question, as he would have been if our Lord had made him the head of the Church, but that it was settled by St. James. As a matter of fact, St. Peter gave no decision; for Scripture tells us that he only gave an opinion as the rest did, including Barnabas and Paul.

In fact, far from the Council being called together to hear the decision of St. Peter, it was called for the sensible purpose of having a general discussion on a most important point; and St. Peter simply gave his opinion as the others did. How, in the face of this narrative, any Pope can claim to do what St. Peter did not do is marvellous. The circumstance certainly may be pointed to as an evidence that the whole Church assembled in Council has a power to decide controversies; but that is a very different matter from saying that St. Peter had this power exclusively. This modern claim simply places the Popes above St. Peter in power and dignity. If St. Peter had the power granted him by our Divine Lord to give the final decision in matters of faith, here is a case in which he could, and most certainly would, have exercised this power; and the Apostles would have been too well aware of our Lord's teaching to have opposed His claim if such a claim had existed.

But here is Scripture testimony to the undeniable fact that it was St. James, the local bishop, who decided the important question. The very words used by St. James are sufficient to settle the matter. He says "my sentence is." If St. Peter had a right to decide he would have said most certainly the sentence of St. Peter is so-and-so; but there is not one trace of special deference to his opinion in the whole affair, and this is the first Council held in the true Catholic Church. How different in its inception and in its result from the Councils of the Roman Church, which certainly is not Catholic in its following of the Apostles. In this chapter also we find that whatever was decided was not by Peter but by "the Apostles and elders and brethren." (Acts xv.) How different this from Papal rule, which will not even listen to the least suggestion of the brethren. It should be clearly understood by Protestants, and for that matter by Romanists, that the Council which abandoned the infallibility of the Church for the infallibility of the Pope a few years since, not only made the Pope (Pius IX.) infallible, but also made all the Popes infallible who had preceded him. It is by no means clear whether the Pope made himself infallible, or whether he got the Council to do the deed. It is only certain that the deed was done. But it is difficult for the ordinary mind to understand why, if the Pope was infallible all the time, it was necessary to wait till the nineteenth century to discover it, or why, if he was really infallible, he could not have said so himself, and arranged the matter without the Council.

One thing is certain. The Council was not at all unanimous about the same infallibility. It was necessary, however, for the Pope to compel some appearance of unanimity before he could avail himself of the honour which he so greatly coveted. We append here some extracts from the early Fathers of the Church, taken from Roman Catholic writers, which should for ever silence all dispute as to their opinion on infallibility, and Roman claims of jurisdiction.

The earliest mention of Peter's name is in that First Epistle to the Corinthians, chapter v., which is attributed to Clement. Clement is alleged to have been Bishop of Rome from A.D. 92—101, and by some to have been appointed bishop by Peter himself. His testimony is very important. Writing to the Corinthians, he said,—

"Let us have before our eyes the excellent Apostles. Peter, through unjust envy, underwent not one or two, but many sufferings ; and thus being martyred, went to the place of glory that was due to him. Through envy Paul also receives the reward of patience. Seven times he was in bonds; he was whipped and stoned. He preached in the east and west, leaving behind him the glorious report of his death; when, after he had taught the whole world righteousness, and had come to the borders of the west, he suffered martyrdom under the rulers."

Clement says little of Peter, but much of Paul. His mind seems to have been more directed to the mission of the latter than to that of the former, and he makes no distinction of rank between them.

Neither Hermes (A.D. 70), Barnabas (A.D. 73), nor Polycarp (A.D. 108), even mention the name of Peter.

The next writer who names Peter is Ignatius (A.D. 107). Writing from Antioch, he said, "I do not command you (Romans) as did Peter and Paul; they were Apostles, I am a condemned man. They were free, but I am, even this day, a servant." But no reliance can be placed on the correctness of the text of this epistle, for the best critics are agreed that it has been tampered with. It would seem to imply that Peter and Paul taught the Romans, but it does not imply that Peter was Bishop of Rome, any more than Paul; and it should be noted that the Epistle is not addressed to the Bishop of Rome, but to the Christians at Rome.

We next hear of Peter in a fragment of an Epistle written by Dionysius of Corinth to Soter, Bishop of Rome (A.D. 170), preserved by Eusebius :—" So you also, by an admonition so valuable, have again united the planting of the Romans and Corinthians, which was by the hands of Peter and Paul. For both came to visit Corinth, and planted us, both alike taught, and alike went to Italy; and having taught together, they gave their testimony about the same time " (*Ap. Euseb.*, ii. 25).

Irenæus, Bishop of Lyons (A.D. 178-200), tells us that the Church of Rome was founded by "the two glorious Apostles Peter and Paul," and the Apostles having founded and built that Church, committed the sacred office of the Episcopate to Linus. He enumerates by name all the bishops to his day—Eleutherius—whom he reckons as the twelfth bishop, naming Linus as the first bishop. He therefore excludes both Peter and Paul in that capacity. But even in this he is contradicted by Tertullian, who tells us that Peter appointed Clement as first bishop, another of the countless proofs that the "Fathers" did not always agree either in doctrine or chronology.

The "Apostolic Constitutions" represent Linus as having been appointed first Bishop of Rome by Paul, and Clement after the death of Linus by Peter. The date assigned to these "Constitutions" is A.D. 270.

The writings of Irenæus are preserved chiefly in a Latin translation by Eusebius, the ecclesiastical historian. Valesius, a learned Roman Catholic commentator on this work, observes: "Irenæus, as well as Eusebius, says that Peter and Paul laid the first foundation of the Church which was at Rome; but these writers nowhere reckon them among the first bishops of the Church." He also states that "the Apostles had a rank peculiar to themselves, nor were they ever reckoned among the bishops of the Churches."

The works of Cyprian, Bishop of Carthage (A.D. 250), have been mutilated; but though he speaks in eulogistic terms of Peter he distinctly says: "That the rest of the Apostles were even the same that Peter was, being endowed with the like fellowship, honour, and power."

We meet in the writings of this Father, and particularly in the Fathers of the fourth and fifth centuries, the expression "The Chair of Peter." Romanists at once exclusively appropriate the term to the Church of Rome. But the designation was equally applied to Antioch, Alexandria, and other cities. Indeed, it can be easily shown that by the term "chair" doctrine was meant, and, to repeat the words of Augustine in his great work on the "Unity of the Church," "We who call ourselves Christians do not believe in Peter, but in what Peter taught." There is a remarkable passage in one of the Epistles of Pope Gregory I., who wrote at the beginning of the seventh century, addressed to Eulogius, Bishop of Alexandria. Gregory refers to each branch of what he termed the triple See of St. Peter—Rome, Alexandria, and Antioch—as having equal claims with one another both in honour and authority; and in the same Epistle he disclaimed any special honour to himself, inasmuch, he said, as the Bishop of Alexandria, to whom he was writing, was himself one of St. Peter's successors.

We now come to Eusebius, "the Father of Ecclesiastical History" as he is called; for in his great work, which he wrote about A.D. 320, he has recorded every circumstance then extant connected with the history of the Church. He refers to Peter's alleged visit to Rome, which he puts down as during the reign of Claudius. And even here Valesius, his learned Roman Catholic commentator, says Eusebius must be mistaken as to time, for the alleged visit during the reign of Claudius would contradict history, as related in the Acts of the Apostles. And nowhere does Eusebius state that Peter ever was Bishop of Rome, which, if a known fact, he could not have omitted to state. The heading of the second chapter of his third book is "the first (*protos*) that presided over the Church of Rome." "After the martyrdom of Paul and Peter, Linus was the first that was elected to the Bishopric of the Roman See."

Yet we are informed in "Catholic Belief" that Peter reigned in Rome for twenty-five years. There is, as I have said, a proverb, "Lie, and lie boldly." How sad it is that a Church, even nominally Christian, should carry out such principle.

CHAPTER VIII.

HOW THE POPE WAS MADE INFALLIBLE IN THE NINETEENTH CENTURY.

"For a bishop must be blameless, as the steward of God, not self-willed, not soon angry."—TITUS i. 7.

IT is certain, as we have said in the last chapter, that there was very far from being any real unanimity in the Vatican Council on the question of the personal infallibility of the Pope. But what were the opposition to do? The bishops were summoned for the purpose of declaring the Pope infallible, and woe to him who dared to object. We must pause before we condemn those who wished to do so, and did not. Let it be remembered that they had all been brought up from their earliest years in a slavish system of compulsory obedience, that submission to the Pope had been the rule of the Church for centuries. We must take into account the force of multitude, and remember that while the consequences of objection would certainly be serious in this world, it might also bring suffering in the next, according to the teachings of the Church; yet there were some who had the courage of their opinions.

The Bishop of Kerry, Dr. Moriarty, was, to my personal knowledge, one of those who was strongly opposed to the new decree. I heard from his very lips the sad announcement that he had voted against his conscience, and that to his certain knowledge many other bishops had done the same. What a specimen of infallible teaching! Certainly St. Peter would not have required this in the Council of Jerusalem. But this good bishop was not alone in his grief. And here, let it be noted, that remote and careful preparation was made for the declaration of the Pope's personal infallibility some time before the Council was convened, just as remote and careful preparation is now being made for proclaiming it an article of faith that the Pope must be a temporal sovereign. Well, indeed, will it be for those who have the wisdom to note these signs of the times ere it be too late. In August, 1868, the New York *Catholic World*, the mouthpiece of the Romanists in America, in commenting, as in duty—shall we say bound or obliged?—on the recently issued Syllabus, declared that every Catholic must yield obedience to the Pope under pain of sin, when he administers discipline, or issues orders.

The Roman Catholic press of America is taking precisely the same tone in regard to the temporal power of the Pope; and it is perfectly plain to every unprejudiced mind that the great battle for the temporal supremacy of the Pope will be fought out in America. The following extracts from the Roman *Catholic Weekly*, a paper published with full episcopal approbation in Albany, New York State, will show the tendency of Romanists in this direction. It says:—

"Now whilst there may be some difficulty in classifying these gentlemen our friends, there is and can be no difficulty in locating the *Catholic Weekly*. There is no crookedness nor trickery in our title or mission. We are Catholic first, last, and all the time. Our career is to enlighten Catholics of every nationality, and to defend the Church against every comer, no matter who or what he is. We are not, we humbly admit, endowed with that intellectual finesse that, like our friends (?), can draw a hard and fast line between the Church and the Pope, and put him on one side and the Church on the other. To our child-like and simple intellect both are the same. When the Pope speaks, the Church speaks, and when the Church speaks God speaks. We have been always trained to think in this old-fashioned groove, and now that we have grown to manhood we cannot shake it off. The Church would be in a sorry plight if it did not live in the Pope (*sic*). Like a football, it would be kicked about by every political tyrant or intellectual crank. We do not even make the distinctions of the learned between infallible and non-infallible utterances. We are in such awe of his name, his office, and his functions, that to us the least official of his pronouncements is freighted with the will and voice of God.

"To betray him would be the basest of betrayals, to be disloyal to him is a treachery, the blackest among men, to our thinking. Every other consideration is subservient to his authority and the welfare of the Church. What lies beyond this territory is secondary, and incidental. Though we love our country dearly, we love our Church more, and the Pope more. We cannot recognise any aid which our country may give us to reach Heaven, and we do not recognise, we cannot reach that blessed goal without the Church and the Pope."

What miserable, what unchristian words are these: "The Church would be in a sorry plight if it did not live in the Pope." One marvels if the man who wrote these words ever read the Scriptures, which tell us that the Apostles gloried in living in Christ. Truly all this looks but too like the great apostasy, when the man of sin (and many of the Popes have been indeed men of sin) shall sit in the temple of God, showing himself that he is God. Remember that there is no qualification, no words to modify this awful—may we not say?—blasphemy. The utterances of the Pope, whether fallible or infallible, are to be considered as the "voice of God," and to disobey or question is crime. If the Pope approves of incest we must also approve it. If Popes in past ages had innumerable illegitimate children, we must respect their decisions with holy awe when they appoint these children of sin to the highest places in the Church, as Popes have done again and again. Protestants have yet to learn all that is involved in this claim of infallibility.

A belief in the temporal power of the Pope is not, I again repeat, an article of the Roman Catholic faith at present; but there are thousands of men, like the editor of the Albany paper, who are ready to receive it at a moment's notice, and already there are numerous Roman Catholic publications preparing the way actively for its acceptance. But what need is there for a formal proclamation of this doctrine, when it is involved in the very doctrine already proclaimed? The claim of spiritual infallibility made by the Roman Church must not be disputed. But as there is no question of public government, or politics, which cannot be made a religious question, the Pope is practically, to his followers, an infallible authority in all temporal affairs. He claims to be the judge, and a judge from whose decisions there is no appeal, as to whether any political question comes under his jurisdiction or not. What could the most bigoted Romanist desire more?

The constitutions of the United States, and the laws of England, were framed for the general good, and the protection of every individual. The preamble to the constitution of the United States says that its laws were established "in order to form a more perfect union, to establish justice ... and to secure the blessings of liberty to ourselves and to our posterity." Certainly the framers did not foresee a time when the permission of the Pope, and not the approval of the laws of the State, would be necessary even to allow the existence of a body of men united for the purpose of advancing the interest of labour. Yet the American society, known as the Knights of Labour, had to place their regulations in the hands of Cardinal Gibbons, and to submit them humbly for approval, not to the government of the United States, but to the Pope of Rome.

It is certainly amazing how the American people, who profess to set such a high value on their liberty, can allow themselves to be quietly made the slaves of Rome. Dr. Brownson, an eminent writer in the Romish Church, of whom the same Church had a wholesale fear during his lifetime, as he was a man whom they well knew would not hesitate to strike even Rome, if Rome offended him, spoke out very plainly, as most fanatics will do. Authorised by the Church, which certainly applauded him when he made such utterances, he declared that it would be "an intolerable tyranny to be obliged to obey the State, if the State was not under the control of the Church."

Another important outcome of this claim of political infallibility in the government of the world, is the Church's alleged right to punish heretics. The very politicians who to-day are fawning at the feet of the Archbishop of New York, and Cardinal Gibbons, may yet know, to their cost, how Rome can persecute when once she has the power. A Protestant paper in New York expresses its sympathy with Leo XIII. because he was insulted "for the sins of Popes who burned heretics three hundred years ago." Does not the sympathiser know that the law which commands the destruction of heretics, by fire or sword, still exists, and would be put in force if only the infallible Church had the power to do so? This is the extract :—

"Why should this poor old man, who has done nothing but good, be insulted for the sins of Popes who burned rebellious friars three hundred years ago?"

It is the false charity of men like the writer in the *New York Churchman* which is the great help of the Roman Church. The claws of the tiger are there, and they are not blunted. The duty of the Church to persecute is just the same as it was in the days when the hapless Bruno was committed to the flames. The Church of Rome only ceases open persecution because she cannot do it,—the will is there but not the power; but the time is fast coming, through the instrumentality, not of Romanists—for the vast multitude of Romanists are absolutely indifferent to the Church to which they nominally belong—but through the instrumentality of "liberal" Protestants, when Rome will have the power to persecute, and then the Liberal Protestant will fare as badly at the hands of that Church which he has served so well, as the most illiberal radical.

It would be well if Protestants of the extreme "High Church" type could realize how little respect Rome has for them. The more Roman, or, as they are pleased to term it, the more " Catholic " they become, the more ridiculous they appear to Romanists. It is true that Rome sometimes hides her sneers, when there is fear of offending a millionaire, but she does not on that account change her real sentiments. An article which we give below will be amusing to some, and we hope instructive to those who imagine they are approved by Rome, because they are imitating her practices.

The Rev. Philip Fletcher, a Roman Catholic priest, and formerly curate of a Ritualistic Church at Brighton, writes as follows in the *Weekly Register:*—

"Some of these Anglican neighbours have extraordinary impudence. Though they don't live in our house, but have got one of their own, though they don't even intend to quit their own residence and come and dwell in one which has foundations, yet they are for ever poking about our premises, and picking up what they can find; and having found something though it does not belong to them, they carry it off and stick it in their own garden, though it won't grow there, or nail it up on their walls, though it doesn't suit their furniture a bit. Yes, 'his neighbour cometh and searcheth him.' He does, indeed. Now, if they came to search us from good motives, we would not mind. Some of them do, and we are always then glad to see them. We show them over everywhere, and explain the whole plan of the Catholic house and grounds. Such as these come to see if our house is better than their own. It is not difficult to prove to them that it is so, for many of us have lived in that house of theirs, and right glad we are to have got out of it. Nothing but noise, and quarrelling, and brawling from morning to night. A regular babel of confusion. Even those of us who were never inside of it can see and hear what goes on, for the Anglican walls are very thin; and what they see and hear offers them no temptation to seek shelter under that noisy roof. But there are, as I say, others of these neighbours of ours who 'come and search' with no such worthy motive. No; but they want to patch up their own tumble-down dwelling with odds and ends from Catholic sources, in order to make more short-sighted people imagine that theirs is the Catholic Church. So they make raids upon our possessions, and then pass them off as their own, generally, however, breaking them in the process. The Ritualist parson, especially one, goes abroad, and *e.g.*, sees a sacred minister, after a Requiem Mass, bearing the Processional Cross; so when he gets home he has a procession on Sundays, before or after (or probably both) his Sunday High Celebrations, with a bearded clergyman in a Dalmatic and a bad temper (at having to carry what the butcher in a surplice used to do), bearing the cross in front of a long line of processionists. He attends a Pontifical High Mass, and sees some one in a cope in close attendance at the altar; so, on his return, he immediately pops his master of ceremonies into a cope, who flits about delighted with his investiture, and orders people about more commandingly than ever. He sees the red lamp burning before the tabernacle in every Catholic Church, and he thinks, 'How sweet it would be to have the same thing at home;' but having no tabernacle he makes up by having seven red lamps instead of one; and to make the illusion more perfect, has a sham tabernacle painted or carved behind his communion table. He looks into a Roman Missal, and sees that there are no commandments, so he leaves them out at his 'early celebration' (like a naughty boy, 'when nobody is looking'). He notices 'Secreta,' and 'Canon,' and 'Memento for the Dead,' and 'Post Communions,' which are not in the 'Book of Common Prayer;' but that doesn't matter a bit; he soon stitches them in. He happens upon a 'Garden of the Soul,' and finds warm, stirring solid devotions, which are unknown to cold, formal Anglicanism; so he makes up a 'Book of Devotions,' adapted to members of the Church of England, in which he calmly palms off as Anglican devotions what was written by most Roman and utterly anti-Anglican authors; and in order to hinder recognition of their true origin, he mutilates these devotions so as to fit in with Anglican fads and fancies. And then he glories in being 'so Roman,' and no doubt thinks he is a very fine bird, though there are plenty of more knowing birds behind him who are laughing in their sleeves, and out of them, at the foolish jackdaw strutting about in feathers not its own."

I know, and many others know, that the Church of Rome of to-day persecutes as far as she dares, shielded and helped by "liberal" Protestants, who are so very liberal of the lives and liberties of others, and have so very little sympathy for their sufferings. Why cannot Protestants be Protestants, and men? Why do they lie down and worship at the very feet of that power which, whatever toleration it may have for other Protestants, has nothing but words of the utmost contempt for those who are Protestants without liberty, Papists without a Pope, and Catholics without unity?

"Popular feeling," says a Protestant writer, "is mostly for the Pope." I was in Rome not long since, and I know, for I took the trouble to inquire even then, Romanist as I was, and I solemnly declare that "popular feeling" was altogether against the Pope. Against himself personally there was not a bad feeling, but he represents a system which the Roman and Italian people know too well has been the curse of their country, and as the administrator of that system he is justly hated. "The Pope," says this writer, "has done nothing but good." Is it then good to show the whole world how he sympathises with his predecessor in the burning of heretics? Need we say more? A rebellious friar! How easy it is to take away character! Just so Dr. McGlynn is "a rebellious friar;" and presumably this writer in a first-class paper, representing the opinion of the whole Episcopal Church of the United States, would like to assist Archbishop Corrigan in burning him alive also, before the City Hall in New York, and he would be able to command the assistance and the sympathy of a considerable number of men who agree with him in their condolences with the Pope, because the people of Italy have shown their respect for a martyr of liberty.

But these ardent "Protestant" sympathisers with the Pope are the veriest heretics in his eyes, and they would certainly be led to the stake in short order, after an example had been made of Dr. McGlynn and myself, if it was in the power of Archbishop Corrigan to inflict it. Nor do I blame him; he would simply be carrying out the orders of the infallible Church to which he belongs. Has he not shown how he would like to punish, if he dare, when he sentenced a priest to ten days' imprisonment, and penance in a monastery, and this in free America, because he said one little word in disapproval of the way in which Dr. McGlynn was treated? The Archbishop sentenced a sister to Blackwall's Island as an insane person, because, according to her statement to myself, she had denounced conduct which she justly considered shameful between a priest, and the Lady Superior of the convent where she was a nun. If men cry, Peace, peace, where there is no peace, it would matter little if they were the only victims of their folly, but the danger will not end with their lives. It may require another generation of "liberal Protestants" to secure for Rome the full power to persecute.

Protestants of this class, and every intelligent human being, should know that the Church of Rome requires every bishop to take a solemn oath at his consecration to persecute heretics. The oath has been published, and—to his credit be it said—by a High Churchman, who has the common sense to see that the Church of England gains no respect from Rome, nor strength for herself, by laying herself at the feet of the Pope.[*]

The editor of the document from which I quote, the Rev. John M. Davenport, comments thus on the velvet-paw policy of Rome :—

"The cities just named have bitter experience of this velvet-paw treachery. They have harboured a religion all smiles and affability while in low estate; they have been flattered into giving it pecuniary and political aid; they have with kindly spirit patronised its bazaars and lotteries; and yet what is the return? Exchange of kindnesses? Far from it. It combines to plot

---

[*] This important document can be obtained from the publisher, George A. Knodell, St. John, N.B. It can also be seen in the latest edition of the "Roman Pontifical."

against and crush its benefactors, and to boycott them out of office and existence. Boston is the only city of the four which has revolted somewhat successfully against the tyranny. New York groans under its papal fetters, and a press controlled by the Roman Catholic Church. Quebec has become almost wholly Roman by the exodus of the rising generation of English people, not strong enough to withstand the trade boycott, while the non-Roman population of Montreal is outnumbered by the Roman in the proportion of three to one; and yet the minority have to pay more taxes than all the rest put together, as the Roman Church, though rolling in wealth, has managed to exempt its vast property from taxation."

In September, 1851, the *Rambler*, a Roman Catholic Magazine published in England, wrote thus :—

"A Catholic temporal government would be guided in its treatment of Protestants and other recusants solely by the rules of expediency. . . . None but an atheist can uphold the principles of religious liberty. . . . Shall I hold out hopes to my fellow-countryman that I will not meddle with his creed if he will not meddle with mine? Shall I lead him to think that religion is a matter of private opinion, and tempt him to forget that he has no more right to his religious views than he has to my purse, or my house, or my life-blood? No. Catholicism is the most intolerant of creeds."

The Shepherd of the Valley, a paper published under the auspices of Archbishop Ryan of Philadelphia, a prelate who is fêted, or, as a local paper says, "dined and wined" by all the leading Protestants of

Philadelphia, has published the following pastoral instruction of the Archbishop. We only wish it could be read in his presence and in the presence of those who, by patronising him in society, are helping to hasten the time when he will be able to persecute as he declares he is bound to do, and as he has sworn in the oath which he took when he was made bishop that he will do. Here are his own words:—

"We maintain that the Church of Rome is intolerant, that is, she uses every means in her power to root out heresy; but her intolerance is the result of her infallibility. She alone has the right to be intolerant, because she alone has the right. The Church tolerates heretics where she is obliged to do so, but she hates them with a deadly hatred, and uses all her power to annihilate them. If ever the Roman Catholics in this land should become a considerable majority, which in time will surely be the case . . . then will religious freedom in the Republic of the United States come to an end. Our enemies know how the Roman Church treated heretics in the Middle Ages, and how she treats them to-day whenever she has the power. We no more think of denying these historical facts than we do of blaming the holy God, and the princes of the Church, for what they have thought it good to do."

The following are the words, in Latin and English, by which every Roman Catholic bishop pledges himself to persecute every Protestant:—

"I WILL, TO THE UTMOST OF MY POWER, PERSECUTE AND ATTACK HERETICS, SCHISMATICS, AND REBELS AGAINST THE SAME OUR LORD (THE POPE) OR HIS AFORESAID SUCCESSORS."

"Hæreticos, schismaticos, et rebelles eidem Domino nostro, vel Successoribus prædictis pro posse persequar, et impugnabo."

What would the Roman Catholic Church say if the ministers of any Protestant denomination were to make such a vow at their ordination? What a cry there would be of bigotry and oppression! But because all this, and a great many other things, are not suspected by unsuspicious Protestants who, not doing these things themselves, never dream that they are done by Romanists, and because the same Romanists very wisely use the Latin tongue to conceal their deeds of evil, they can afford to lie about their teachings, and thereby deceive the world at large. Let it be remembered that it is a part of the teaching of the Roman Church that faith need not be kept with Protestants under any circumstance whatever; and let Protestants who know these things beware lest God shall call them to a terrible account, at the last day, for supporting such a system of lies and imposture.

Again, be it remembered that Roman Catholics are bound, not by what they may say in society, or to converts who are too often, as I was myself, easily deceived, having no suspicion of even the possibility of such falsehood. The Roman priests and bishops are bound by the dogmatic teaching of their Church, and we have a right to judge them by that teaching, and by it only. A man has no right to refuse to be judged or bound by the laws of the Church to which he belongs, above all in the case of the Church of Rome.

The subject is one of so much importance, that I give the following extracts from St. Thomas Aquinas, and be it remembered that he is no obsolete authority, he is still the "angel of the schools," and the great authority in all matters of theological teaching in the Roman Church. What he says, Rome says; for Rome has put the seal of her strongest approbation on his teaching, and the present Pope has especially approved it.

"Though heretics must not be tolerated because they deserved it, we must bear with them till, by a second admonition, they may be brought back to the faith of the Church. But those who, after a second admonition, remain obstinate in their errors, must not only be excommunicated, but they must be delivered to the secular power to be exterminated." ("St. Thomas Aquinas," p. 90.)

At p. 91 he says:—"Though heretics who repent must always be accepted to penance as often as they have fallen, they must not, in consequence of that, always be permitted to enjoy the benefits of this life. . . . When they fall again they are admitted to repent. . . . But the sentence of death must not be removed."

Later on in the same article all dealings with heretics are positively forbidden.

The Council of Lateran, held in 1215, decreed as follows:—

"We excommunicate and anathematize every heresy that exalts itself against the holy orthodox and Catholic faith, condemning all heretics, by whatever name they may be known . . . for though their faces differ, they are tied together by their tails. Such as are condemned are to be delivered over to the existing secular powers to receive due punishment. If laymen, their goods must be confiscated; if priests, they shall be degraded from their respective orders, and their property applied to the use of the Church in which they officiated. Secular powers of all ranks and degrees are to be warned, induced, and if necessary compelled by ecclesiastical censures to swear that they will exert themselves to the utmost in defence of the faith, and extirpate all heretics denounced by the Church who shall be found in their territories. And whenever any person shall assume government, whether it be spiritual or temporal, he shall be bound to abide by this decree.

"If any temporal lord, after having been admonished and required by the Church, shall neglect to clear his territory of heretical depravity, the Metropolitan and Bishop of the province shall unite in excommunicating him. Should he remain contumacious a whole year the fact shall be signified to the Supreme Pontiff, who shall declare his vassals released from their allegiance from that time, and will bestow his territory on Catholics, to be occupied by them on the condition of exterminating the heretics, and preserving the said territory in the faith.

"Catholics who shall assume the cross for the extermination of heretics shall enjoy the same indulgences, and be protected by the same privileges, as are granted to those who go to the help of the Holy Land."

And with all these stern realities, and the fact before the eyes of the whole world, that the present Pope has endorsed the conduct of his predecessor in burning heretics, we yet find the following in the *New York World:*—

"When the Pope of Rome celebrated his jubilee about a year ago there were sent to him no congratulations, from any source, more cordial than many which had a Protestant origin. This fact did not indicate any tendency of Protestantism towards Romanism (?); but it showed that the personal character of the sovereign Pontiff commanded respect, even affection, from many Christians who entirely decline to sanction his ecclesiastical claims. Understood in that sense, a hearty concurrence may be given to what Cardinal Ryan said at the recent anniversary dinner of the Catholic Club in Philadelphia, 'Many Protestants who have met the Pope, while not religiously Catholic, are personally Papists.'"

If these men who are not "religiously Catholic," but are "personally Papists," are not prepared to be altogether personally, relatively, and absolutely Papists, they will meet with the same fate as Bruno, as soon as Rome can inflict it, and all their previous concessions and liberality will not save them.

But Rome distinguishes "infallibly" in the matter of secret societies. Why indeed should she not do so, when she claims that all power has been given to her, in heaven and in earth? The world has rung with the story of the shameful murder of Dr. Cronin. What has Rome to say about this matter? It would be wise if those who are so sure that Rome is the friend of law and order would read the signs of the times, and see for themselves the conditions under which she assists to keep or break the public peace.

The history of the way in which the Knights of Labour have been and are controlled by the Church of Rome is well worthy of the consideration of those who would read the signs of the times. This organisation has no religious or political standing or aims. It is simply a body of men united for the purpose of mutual advantage, and for the protection of their own commercial interests. Scarcely had this organisation been formed when the "Church" interfered. The head of the organisation, Mr. Powderly, is a more or less devout Roman Catholic; and this fact of course gave the Church the much-desired thin end of the wedge. But it is perfectly amazing, and it is an undeniable evidence of the power of the Roman Church in America, that a body of men who are a non-religious organisation should be obliged to place themselves slavishly at the feet of the Pope. If anything could open the eyes of the Protestant people of America to the danger to the Republic, from the aggressions of Rome, this most certainly should do so.

Although Mr. Powderly had the talent to organise, and even to control his organisation, he was a child in the hands of the "Church." To her mandates he was required to bow down abjectly, and he did bow down. No doubt he was made aware of the inevitable consequences of doing otherwise. Now it should be again observed that the Knights of Labour are not a Roman Catholic organisation; at least they were not, and were never intended to be such in their inception. A large minority, if not a fair majority, are Protestants. What matter? They also must bow to Rome, and they have done so. The inner secret of the power of Rome over this organisation will probably never be known, but quite enough has been made public. Possibly Mr. Powderly was threatened with the loss of his power in the organisation if he did not obey orders. Rome has more ways of enforcing her commands than men suppose, who do not know her inner workings. She can make herself felt from the throne to the hovel, and she does make herself felt. Not for the welfare of the people—for what people have ever prospered under her rule?—but for the supposed advancement of the Church. Not for the advancement of the kingdom of Christ, for He has distinctly condemned her in advance, when He said, "My kingdom is not of this world;" and her whole desire is to rule the kingdoms of the world.

Whatever may have been the motive or cause of Mr. Powderly's degrading submission, there is no doubt about the fact. It is possible to understand his action in the matter, but how can we account for the submission of a large body of men who are not Roman Catholics? The heads of the Church of Rome in America, in view of this, and many such evidences of their power, may well boast in Rome that they have the people of America under their feet. Imagine for one moment a body of English working men submitting the rules of their organisation to the Pope for his approval, and waiting in abject submission till he was pleased to set the seal of his approval on them. It was said at the time, and I believe with truth, that if Powderly had held out and refused to submit the rules of the society, Rome would have succumbed. She always knows just how far she can go, and she very seldom risks going farther. She has on her side American men of capital who work for her, and with her, in the fond delusion that she will protect the millionaire, her kingdom and interests being like his, of the world. But the millionaire, if he took time to read history, would soon learn that the expected protection will be withdrawn when the Church of Rome becomes strong enough to crush him, as well as the working man. Millionaires are generally willing to give a tithe of their wealth to protect the rest; and no doubt the rich employers of America are only too well pleased to have the working men who belong to the Knights of Labour under the control of Rome.

As the matter is of such importance, we give the facts from a Roman Catholic paper, the New York *Freeman's Journal*, which now dispenses the dynamite of the Church under the editorship of Pat Ford, whose name has become notorious as the advocate of material dynamite.

The following is the letter of the Cardinal Prefect of the sacred congregation to Cardinal Gibbons, embodying its decree in regard to the American Knights of Labour:—

"ROME. *August* 29*th*, 1888.

"MOST EMINENT AND MOST REV. LORD,—I have to inform your Eminence that the fresh documents relative to the society of the Knights of Labour, which have been laid before the Sacred Congregation, were examined at its meeting held on Thursday, August 16th, of the current year.

"Having carefully studied these documents, the Sacred Congregation orders that this reply be made:— That, judging by all that has hitherto been proposed to it, the Knights of Labour may for the present be tolerated. The Sacred Congregation only requires that the necessary corrections be made in the statutes of the organisation, in order to explain what might otherwise appear to be obscure, or be interpreted in a wrong sense. The modifications should especially be made in those passages of the preamble of the rules which refer to local association; the words which in these passages savour of socialism and communism must be corrected in such a manner as to make them express simply the right given by God to man, or rather to mankind, to acquire by legitimate means, respecting always the rights of property enjoyed by every one.

"I am happy to be able to inform your Eminence that the Sacred Congregation has praised highly the resolve of the Bishops of the United States to take heed, in concert with itself, lest there creep into the society of the Knights of Labour, and other similar organisations, anything contrary to justice and honesty, or not in conformity with the instructions given as to the Masonic sect.

"In confirming and supporting you in this excellent project, in the name of the Sacred Congregation I pray you to accept the assurance of our respectful and devoted sentiments.

"Your Eminence's very humble servant,
"JOHN CARDINAL SIMEONI, *Prefect.*

"To His Eminence CARDINAL JAMES GIBBONS, *Archbishop of Baltimore.*"

The New York *Sun* published the condemnation, by the Tribunal of the Roman Inquisition, of the doctrine proposed by Mr. Henry George, abolishing private property in land, and giving the further direction that, if the Society of the Knights of Labour would be tolerated by the Roman Catholic Church, they must correct any expression of agreement with the views of Mr. George. The following letter from Cardinal Gibbons to Archbishop Elder of Cincinnati was the result:—

"CARDINAL'S RESIDENCE,
"408, *N. Charles St., Baltimore, September* 25*th.*

"YOUR GRACE,—On receipt of the letter of which the enclosed is a copy, I wrote to Mr. Powderly requesting him to come and see me. He came on the 24th inst.

in compliance with my invitation, and cheerfully promised to make the emendations required by the Holy Office, and expressed his readiness to comply at all times with the wishes of the ecclesiastical authorities, Very faithfully your friend in Christ.

"J. Card. Gibbons.

"Most Rev. Dr. Elder, *Abp.*, *Cincinnati.*"

But this is not all. Would it be believed that a set of Roman Cardinals, not one of whom, as I can testify from my own personal knowledge, can read one word of English, could have the impertinence to tell the English-speaking and English-thinking men of the great American Republic that their organisation "may be tolerated for the present"? Nothing can be done until certain words, of which these Cardinals do not understand one single sentence in the language in which they are written, are altered to suit their pleasure. And this in the nineteenth century! If such things can be done now, no statement of the claims of the Church, or of the abject submission of the people to it in the Middle Ages, should surprise us. Indeed there was a good deal more resistance to Rome then than now. Talk of the exaction and tyrannies of Imperial Rome towards her colonies; they were as nothing compared to the demands and exactions of modern Papal Rome. The Inquisition is practically established now in America, as Cardinal Gibbons plainly states, for the "Holy Office," to which he refers in the above letter, is one of the names of the Inquisition. For the present it "tolerates;" it will burn whenever it will be safe to burn. It should be observed that in all this business of regulating American affairs there is not one word of reference to the opinions of the people of America. As for the Government, it is simply ignored. It is a matter of no account.

But if Rome exercises her power over the government of America, and dictates to the American working man just how far he may go in claiming his rights, and just what words he may use in his charters of incorporation, there are Societies with which Rome does not interfere, partly because she dare not, partly because she knows that the time may come when she can make use of these societies for her own advancement.

The Clan-na-Gael goes on her murderous way with the full approval and blessing of the "holy" Roman Catholic Church. Certainly it is a very blessed thing for this world to be a "faithful child" of holy Church. If you have private or public grudges, and want to avenge them, you need not fear, if you submit to the Church in essentials, that you will find any interference with your plans in such trivial matters. I am serious; the subject is far too serious for jest. I am stating facts; and the fact that these facts are startling, should not blind us to them or to their consequences. I do not ask any one to take my word for these assertions. The case is before the public. When has the Church of Rome said one word, in America, to censure the Clan-na-Gael, or any other Irish secret assassination society? If anything has been said it has been in so low a whisper that no one has caught the sound.

The truth is, that Rome dare not interfere with the secret societies of the Irish people. It is only Protestant societies which she rules and regulates. The determined attitude which the Irish have taken against any interference of Rome in their political affairs has had its due effect. Rome cannot do without Ireland; above all, it cannot do without the Irish people in

America, and Rome acts accordingly. The facts are before the public. I do no more than to draw public attention to what already exists.

A short time since, Father Murphy of Kilmeen, Ireland, was sentenced to four months imprisonment for violating the law, in connection with the eviction of one of his parishioners. He appealed against the sentence, and after a long and careful hearing the case was fully proved against him. The magistrate, anxious not to offend the "priest" (an easy offence to commit, the consequences of which are well known to all those who administer justice in Ireland), offered to remit the penalty if the priest would apologise, and promise to refrain from such conduct in the future. But the priest would do nothing of the kind. He knew too well the value of an imprisonment, and the capital it would make for him when his sentence was ended. But what of the Pope? Never a word is said in approval, no matter how mild, of all this; it is only the Protestant institutons of America which come under the personal control of Rome, and whose members must submit to have even the very wording of their rules criticised and altered as the Pope pleases.

The very idea of denouncing in any way the Clan-na-Gael murders has been laughed to scorn by Archbishop Corrigan's organ, the New York *Freeman's Journal*. I give the very words of the paper:—

"For real cheek and presumption, evidently begotten of ignorance, we commend the editorial of the *New York Press*, in which the Catholic Church is asked to thunder from its pulpits against its miscreants guilty of the deed."

Of course it would not do to approve too openly of the assassination of Dr. Cronin, who seems to have been the only practical Catholic of the lot, and who from that point of view should have had some claim to the sympathy, if not the protection of his Church. But the Clan-na-Gael are too powerful a body to be offended, and too many of its members are implicated in this disgraceful affair, to admit of the condemnation of the society as a whole. But let it be supposed for a moment that the Knights of Labour had assassinated a member of that body, and above all if that member had been a Romanist, what torrents of righteous indignation would have been poured forth on the leaders, and on every member of the organisation. Rome is fine at virtuous indignation when the shortcomings of other people are concerned, or when there is political capital to be made out of the condemnation of her own children.

Rome is wiser in her generation than the children of light. Why should not the Papal Church "thunder from her pulpits" against the evildoers who are her children? But see how gently these men are spoken of; they are only "miscreants." Perhaps these very "miscreants" have sat at the feet of the editor of this paper, and learned from him the doctrine of spreading the lurid light of assassination. "Spread the light." Send dynamite to blow up the "English enemy." Kill; destroy. Let innocent men be murdered with the so-called guilty; no matter. The innocent must suffer sometimes, even in legalised war. This was the teaching of the "Spread the Light" paper, still, we believe, owned by the editor and proprietor of the New York *Freeman's Journal*, the leading Roman Catholic paper in that city. No wonder the editor treats the Chicago murderers as men and brothers; they are merely "miscreants," a mild word, which may be used in jest even to describe some boyish freak. Why should the Catholic Church be asked to denounce these devoted sons of Ireland and of Rome ? One Cronin more or less; what matter, when the thousands who are left have to be considered, and the political influence which they wield ? Truly of such are the kingdom of earth ; what matter about the kingdom of heaven ? Here is the opinion of Archbishop Corrigan, for no paper under his authority would dare make any statement contrary to his will.

We give another paragraph from this official organ of the Roman Church, and let there be no mistake on these subjects. If the Pope with one word could stop the circulation of the Bible in France, he could as easily have stopped the circulation of the dynamite *Irish World* in New York. It is easy to prevent the circulation of the Bible, but to say a word to the editor of a powerful paper, like the New York *Freeman's Journal*, is quite another matter.

"The Chicago Clan-na-Gael revelations is a bad business for all concerned, as well as for the cause in whose name the actors are supposed to have worked ; but there may be some good in the lesson taught by it, that will compensate for the chagrin which all true friends of Ireland must feel over the sad affair."

All true friends of Ireland must feel "chagrined," and it is a "sad affair;" and this is all the holy Catholic Church, as represented by Archbishop Corrigan, has to say of a foul and brutal murder. It is not unfair to suggest that the "chagrin" (a curious word to use in describing the utter abhorrence which every true Christian should have for such deeds) may be, not because the murder was committed, but because it was found out; and it is worthy of note that the writer thinks that "the good in the lesson" will compensate for the sad little affair of the murder. What words are these for Christian men to use unreproved, and in the name of the Roman Church, which claims such exceptional holiness !

But there are many reasons for the quiet condonement of any evil which the Clan-na-Gael may do. The Clan-na-Gael is rich, and Rome has a supreme respect for wealth. She craves money as no other Christian community ever craved it, and she works for it as no other Christian community ever has worked for it. She is far too wise to risk the loss of money, or of the friendship and support of those who have it, and who may find it to their interest to have the shield of her protection thrown over their evil deeds. Here is a statement worth the careful attention of those who may wish to know just how the Roman Catholic Church stands in this matter :—

"F. W. Dunne, a leading Chicago Irishman, who was expelled from Camp No. 16, Clan-na-gael, for charging Alexander Sullivan in 1882 with using $85,000 of the funds of the organisation in paying his debts, is out with a statement. He says :—

"'The present strength of the organisation is 22,000, and it has been in existence for twenty-two years. To estimate the numerical strength of the organisation one-half its present strength will be moderate.

Yearly dues, 11,000 men at $6, $66,000 ; for twenty-two years	$1,542,000
Initiation fees, 11,000 men at $2	22,000
New members, to fill vacancies, 21,000 per annum, at $2 each	42,000
Special calls, twenty-two years, say five calls, averaging $5 per head, or 55,000 for each call . .	275,000

Brought forward	$1,881,000
Annual picnics, say $40,000 per annum, or $100 for 400 camps, for twenty-two years	880,000
Skirmishing fund, obtained by Ford and Rossa	103,000
Total	2,864,000
Deduct hall rent, say 400 camps at $100 per year, for twenty-two years	880,000
Total	$1,984,000

"'You will see,' continued Mr. Dunne, 'what a haul the Triangle has had. I content myself with making this statement. I challenge Alexander Sullivan, or Father Dorney, to disapprove anything I say. The courts are open to the former if I libel him. As a Catholic, I will appear before the Archbishop to prove everything I say against Maurice J. Dorney as a priest.'

"Father Dorney, the associate of Sullivan and Egan, is being denounced on all sides. It will be remembered that he was appointed to examine Sullivan's accounts, and he pronounced them all straight, after the money had disappeared. And now the Clan-na-Gael demands his 'removal' (not as Cronin was removed, however) by the Archbishop. A telegram from Chicago says: 'Clan-na-Gael, Camp No 52, United Brotherhood, held a special meeting on Saturday night, at Forty-Second and Halsted Streets. It was an important meeting in many respects. The object was to discuss the part taken by the Rev. Father Dorney in the Cronin matter, and also his denial of the fact that he is a Clan-na-Gael, and that he was, if he is not now, a member of Camp 16. When these charges were first made against Alexander Sullivan by Dr. Cronin, Camp No. 17, which then met at Fourty-Fourth and Halsted Streets in the Town of

Lake, demanded an investigation. Dorney acquitted Sullivan of all sharp practice.'"

If a Protestant clergyman of any denomination had even been named in such a connection, what an outcry there would have been in every Roman Catholic paper all over the world.

The Pope has certainly denounced assassinations and outrages now and then in Ireland, under pressure from the English Government. But he changed the subject, with a promptness which would be amusing if the matter was not so serious, when he found that the Irish people would cut off the supplies if they were interfered with. All the world knows that it has taken all Archbishop Walsh's tact and popularity to keep the peace between the "faithful" Irish and the Pope. Indeed nothing could well be more undignified than the Papal proceedings in this matter. But to interfere with the free right of the Irish American, to assassinate any one who is pleased to denounce fraud, is quite another affair. And yet there are Protestants, and Protestant capitalists, who think that the Church of Rome will protect them from the "mob" if they extend their protection to the Pope's representatives in America. When the Pope has not been able or has not been willing, to protect Irish men of honour like Dr. Cronin of his own communion, and Irish landlords, Protestant or Romanist, from assassination, the American millionaire might know that he will find himself deserted when he most needs help.

It is interesting and instructive to observe who the men are whom Rome delights to honour. The *New York World*, a paper which cannot be charged with any anti-Romanist sympathies, has the following paragraph. It might have added one more to the "two great" and good men, all devoted Roman Catholics, of whom America is so justly (?) proud, and who are so much honoured by the Roman Church. Sullivan, the iceman, who is accused of the Cronin murder, has been no doubt accidentally omitted.

"The United States of America has two great Sullivans. One knocked a man down, and shot him dead as he was rising. An American judge held that, having been knocked down, the man would naturally be angry, and might desire to injure Sullivan; therefore the shooting was done in self-defence. This Sullivan also sent dynamiters to England to blow up and mangle innocent women and children. The other Sullivan is a brute who thrashed his wife, and knocked a waiter-girl down. He is to meet a good man in a few days. It is to be hoped that nothing will occur to interrupt the proceedings. The United States is justly proud of its two Sullivans."

The same paper adds significantly:—

"Labouchere says Sullivan had nothing to do with the Cronin murder. Davitt says the same thing, and Pat Ford says ditto. How do they know? If they are positive that Sullivan had nothing to do with it, it may not be too much to say that they must know who had."

Pat Ford, it will be remembered, is the—we had almost said infallible—successor of the late Dr. Brownson, and of Mr. Egan (not the dynamiter, but a namesake), promoted to Chili regions, who is now teaching the young idea how to—well, suppose we say shoot, in one of the many Roman Catholic "Universities" in this happy land. But what matter? Are they not all faithful sons of the "Church"? And if they are not prepared to live for it, they will be ready, when called on, to fight for it, which is of far more consequence. Decent men like Cronin could only live for their faith, and are not worth counting or encouraging.

After all, it is far better, in the Church of Rome, to be a murderer than a heretic. There is no chance for the heretic, but for the murderer there is every hope, especially if he belongs to any powerful body of men who cannot be interfered with without dangerous consequences. Bishop Foley thus disposes of heretics:—

On the 31st of December, 1869, Right Rev. Bishop Foley of Chicago swore before the civil court at Kankakee, that the following sentence was an exact translation of the doctrine of the Church of Rome, as taught to-day in all the Roman Catholic seminaries, colleges, and universities, through the "Summa Theologica" of Thomas Aquinas (vol. iv., p. 90):—"Though heretics must not be tolerated because they deserve it, we must bear with them, till by a second admonition they may be brought back to the faith of the Church. But those who, after a second admonition, remain obstinate to their errors, must not only be excommunicated, but they must be delivered to the secular power to be exterminated."

A priest in New York diocese was threatened with all sorts of ecclesiastical pains and penalties, if he assisted me in any way in my efforts to help emigrant girls, though the work had been specially approved by the Pope. But to be a Sullivan, and a slogger, is quite another affair. Priests are quite at liberty to follow their inclinations, and to show all honour to the "big fellow." We are informed in the *New York World* that :—

"Father Bonlow, the pastor of the little Roman Catholic Church in Belfast, is about the only regular visitor. He doesn't bother the boys talking about theological matters, and Muldoon gives him $100 a year for the Church, and they call it square. The priest likes to go over in the lounging room Muldoon has fitted up in the stable, where John L—— pounds the bags, wrestles, has his baths and is rubbed down. Slogging, wrestling, and episodes of the ring generally are the favourite topics of conversation, and Father Bonlow can give points to many sportsmen on these subjects."

It is indeed difficult to know what the "Church" will not "square" if the money to square with is only forthcoming. Happy Sullivan to fight under such blessed auspices! But we are also told that his pugilistic opponent, Kilrain, was by no means behind in the race for priestly favour. He, too, had the "special blessing" of the Holy Catholic Church. And Sullivan was met and blessed by priests on his way to the brutal exhibition, where he did such honour to his faith and country, as a prize fighter.

In a report from Ottawa, published in the *New York World*, the Deputy Minister of Justice says :—

"The American people are now beginning to realize the dangerous element they have among them in the Clan-na-Gael society, the influence of which society defeated the Extradition Bill in the United States Senate. The Dominion Government has evidence that this society a year or so ago had planned the destruction of the Parliament buildings here and the assassination of Lord Lansdowne, then Governor-General. We discovered the plot, and frustrated their murderous designs; and it is hardly to be wondered that any member of the society against whom there are strong evidences of complicity in murder should not expect much leniency from the executive at Ottawa."

It is strange if the Government at Ottawa is aware of the guilt of the Clan-na-Gael, and knows what a menace it is to society, that the Roman Church should have such warm supporters in that country.

Here is the history of another good Catholic, with whose career the Church seems quite satisfied. Is it any wonder that Roman Catholic young men with any self-respect are beginning to be ashamed of their Church, as a writer in the (Roman Catholic) *Richmond Visitor* declares? The editor of that paper says :—

"The want of due respect for the clergy is very noticeable among our young people. Among the boys especially is this lack of courtesy most marked. Young men fail or refuse to recognise their own pastor on the street. Young boys will hide and seek to avoid meeting with their parish priest. This is not right. It could not fail to discourage the most sanguine priest were such a thing possible. It must certainly render his work less pleasant, to feel that those in whom he is most interested, endeavour to shun him on the streets. It is all foolishness to think that the priest does not know them. He has nothing else to think of but those entrusted to his care. Young people, respect your clergy; by so doing you will respect yourselves."

The bishop of the diocese where there is such a

lamentable state of things as that described above is the right Rev. Dr. Keane, the present Rector of the new Roman Catholic university in Washington. It will be interesting to see if he will be able to secure all the respect he desires, from the young men whom he expects to graduate in his university. If he could not obtain for himself and his priests even the common courtesies of life in his own diocese, and when they were under his own pastoral control, and taught in his own schools, it is scarcely to be expected that he will fare better with others. But what a revelation this is of the inner life of the Roman Church.

The Roman Church professes to rule for God; the result of her rule shows that she rules for the devil. Everywhere that she has obtained power there is the same record of violence and crime. Look at Ireland. Look at New York and Chicago. In these places Rome has more power than in any other country in the world; and what is the result? As regards Ireland, I will speak later and give facts which cannot be disputed. As regards New York, the records of the police courts ought to make every honest Romanist blush for shame. Gangs of ruffians with Irish names, which tell their nationality, and with medals or scapulars which tell their creed, make certain parts of New York hideous with crime. And what does the Church of Rome do for their improvement? An Irish judge has stated lately that he sentences from ten to fifteen thousand criminals every year in New York, and there are few indeed of these who are not members of the "holy" Catholic Church. God help them! I do not here say one word of reproach to the Irish for Irish crime; but I do say, in the words of the late Dr. Moriarty, that eternity will not be long enough, nor hell hot enough, to punish those who have deliberately deceived these unhappy people.

I might fill the present work and volumes more if I gave anything like a history of Irish crime in New York, simply taking the facts from the daily papers. I have a personal knowledge of the workings of some of the Roman Catholic institutions in New York. Protestants who do not inquire into details, and who do not know facts, are lost in amazement at the number of charitable institutions which are supported (as they think) by the Roman Catholic Church. As a matter of fact, they are supported to a great extent by Protestants, who are taxed—and obliged to pay the tax, too—for the support of these institutions; whose existence would not be necessary if the poor Roman Catholics were taught to believe in the Gospel, instead of the Papal Church. Sometimes these men commit murder too openly to be shielded by the Church, or by the saloon keepers, who are in such high favour with the Romish bishops.

The Roman Catholic Church obtained her great foothold in the United States after the civil war. However priests may quarrel with each other, and even with their bishops, they always unite in the most extravagant laudations of their Church. During the war the sisters did good service with other ladies in nursing the sick. The Roman Church, wise as the serpent, has kept before the public, and worked it for all it was worth. The Americans are a generous people, and they responded to the appeals which were made after the war, on behalf of the sisters, promptly and largely. The thin edge of the wedge was got in well, and Rome knows how to keep it there. It was made to appear a crime of the first magnitude to refuse a "sister" anything, and the charm has worked till to-day. It has become now a political necessity. At Washington no politician, no matter who is President of the United States, dares to refuse the tax which the sisters go round to collect every month, or oftener. Picture to yourself sisters being allowed to visit the British Museum, Whitehall, the Houses of Parliament, and all the public and private offices of London every month, and *demand money*, and then you can understand the state of affairs in " free America." In fact, the country is very far from being free in many respects, and it is a mere question of time when it will be bound hand and foot by Rome.

But why are all these public appeals necessary? The sisters who educate are well provided for. They charge very large fees for educating the rich, and they are splendidly paid for educating the poor. The amount of public money which is bestowed on the Roman Catholic convents in America would hardly be credited; and what is the result? Far from decreasing crime it increases. Here is a case. Lizzie Ahearn comes from Ireland, and is living out in New York. She has a child; she gets ill, and cannot provide for it. It is taken from her to the New York Roman Catholic Foundling Asylum, which is a favourite institution with the New York Archbishop, who is loud in his praise of the foundress, Sister Irene. I tried to establish institutions to prevent crime, but that was a crime, and I was pursued by all sorts of ecclesiastical opposition. But to establish a place where crime can be rewarded, and where it can be practically encouraged, is a great virtue; and the sister who undertook to care for the illegitimate children of New York Roman Catholics, has a high place in the estimation of Archbishop Corrigan and his clergy, and no doubt they do well to be grateful.

To me it seemed that to have looked after this friendless emigrant girl, and to have protected her on her arrival in this country, would have been a far more meritorious work than to have provided for her when she fell.

CHAPTER IX.

THE TEACHING OF THE BIBLE AND THE TEACHING OF THE CHURCH.

"Not giving heed to Jewish fables, and commandments of men, that turn from the truth."—Titus i. 14.

THE vital difference between the Roman Catholic religion and the Protestant is simply this. The Protestant relies on the Scripture as the first, and the last, court of appeal in deciding controversy. The Romanist, on the contrary, looks to the Church as the only court of appeal. The Romanist justifies his exclusive appeal to the Church on the ground that the Church has been appointed by Divine commission to teach all nations, and therefore if there is a difference between the Church and the Bible, the Church must decide, as it is above the Bible. And the Romanists enforce their claim on the ground that Protestants have so many different opinions, all taken from the Bible, that obviously the Bible cannot be intended to teach us what to believe, as its meaning may be so variously interpreted.

This argument, like many similar ones, looks very plausible until it is thoroughly sifted. In the first place, Protestants are all agreed on the plan of salvation, which rests on Christ alone. Roman Catholics have many plans of salvation, which rest on many sources and saviours. It is very much to be regretted that

Protestants in their controversies with Romanists do not know what a large latitude is given to the Church in the matter of truth. Priests who are trained to evasion make statements—I had almost said unconsciously—without due regard for truth. The Roman Catholic laity know very little about their own religion, and they know worse than nothing about the Protestant religion; hence arises one great difficulty in arguing with a Romanist. Its chief value is to make him think, which is certainly a great gain.

A Romanist who has been taught to believe that a Protestant has no real religion is amazed when he comes into contact with Protestants, and finds that they are Christians, and that far from not believing in God, they only desire that their Roman Catholic brethren should believe in Him aright. Once a Romanist is convinced that he has been deceived, the way is opened for his further enlightenment; but it is difficult indeed to make him doubt the sincerity or the honesty of his teachers, a point which should never be forgotten.

Protestants, then, should remember that the Roman Catholic laity, when discussing religion with them, are honest as far as they know; but they should remember also that Roman Catholics are deceived themselves on the most important points. Take, for example, the permission to read the Bible. The Romanists, in controversy with a Protestant friend, will declare most positively that the Church does not forbid the unrestrained reading of the Bible, and the Protestant who is sincere himself, will not suspect that the Romanist is himself ignorant of the true teaching of his Church. Yet such is the case. There has been an evidence of this quite recently on an important subject.

A French Roman Catholic gentleman, very famous

as the author of a work on Lourdes, where an apparition of the Blessed Virgin was said to have taken place some years since, published a French translation of the Bible. It was certainly a bold step to commence such a work, but his position seemed almost unassailable. He obtained the highest approval from the Pope in writing, as well as from his own ecclesiastical superiors. The book was selling by hundreds of thousands, when all at once the crash came without previous warning. The book was forbidden by the same infallible authority which had so lately commended and approved it. Certainly it is a great thing to be a Pope, for a Pope, and a Pope alone, has the privilege of having half-a-dozen infallible minds, all equally warranted to be the truest, and each is looked upon, by his deluded followers, as inspired by the Holy Ghost. If the consequences of this to millions of the human race were not so infinitely sad it would be very amusing. As it is, it is too near tears for laughter. How any one with common sense, which is even approaching sound and sane, can fail to see the folly of all this, can only be explained on the Scripture statement that God sends some persons a strong delusion, so that they will believe a lie. It is noteworthy, too, that those who so easily accept the lies of Rome are too often of the very class on whom this judgment of believing a lie is predicted. They are those who have "pleasure in unrighteousness," men who bow down to Rome because she fosters their pride by promising them wealth, political distinction, and social advancement.

It is, as we have said, quite necessary for the Pope to be infallible, and it is extremely convenient. No matter what he teaches it is right; it is, so he vainly thinks, the voice of God which speaks. At one moment this voice may sanction incest, and at the next moment reprove it. One day he may permit the circulation of the Bible, and at the next he may forbid its circulation. What an easy time a Pope has! So infallible are his utterances, that no matter how often he may change his opinions, no one dare say that he is mistaken. And let it be remembered that this is no fancy picture, or exaggerated statement of mine.

What a contrast between the teaching of the Apostles and the teaching of Rome. The modern successor of the Apostles gives his most powerful support to the circulation of a book of miracles written in honour of the Blessed Virgin. The people may read this, but the book which contains the history of the miracles and the Gospel of Christ is forbidden. Ought not this fact, which is too public for denial, to convince the world of the unchristian character of the teaching of the Church of Rome? But it is necessary that Protestants at least should be deceived as to the real teaching of Rome. This is not a difficult matter. They meet a Cardinal in society; to them he is all courtesy and affability. He seems such a "nice fellow," no nonsense about him. They do not doubt his sincerity. Why should he say one thing to them, and say another in private? Why, indeed, except that the Church to which he belongs finds it convenient to deceive you, and even prevent you from having the least suspicion that you are being deceived?

There has been a considerable stir made about this sudden and very decided suppression of the Bible in France. People say, "Here is another evidence that the Church of Rome will not allow the Bible to be read," so it is necessary to prepare a little nice ecclesiastical dust to throw in the eyes of the public;

and who is better fitted to do this than the courtly mannered, if humbly born, Cardinal of Baltimore? He will be believed, and listened to, if others are not. But how little his hearers know that when the Cardinal goes into the pulpit in his cathedral, and tells every one to read the Bible, he leaves the ink scarcely dry on the paper whereon he has written for publication these words: "God never intended the Bible to be the Christian rule of faith, independently of the living authority of the Church" (Cardinal Gibbons' "Faith of our Fathers").

In this work, which has been written not only for Roman Catholics but for Protestants, there is one entire chapter devoted to the uselessness of the Bible. In fact, according to this veracious Cardinal, the Bible was only written to be a snare to us, and the less we have to do with it the better. Certainly it is a dangerous book when it is used to oppose Rome, for it is very plainly against her claims. It would seem that instead of the Holy Scriptures having been written to make us wise unto salvation (2 Tim. iii. 4), they are likely to become a trap to ensnare our souls. The Cardinal's contention in his book is briefly this. The Jews did not consult their Scriptures in order to make them wise unto salvation; they referred, not to the Scriptures, but to the high-priests for decisions. In proof of this statement the Cardinal quotes Deut. xvii. 8, a passage which clearly refers to ordinary events, or rather to the extraordinary events of life, in which case the Jews were told to apply for advice to the priests. The Jews, he said, did not want the Scriptures, and why should Christians want them?

It does seem as if there must be a strong motive in this constant depreciation of Scripture. It does not seem to matter that St. Paul commended Timothy for studying the Holy Scriptures from the time he was a child. The Cardinal asserts that "Jesus himself never wrote a word of Scripture." To reply to this blasphemous insinuation would seem almost unnecessary. It is quite true that Jesus did not write any part of the Bible, but we know that the Bible contains His very words; and it is almost too horrible to find a man who professes the Christian religion quibbling over such statements. Alas! the words of Jesus, we must fear, are of very little moment to this dignitary of the Roman Church in comparison with the words of his Church. In an age of agnosticism and doubt the very words of Jesus Christ Himself are treated as of no moment, and that by one who professes to be a Christian, and who is constantly denouncing Protestants for inconsistency.

The outcome of his whole argument is the utter worthlessness of the Bible. If it is only to be interpreted by the Church, and if the laity are not capable, no matter whether ignorant or learned, of understanding it, one wonders why it was written. As a fact, the Church has never given an infallible explanation of a single chapter of the Bible. After this we cannot be surprised that so many of the nations, over whom the Church of Rome once had unlimited control, have become infidel. I can only marvel that this chapter in Cardinal Gibbons' "Faith of our Fathers" has not been made use of by infidels as the strongest argument ever penned against the Christian religion. What a farce religion would be if the Bible was the utterly useless, and decidedly misleading, book which he would have us believe! And what a sneer at the very preaching of Jesus recorded therein is contained in the way in which His words are so spoken of! If all

Scripture is to be understood by the interpretation of the Church, are we, then, to place Jesus Christ Himself at the feet of the Pope, and require that He shall submit the meaning of His own words to men who have been amongst the vilest breakers of His commandments? Truly the Son of man is crucified afresh in the Church of Rome century after century.

But this is not all. In this same book we find the statement that the words of our Divine Lord in John v. 39 do not mean what they say. Cardinal Gibbons admits that there is such a passage in the Bible as "Search the Scriptures; for in them ye think ye have eternal life; and they are they which testify of Me." He says this is triumphantly quoted in favour of private interpretation of the Bible, "but it proves nothing of the kind." It is almost useless to controvert this assertion. Those who have Bibles can see for themselves, by reading the whole passage, how cleverly the denial is framed. In the last verse of this very chapter our Lord reproaches the Jews with not believing the writings of Moses; and yet this poor Cardinal would have us believe that our Lord did not mean what He said when He gave the command to search the Scriptures. It is pitiful to see the subterfuges, the evasions, the explanations which explain nothing, to which the Cardinal is driven to uphold the unscriptural teaching of his Church.

But let us suppose for a moment that he is right, and that the Bible is of no use except as a mere record of fact—if indeed it is of use even so far, since the plainest and most sacred facts, the very recorded words of our Lord, may be made to mean whatever the Church pleases—what ground has the Church for its authority? Take, say, the Bible—if it is as worthless to the world as the Cardinal would have us believe—and what have we left? Nothing but "tradition" and the Fathers.

Now this is an important point in the controversy. It is evident, even to the cool self-assertion of Roman controversialists, that the Pope cannot stand like Mahomet's coffin, between heaven and earth. Even an infallible Pope must have some ground on which to place his infallibility. He cannot come forward and say, "I am infallible; you must believe me, because I say so." Practically this is what Rome does say, but it is delicately modified. Rome declares that the Bible says that St. Peter was the head of the Church, the rock on which the Church was founded. Now we let pass the bare assertion which this claim makes. It is true that Rome says so, but it is also true that a large number of the Fathers of the Church say that this is not the true interpretation of the passage in question. But let that pass also. Where, we ask, is there in the whole of Scripture one solitary word which says, or even implies, that St. Peter was to have for his successors a series of infallible Popes? Let Rome prove this, and the case is ended. The only text on which Rome attempts to base this claim is the one in which our Lord promises to be with His Church to the end of the world. This text is worth careful examination, in view of the use which has been made of it. (Matt. xxviii. 19, 20.) "Go ye therefore, and teach all nations, baptizing them in the name of the Father, and of the Son, and of the Holy Ghost: teaching them to observe all things whatsoever I have commanded you: and, lo, I am with you alway, even unto the end of the world." Now where is there one word in this text which even infers that St. Peter should have successors who should be infallible? The inference which Rome draws from this text is simply absurd.

The Apostles were to teach all things which Christ commanded them; but St. Paul tells us that if an angel from heaven should preach any other gospel to them than that which he had preached he should be accursed. Now how were the disciples to judge of this, unless they used their own reason? We find also that there were such serious differences of opinion between the Apostles themselves, that most certainly no one Apostle had the exclusive power to decide all matters of controversy; and if St. Peter had not this power—and the Bible narrative plainly shows that he had not—how could the Pope have what St. Peter had not?

But there is a deeper depth of unbelief—and shall I say blasphemy?—into which the Cardinal has fallen. He says plainly that though "most Christians pray to the Holy Ghost, the practice is nowhere to be found in the Bible." If he believes the Holy Ghost to be God, why should he make any such remark? We shall be told next that the doctrine of the divinity of the Holy Ghost is not declared in the Bible, and that it remained for the Church, which does so many wonderful things, to declare the Holy Ghost to be God. He says that "fools rush in where angels fear to tread," and we agree with him. His description of the exact value of the Bible as an authority is of a piece with his declaration about the Holy Ghost; and, by the way, it should be noted that if the doctrine of the divinity of the Holy Ghost is not in the Bible, as Cardinal Gibbons implies, that Church, and that Church alone, has the power to declare the Holy Ghost God. Yet such is the unconscious absurdity of the argument, that the Roman Catholic Church bases all her claims on the supposed exceptional gifts to her of the Holy Ghost. So she first declares the Holy Ghost Divine, and then declares that she is inspired by the Holy Ghost. This chapter ends with a stupendous falsehood. The Cardinal writes:—

"After his ordination every priest is obliged in conscience to devote upwards of an hour each day to the perusal of the Word of God. I am not aware that clergymen of other denominations are bound by the same duty."

I do trust that some minister of the Gospel, whose public position will prevent the Cardinal from refusing a reply to, or trifling with him, will ask him to state where the authority is to be found for this assertion.

When, where, and under what circumstances are priests obliged to spend an hour every day in the perusal of God's Word? They are certainly obliged to read the Breviary, as the Roman Catholic prayer-book for priests is called, but there is little indeed in this book of the word of God. Every Protestant who reads the Cardinal's book will conclude that his statement is true; but how far it is from being even approximately true no one knows better than the very reverend falsifier. It is a time when plain words are best. I have heard priests complain again and again of the tissue of lies and legends which they are obliged to recite daily from their Breviary, which contains besides only a few texts of Scripture and a few psalms.

We have remarked that when the Bible published in France by M. Lassarre was forbidden by the Pope, after it had been approved by him, there was a great outcry, especially in this country. After the Protestant press had got hold of the facts they could not well be denied, and even the Roman-controlled press in America could not be induced to hush up the scandal altogether. Something had to be done, and the veracious Cardinal was just the one to do it. Accordingly he preached a sermon in his cathedral at Baltimore, in which he uttered more heresy than he could do penance for in the course of ten lifetimes. But what matter? It was all for the Church. And had not the Church given him its highest honours, and might he not even yet aspire to the highest honour of all?

Now in his book, from which we have made some extracts, he has said in plain terms that the Bible is of very little use to any one. Here are his own words: "It was by preaching alone that Christ intended to convert the nations . . . no nation has ever yet been converted by the agency of Bible associations." Further he says on the same page that "Christ never commanded His Apostles to write a line of Scripture." But some one who knew the Bible better than this Roman Cardinal must have called his attention to the inexpediency of allowing this flagrant falsehood to continue in print, for he has added in a footnote, "except when He directed St. John to write the Apocalypse;" as if there could be exceptions, as if the one great fact that all Scripture was given expressly for our instruction was not sufficient evidence that we should have it placed on record. The New Testament writers were moved to write by God the Holy Ghost, and surely that is sufficient for any ordinary Christian. In the eagerness of the Cardinal to clear his Church of the blame and shame of suppressing the Bible, he has let himself run into heresy; and if he ever becomes Pope, it will be a curious question whether he can validly hold the infallible throne after such a lapse.

There are two things which the Roman Catholic

Church has always found necessary for its existence, and these are the power to persecute and the power to curse. She cannot persecute unless she has temporal power, which will enable her to torture, or imprison, or kill those against whom she has any cause of complaint; hence her great desire to obtain temporal power. But she is free to anathematise and curse; and a careful glance at the history of the Church of Rome will show that she only restrains herself from these weapons when she is afraid of public opinion being too strongly against her.

But in the matter of cursing she is not restricted to the cursing of individuals. She curses the holders of certain opinions, and she pronounces the opinions accursed as well as the persons who hold them. This is a subject little thought of, or understood. As the Church of Rome has found that the reading of the Bible is a great hindrance to the success of the Roman Catholic religion, she has at different times cursed the readers of the Bible, and the reading of the Bible also. This of course she denies; but look at her official documents, and the case is proved against her. Cardinal Gibbons has written and published a book on the Roman Catholic religion, a chapter of which is, as I have said, occupied in showing what a useless and mischievous book the Bible is, and he has also preached a sermon in which he has praised the Bible, and advised people to read it. Now, as the matter is very important, we place here side by side a series of propositions which the Pope has cursed, in his "infallible" Bull *Unigenitus*, and a series of extracts from the sermon of Cardinal Gibbons, which will show that he has deserved the curse of his own Church, for he has actually declared to be true what his Church has affirmed to be accursed.

The condemned and accursed propositions will be found on the left-hand side of the page, and the cardinal's propositions facing them on the right-hand side.

PROPOSITIONS CONDEMNED BY THE BULL *Unigenitus*.	PROPOSITIONS AFFIRMED BY CARDINAL GIBBONS.
"It is useful at all times and in all places and to all sorts of folk to study the Scriptures, to understand their spirit, and the piety and the mysteries they teach. "This study of Holy Writ... is for all the world. "The sacred obscurity of the word of God furnishes no excuse even to laymen for neglecting to read the same. "The Lord's Day should be hallowed by pious reading, especially of the Holy Scriptures. "To forbid the reading of the Scriptures, more particularly of the Gospel, to Christians is to interdict for children of the light the use of light."	"I strongly exhort you to sanctify this season of Lent by studying the Bible at least ten or fifteen minutes every day, especially the New Testament and the Psalms. "The Scriptures ought to be the garden of the priest, as said St. Charles Borromeo, and of the laity as well. What is good for the one is good for the other. "You can study and ponder over it in your homes till it impresses itself upon your heart. No other agency has produced such a revolution in society as the Bible. "We should be always ready when temptation comes with the Scriptures in our hearts, for they are the best antidote for sin."

But there is, if possible, a deeper depth. The official organ of the cardinal, published in Baltimore, chimes in with the amazing assertion that the reading of the Bible is the cause of modern paganism. What a terrible state of things when the sacred book of the Christian has become such a menace to Christianity. It is curious how Romanists overlook the fact that it is in Roman Catholic countries, where tradition and the Church is put before the Word of God, that infidelity most of all flourishes. It is because people do not believe the

Bible, and not because they read it, that infidelity increases. As the matter is so serious, we give the very words of the *Catholic Mirror*, the Cardinal's organ:—

"The development of the modern paganism that is spreading on every hand among non-Catholics is the logical result of an open Bible as the sole rule of faith. Catholics have never been dependent upon it for authority in the practice of their religion."

But there is yet the consideration that the Fathers do not agree among themselves. By the Third Article of Pope Pius' Creed every Roman Catholic priest must "promise, vow, and swear most constantly to hold and profess" as follows:—

"I also admit the Scriptures, according to the sense which the holy Mother Church has held and does hold, to whom it belongs to judge the true sense and interpretation of the Scriptures; nor will I ever take and interpret them otherwise than according to the unanimous consent of the Fathers."

And now let us see what was the teaching of the Fathers on this subject. The article, like many others from the same source, is anything but clear. First, the Church is held to be the true and only interpreter of Scripture, and then the Fathers are declared to be the interpreters. At the fourth session of the Council of Trent, held April 1546, a decree was passed in which it is enacted, "that in order to restrain petulant spirits, no one relying on his own skill shall in matters of faith and of morals pertaining to the edification of Christian practice, wresting the sacred Scriptures to his own sense, dare to interpret them contrary to the unanimous agreement of the Fathers."

Now if there is one enactment of the Church by which the Roman Catholic is more bound than another it is by the decrees of the Council of Trent. The decree on the subject of the authority of Scripture is one which deserves special notice. The circumstances under which it was enacted should also be recalled. This Council was convened for the purpose of checking the advance of liberality of thought then inaugurated, under the pressure of the Protestant Reformation. Every care was taken as to the very words in which its decisions were made. Rome was seriously alarmed at the appeal to Scripture made by the Reformers, and at the spread of Gospel light.

It should be observed that there is a great difference between the tradition which is purely oral and the tradition which is written. The first decree on tradition was passed in the First Canon of the Fourth Council of Constantinople, A.D. 869, reputed the Eighth General Council; but this Canon clearly pointed out a tradition presented in the records of the Church, and handed down by a succession of witnesses, and not the oral tradition now claimed by the Roman Church. Of Ignatius, Bishop of Antioch (A.D. 70), the historian Eusebius said: " He exhorted them (the Churches) to adhere firmly to the tradition of the Apostle, which for the sake of greater security he deemed it necessary to attest by committing it to writing."

The earliest Latin Father, Tertullian, an African (A.D. 194), while he set great value on custom and tradition, appealed to the Scriptures alone as of authority. In arguing with the heretics he demanded from them proofs from Scripture.

" If it is not written, let him fear the curse allotted to such as add or diminish."

The passages from the early Christian writers which insist on the Scriptures as alone of authority in matters of doctrine are so numerous, and so well known, that it is at the present day almost labour and time lost to repeat them; they are to be found in almost every Protestant controversial work. I shall nevertheless transcribe a few of them merely as illustrations. What could be more striking than the words delivered at the First General Council of Nice (A.D. 325) by Eusebius, Bishop of Cæsarea, in the name of the three hundred and eighteen bishops then assembled? He says:—

"Believe the things that are written; the things that are not written neither think upon nor inquire into."

Gregory, Bishop of Nyssa (A.D 379), says:—

"Let a man be persuaded of the truth of that alone which has the seal of the written testimony." And again he wrote: "Forasmuch as this is supported by no testimony of Scripture, we will reject it as false."

And Cyril, Bishop of Jerusalem (A.D. 356), places the matter very clearly before us. He says:—

"Not even the least of the Divine and holy mysteries of the faith ought to be handed down without the Divine Scriptures. Do not simply give faith to me while I am speaking these words to you; have the proofs of what I say from the Holy Word; for the security and preservation of our faith are not supported by ingenuity of speech, but by the proofs of the sacred Scriptures."

Jerome, a Presbyter of Rome (A.D. 382), says:—

"The Church of Christ, which has Churches in the whole world, is united by the unity of the Spirit, and has the cities of the Law, the Prophets, the Gospel, and the Apostles; she has not gone forth from her boundaries, that is, from the Holy Scriptures."

"Let not these words be heard between us, I say, or, You say, but rather let us hear 'Thus saith the Lord;' for there are certain books of the Lord in whose authority both sides acquiesce. There let us seek the Church; there let us judge our cause. Take away therefore all those things which each alleges against the other, and which are derived from any other source than the canonical books of Holy Scripture. But perhaps some will ask, Why take away such authorities? Because I would have the holy Church proved not by human documents but by the Word of God.

The New York *Churchman*, the organ of the Episcopal Church in America, writing on this subject, says:—

"The Cardinal has probably a 'dispensation' to say what he chooses to the unutterably gullible Americans; because nothing is easier than to make him recant and withdraw when these concessions have served their purpose."

Mr. C. H. Collette, in his valuable pamphlet, "Is Dr. Manning a Loyal Englishman?" gives quotations from the essays of Dr. Doyle, well known as a controversialist and bishop of the Roman Catholic Church in the early part of the present century, which show how very little opinion he had of the infallible utterances of the Popes on Scripture interpretation :—

"As to the arguments from Scripture or tradition adduced by him (Pope Gregory VII.), or by any of his successors, in support of their temporal claim, they are such as will amuse, or rather excite the pity of a serious mind. One (Pope Boniface VIII.) wisely observed that because an apostle said to our Lord, 'Behold there are two swords here,' the Popes have a right to depose kings. Such an inference might appear plausible to him who was already resolved on an usurpation of right; but a Christian is forced to blush at such a profanation of the Word of God. Gregory . . . quotes from St. Paul to the Corinthians. (1 Cor. vi. 3.) 'Know you not that we shall judge angels themselves? how much more worldly things?' and from this passage he claims to be invested with power of invading the rights of kings and emperors, nay, of remodelling the state of society throughout the world . . . but to offer arguments against such theories is too humiliating to the common sense of men."

With one more evidence of the small respect which the Church of Rome has for the Scriptures, and of the way in which she mutilates the Bible to serve her own purposes, we shall conclude this part of our subject.

If there is one subject more sacred than another, and with which it might be supposed that Rome would not tamper, it is the commandments of God. I had often heard, when young, that the Roman Catholic Church in her catechisms left out part of the ten commandments. When I was considering the question of entering the Roman Catholic Church, I asked the priest to whom I went for instruction if this was true. He denied it indignantly, and of course I believed him. I had yet to learn that you cannot depend on the truth of one single word which a Roman Catholic may say, when controversy is in question. I know that this statement will shock many Romanists, but, as in other cases, the question is not whether the statement is very shocking, but whether it is true. Romanists have been again and again detected in false quotations, and in the most barefaced forgeries, and when detected they have simply gone on repeating the same falsehoods as if they were facts.

There is of course always an object to be gained in all this, but the object is not truth. It seems utterly amazing that any man should wish to deceive others, or lend himself to such deliberate lying that it is very difficult for honest men to believe it exists, even when the evidence is plainly before their eyes; and it is to this unwillingness of honest men to believe others capable of a barefaced deceit, of which respectable and self-respecting heathen would be ashamed, that Romanists owe the toleration which their religion has received from Protestants.

Would to God that Roman Catholics examined for themselves the foundations of their religion. The Roman Catholic Church is like a family with a bad reputation, which requires concealment. It cannot bear the light because its deeds are evil. Honest men are not afraid to meet facts, or to have them known. When a Roman Cardinal can write about the Bible, as Cardinal Gibbons has done, it is all over with Rome. When so many shifts and evasions are necessary to prove that the Bible was not intended for ordinary use, there must be a deep reason for this evasion. There is a very grave difference between St. Paul and Cardinal Gibbons on this subject, and I for one must admit that I prefer to be guided by St. Paul. (2 Tim. iii. 16, 17.) "All Scripture is given by inspiration of God, and is profitable for doctrine, for reproof, for correction, for instruction in righteousness; that the man of God may be perfect, thoroughly furnished unto all good works."

Plainer words could not be used than these. The miserable subterfuge by which Cardinal Gibbons and men of his class try to make it appear as if the Scriptures of the Old Testament only were referred to is beneath criticism, and should be condemned, as it deserves, by every Christian. The words of the Apostle are "all Scripture." The words of the Apostle are that the Scriptures are given by inspiration of God; and yet this Cardinal tells his poor people, who are not even allowed to test the truth of his statements, that they are merely on a level with the pastoral letters of bishops ("Faith of our Fathers," p. 102), and adds the false testimony against the Apostles that they never circulated the Scriptures, and yet these words of St. Paul to Timothy must be well known to him.

Yes, they are known to him, they are known to God, but they are not known to the poor Romanists, who would not for one moment suppose that a "Cardinal" of their holy Church would be guilty of deliberate deceit. If this does not come under the Bible condemnation pronounced on those who add to, or take from, the Word of God, Scripture has no meaning.

The worship of idols, or of deceased persons, is so plainly condemned in the Bible, and so openly practised in the Roman Church, that it is no wonder that Rome is driven to hide the evidence against herself, and this she does by mutilating the commandments. I repeat again, that when I was solemnly assured by a Jesuit Father that the Roman Church did not mutilate the commandments I believed him. I have got wiser since. Facts are the best of all arguments, and here are the facts.

Now the first thing which the Romish Church had to do was to make the translation of the first commandment suit the teaching of the Church. An honest Church would have suited her teaching to the commandments. The words on which so much depend are these : " Thou shalt not make unto thee any graven image . . . thou shalt not bow down thyself to them nor serve them." The Romanists alter the word "image" to the word "thing." I cannot see what is gained by this, for the conclusion is all the same, and that conclusion Rome has not dared to deny. The words of the Bible are too plain. The circumstances under which the commandment was given are quite sufficient to decide the question, even if it was more complicated than it appears. God is a jealous God; He will not share His glory with another. Indeed, if He did, we might say with all reverence that He would not be God. The Jews of old were quite as much inclined as the Romanists of to-day to worship anything except God.

And no doubt another Roman Catholic reason for forbidding the reading of the Bible, and trying to explain away its value, is that it contains such clear denunciations of the idolatry into which the Jews fell, and records the terrible punishments inflicted on them for their lapses into idolatry. A clear knowledge of this might raise inquiries in the minds of Roman Catholics, which the Church might not find it convenient to answer. Those who engage in controversy with Rome should ask for plain answers to plain questions, even if it takes many hours to make a Romish priest give one. Subterfuge, evasion, deceit, are the weapons of Rome. Protestants have no need of such weapons, but let us see that we are not fooled by those who are adepts in the use of them.

The catechism used, and in Ireland used exclusively,

commonly known as Butler's Catechism, has the commandments in the following form :—

"I am the Lord thy God; thou shalt not have strange Gods before Me.

"2. Thou shalt not take the name of the Lord thy God in vain.

"3. Remember that thou keep holy the Sabbath day.

* * * * *

"9. Thou shalt not covet thy neighbour's wife.

"10. Thou shalt not covet thy neighbour's goods."

How awful a deceit to practise on poor helpless children to deprive them of the knowledge of the commandments of God by thus mutilating them. It may perhaps be remembered that in quoting from the catechism used in America, which has been approved by Rome itself, as well as by Cardinal Gibbons, the answer cited to the question, "Can any one be saved out of the Roman Catholic Church?" has these words as part of the reply: "Those who do not seek their salvation in the Roman Catholic Church cannot hope to be saved in a religion of their own make." Now if there ever was a religion to which these words could be applied in real earnest it is the Roman Catholic, for it has been obliged to use all sorts of shifts and evasions to prop up the "religion of its own make." The very commandments have to be altered and omitted. Twenty-nine Roman Catholic catechisms— being those used in England and foreign countries— were examined by Mr. C. H. Collette, the well-known author, and he found that in twenty-seven the second commandment was omitted entirely, while in the remaining two it was mutilated. If this is not a religion of human "make" it is difficult to know what else deserves the term. And why, it should be asked, is there the necessity for this mutilation and suppression of the very word of God? It is done simply and solely to support a system which, if it was founded on the Word of God, if it was Divine, as it claims to be, would certainly not need to conceal from the world the words of the very authority on which it claims to be founded. What should we think of the governor of a province who claimed the right to govern, and yet mutilated and suppressed the very charter of the king under whose authority he professed to act?

The perversion of human nature is the ground of all this evil. Man has always shown a preference for false gods, and strange forms of worship. We see this in the history of the Jewish Church. Rome is only following the course of human nature. In the early Church we find the same temptation to turn from God to idols, and yet there is nothing more sternly reprobated in Scripture. The writings of the Fathers of the Church, far from endorsing Rome's modern doctrine of saint worship, denounce it most sternly, as sternly as did the prophets of old. If the confusion of teaching, and the metaphysical subtleties of the Romish Church, were placed before the public, there is no doubt that it would prove strange reading to many. Romanists make a great boast of their unity, and unfortunately the general public take them at their own valuation. Every doctrine of the Romish Church has been the subject at one time or another of the most acrimonious dispute. The way in which Rome preserves her exterior unity—and her unity is only exterior—may do very well for children, or for those who take all that she says without question, but it will not convince men who use their God-given reason.

The custom of praying *to* the departed unquestionably had its origin in the custom of praying *for* the departed. It is curious and instructive, in view of Rome's departure from the faith once delivered to the saints, to note the progress of Roman Catholic error and invention. Roman Catholics admit that the saints cannot hear our prayers unless they are in heaven, and the Church does not allow, or says that she does not allow, persons to be prayed to publicly unless she has canonised them, or, as we may say, declared officially that they are in heaven. Nor has the Roman Church ever declared how the saints hear us. As they are not themselves omniscient or omnipotent, it is clear that, if they hear us at all, there must be some way, apart from their own faculties, by which they can know what is said to them on earth; and Roman theologians differ on these subjects as they do on so many others.

It is curious, and should be observed, that Cyril of Jerusalem, and other early Fathers who are quoted by the Romanists as authority for praying for the dead, pray *for* the Virgin Mary, the Apostles, and others *to* whom the Church of Rome prays to-day. If these Fathers were not sure, or had not a reasonable hope that certain souls were in heaven, how can the modern Church of Rome be supposed to know better? So true is this and so undeniable, that Cardinal Wiseman was obliged to admit in his published lectures, that "there is no doubt" that the saints are prayed for in the ancient liturgies, as well as all the other faithful departed. This is a frank admission, and we may be sure it would never have been made if there was the least hope of denying it, because its consequences tell so strongly against the Roman theory. But he explains this, which is a clear condemnation of modern saint worship, by saying that it was done before the Church had proclaimed them "to belong to a happier order." The early Christians did not invoke the saints, or even the Virgin Mary. They prayed for the repose of their souls, thus proving that they did not consider them holier than others; and the Roman Catholic Church, according to Cardinal Wiseman and other Romish theologians, had to canonise the saints before they could be invoked. In other words, the Romish Church had to anticipate the day of judgment, and do what God Himself had not done.

There is no trace of prayers to saints in the services of the primitive Church, though there are prayers for the dead—a very different matter. But if there are not prayers to the saints, there is very clear and plain condemnation of the worship of saints. In the edition of the works of St. Ignatius, published by the Benedictines, there is a very remarkable passage, which should set all disputes at rest as to the teaching of the early Church on the invocation of saints and angels. St. Irenæus was Bishop of Lyons, and was martyred in A.D. 165. He says:—

"The Church throughout the whole world does nothing by invocation of angels, nor by incantations, nor by other depraved and curious means, but with cleanliness, purity, and openness, directing prayers to the Lord who made all things, and, calling upon the name of Jesus Christ our Lord, it exercises its powers for the benefit and not for the seducing of mankind."

So strongly does this passage condemn invocation of angels and saints, that the Roman Church is driven, as usual, to explain away facts for the benefit of the faithful, by saying that Irenæus is speaking of the invocation of evil spirits. Now the passage itself is the best refutation of this misrepresentation, for it forbids plainly the "invocation of angels;" and to make the matter still plainer, the reason for forbidding this practice is stated, and this reason applies equally to the invocation of saints. The invocation of angels is forbidden because it is only "to the Lord who made all things" that we should pray, and it is only on the "name of Jesus Christ our Lord" we should call. Thus we see the doctrine of the early Christian Church was exactly the same as the doctrine of the Bible Christian Church of to-day. And I may call all denominations of Christians the Bible Christian Church, for they look to the Bible, and the Bible alone, for their doctrine, while the Roman Church practically refuses to be guided by the Bible, and looks to the Church alone, as Cardinal Gibbons has declared plainly. But there is yet more and equally important evidence as to the opinions of the early Christians.

In the year 366 a sect called Angelites was founded, who were so called because they dedicated chapels to St. Michael. A Council assembled at Laodicea condemned them, and decreed that men "ought not to leave the Church of God and invoke angels." But what avails such plain statements when Rome can teach what she pleases? This decree being far too plain to suit a Church which appeals to antiquity when antiquity agrees with her, and corrects antiquity when it does not agree with her, in some Roman Catholic editions of the acts of this Council the passage was altered to read "angles" instead of "angels." The silliness and absurdity of this change did not matter when Rome had a point to gain. St. Augustine says :—

"Let not our religion be the worship of dead men,

because if they lived piously they are not disposed to seek such honours; but they wish Him to be worshipped by us by whom, being enlightened, they rejoice that we are deemed worthy of being partakers with them. They are to be honoured, then, on the ground of imitation, not to be adored on the ground of religion; and if they lived ill, wherever they be they must not be worshipped. This also we may believe, that the most perfect angels themselves and the most excellent servants of God wish that we, with themselves, should worship God, in the contemplation of whom they are blessed. . . . Therefore we honour them [Angels] with love not with service. Nor do we build temples to them; for they are unwilling to be so honoured by us, because they know that when we are good we are temples of the Most High God. Well therefore is it written that a man was forbidden by an angel to adore him."

It should be said that this passage is given in the Roman Catholic (Benedictine) edition of St. Augustine's works.

We may add here a few passages from the undisputed writings of the Fathers, showing what their teaching was on the important subject of the reading of the Scriptures.

Eusebius, Bishop of Cæsarea, in the name of the 318 bishops assembled at the first General Council of Nice (A.D. 325), said:—

"Believe the things that are written; the things that are not written neither think upon nor inquire into."

Gregory, Bishop of Nyssa (A.D. 379), says:—

"Let a man be persuaded of the truth of that alone which has the seal of the written testimony."

And again he wrote :—" Forasmuch as this is supported by no testimony of Scripture we will reject it as false."

And Cyril, Bishop of Jerusalem (A.D. 356), places the matter very clearly before us. He says :—

" Not even the least of the Divine and holy mysteries of the faith ought to be handed down without the Divine Scriptures. Do not simply give faith to me while I am speaking these words to you; have the proofs of what I say from the holy word; for the security and preservation of our faith are not supported by ingenuity of speech, but by the proofs of the sacred Scriptures."

Jerome, a Presbyter of Rome (A.D. 382), says :—

" The Church of Christ, which has Churches in the whole world, is united by the unity of the spirit, and has the cities of the Law, the Prophets, the Gospel, and the Apostles; she has not gone forth from her boundaries, that is, from the Holy Scriptures.

" In them (the Scriptures) we have learned Christ, in them we have learned the Church.

CHAPTER X.

CONVENT LIFE

"I will therefore that the younger women marry, bear children, guide the house."—1 TIM. v. 14.

THERE are few subjects of greater interest to the world at large than that of convent life. A certain mystery surrounds it, and it is not only the young who are attracted by mystery. Is it true, people ask, that these poor sisters are shut up for ever from their friends? that they are cruelly treated? that they live immoral lives? that they are half starved? that they are unhappy? that—but there is no end to the questions that are asked on this subject, and very often people who only wish to know what is true are sorely perplexed to know what to believe, because they hear such contradictory statements.

The subject is one of great importance, and deserves the most careful investigation. As far as I am personally concerned, I can only say that I have had thirty years' experience of convent life, and that whatever I say, good or bad, for or against, is the result of this long experience. It is no wonder that there is so much perplexity and misunderstanding. So many Protestant parents send their children to convent schools, where they are happy and well treated, that an idea has spread naturally that sisters have been very much maligned and misrepresented, and that the life of a sister is quite different from what has been supposed by Protestants of a past generation.

Young people respond naturally and quickly to affectionate treatment, and certainly the children of the upper class receive nothing else from the sisters. Quick as children are to make observations, their impressions are limited to what comes very plainly and directly under their eyes. Their observations are naturally superficial, and they have all the self-confidence and ignorance of childhood. The parents often do not look beyond the surface. The sisters are kind to the children, and that is quite enough to win the parent's heart. And so the evil goes on year after year; and some day, when the parents find the result has been that the child is so won by the sisters that she cares no longer for home or friends, and that she too desires to live the life which has been pictured to her as so beautiful, in the days when impressions are so easily made, they are amazed and angry, and denounce the sisters, and the Church, and their own child also, for what, after all, is but the natural consequence of their own action, a consequence which it was simply their own fault that they did not foresee. Perhaps experienced friends, perhaps a faithful minister, had warned them long since of the risk which they were running in placing their children under such influences, but all had been in vain. It was so "convenient" to send the child to the sisters. Other children might be influenced to their hurt, but their child would be surely safe. These parents did not realize that it is dangerous to play with fire. It was so much cheaper to send their child to the convent school; it was cheaper for time, but what about eternity? But they found, to their cost, to their lifelong sorrow, the fatal mistake which they made. They placed their child deliberately in danger, and when the harm was done they blamed every one, except themselves.

But even when this result does not follow, other results must ensue, which are scarcely less dangerous, scarcely less fatal. As we have said, it is but natural that children sent to convent schools should love the sisters. And what is the result? We are very slow to think evil of those whom we love, or from whom we have received any benefit. Impressions are often far stronger than arguments, and the impressions of childhood, being unreasoning, are more difficult to eradicate than those which are tempered by experience in later years. Besides, the child, when she comes to reflect in after life, will say: "Well, I was so many years in a convent school, and met the sisters every day, and I saw nothing wrong, therefore all these stories about them must be untrue." When grown up she does not reflect on the very important fact that anything which might have scandalised her was necessarily and carefully kept from her knowledge. So she is worse than ignorant. A person who never was in a convent school, who never associated with sisters, would not have any prejudice in favour of convents, and would not therefore be so likely to listen to the seductions of Romanism. For in truth it is a religion full of seductions. There is such an apparent sanctity of life. There is such an apparent sanctity of practice. There are such seductive appeals to the senses, for it is a religion of the senses. There is such an apparent, though not real, unity of religious belief.

Why is it that Christian men and women, who profess to believe the Gospel, sanction and even help a Church which proves its anti-Christianity so plainly by its worldliness? You have an open Bible and know that the Word of God has a greater value than a "pastoral letter" of Pope or bishop. You who have the law and the testimony, why do not you ask yourselves plainly, Is this a Christian Church? It is not a question of what man says, but of what God says. Understand plainly, and once for all, that Rome has abandoned the Bible as the sole rule of faith. There are too many things in the Bible plainly against Rome for Rome to allow it to be read freely.

Ask yourself the plain question, What is this Church founded on, if it is not founded on the Word of God? We read in the Bible that in the last days perilous times shall come, that the cry will be, "Here is Christ, and there is Christ." Even the very elect may be deceived for a time. If this is so—and it must be so, because God says it, and we at least will not yet abandon God for the Pope or any man—what care should we not take that we may not also be deceived? If we once abandon the Bible, where will the matter end? Keep to the one plain fact. Remember the teaching of the Church of Rome is unchangeable, and that it has said plainly that the Bible alone is not sufficient for our salvation. No matter what specious arguments may be used to enforce this claim, we know it is directly against the plain teaching of Scripture itself.

This may seem a digression from the subject of the present chapter, but it is far from being so. Our object is to show the danger of Roman Catholic schools for Protestant children, and not the least danger is the absence of all religious teaching. One of two things the sisters must do. Either they must break their solemn promises to the parents of the children committed to their charge, and teach these children the Roman Catholic religion, or they must teach them no religion. Roman Catholics are very fond of denouncing public schools as "Godless schools," but the real Godless schools are Roman Catholic.

No educated Roman Catholic will deny that it is a mortal sin, that it is a sin which, if not repented of, will consign the person who has committed it to eternal damnation, to teach any child, be he Romanist or Protestant, any religion but that which is taught, allowed, and approved by the Roman Church. This very subject was the cause of the fiercest debate in Ireland within living memory.

The English Government was very properly anxious that the rising generation of the Irish nation should have the benefit of a liberal and thorough education. But how to accomplish this most desirable object, without raising a storm which could not be easily quelled, was a problem which statesmen had to decide. At last a plan was arranged which it was hoped would combine piety and patriotism, and satisfy all. National schools were established wherein the Irish children were to be taught everything, except their own religion, and the history of their own country. The national schools are now an accomplished fact, and it is not a little curious to note how the excitements of one generation are forgotten in those of the next. Those national schools were warmly supported by the far-seeing Protestant Archbishop of Dublin, Dr. Whately.

After fierce contention on both sides, a compromise was agreed upon, and a Concordat was arranged, the terms of which were that no religion whatever was to be taught in the schools during the regular school hours. But certain short times were fixed during the day, in which religious instruction could be given to those whose parents wished them to receive it; and a strict rule was made and enforced, that children were not to be present in the room when instruction was given to other children of a different denomination. There was, in fact, a conscience clause, which was more or less strictly observed.

Now it is to the working of this conscience clause that I wish to call particular attention, and I may add here that I speak on these subjects from years of personal knowledge and experience. The great contention of Romanists on the school question is that religion should enter into every study, or rather, that every subject should be taught according to the Roman Catholic view of such subjects. For instance, to take an historical example. A Roman Catholic who was teaching history in the fifteenth century would have been obliged by the Church to teach that Joan of Arc was a very wicked woman, who had been justly condemned by the Church for her many crimes, and for trying to save her country in consequence of certain supernatural revelations, all of which were delusions. A Roman Catholic teaching history to-day would be obliged to teach that this same unfortunate woman, who was burned alive by the inhuman cruelty of the ecclesiastics of the fifteenth century, was a great saint, for whose canonisation every effort should be made, and that her revelations should at least be treated with respect. Hence what is right to be taught even on historical subjects must vary with the varying opinions of those who for the time being represent the "infallible" and unchanging Church.

The same holds good in religious matters. In the

Irish national schools, during the school hours, except for a very brief space of time, the schools are "godless" as far as they well can be, for every sign and symbol of a religious nature is removed or carefully hidden. During the entire of the school hours, with a very brief exception, no religion of any kind is allowed to be taught. The amount of lying, deceit, and "pious fraud" which is committed to evade this rule and to do away with the obligations of this miscalled "conscience clause," would be impossible to a respectable heathen, or to any one except a Roman Catholic priest, who, whatever may be said to the contrary, certainly practises the axiom that the end justifies the means.

The much-enduring Inspectors of these national schools, whether Roman Catholic or Protestant, are obliged, or are supposed to be obliged, to see that the "conscience clause" is strictly enforced. But what can they do? The National Board, as the governing body is called, is entirely under the control of the Roman Catholic bishops. The position of Inspector is much desired, and there is short shrift for the man who has the courage to object to any arrangement that has the approval of the parish priest.

It should be remembered that a very large proportion of the Irish national schools are under the care of sisters, or, as they are called in Ireland, nuns; and it would be considered absolutely profane, and too horrible to be endured, if the Inspector should say one word of disapproval of anything which these sisters may do. Therefore all kinds of pious frauds are carried on freely, and the children who know the rules well are habitually taught lessons in deceit. I cannot see that it is any less deceit because it is done for the greater honour and glory—shall I say of God, or of the Roman Catholic religion? Statues of the Blessed Virgin are kept covered up, or in presses. The sign of the cross is made when the Inspector is not present, and is not made, or only made surreptitiously, when he is on the premises. And worse still, the children are taught to consider their religion persecuted, because these things cannot be done openly during school hours.

If this kind of education is not godless it is certainly most demoralising. I doubt if anything could be more so; and yet we find American Protestants in full sympathy with Roman Catholics in their opposition to the public schools of the United States, in which at least open deceit and lying is not taught. Do Protestants realise that if Roman Catholics had schools of their own in America, under nominal Government control, the very same system of deceit which exists in Ireland would be taught in some form or other, and that American citizens would soon become as demoralised as Europe has become?

It is indeed very much to be regretted that Protestants do not know more about the inside life of the Roman communion. Even most Roman Catholics are deplorably ignorant both of the doctrines and the practices of their own Church. As this may seem, and indeed is a strong statement, I give a brief explanation. As for the doctrines of the Roman Catholic Church, Roman Catholics are so sternly forbidden to reason or argue, or even think for one moment, that they simply learn the catechism, and believe what it teaches without the least inquiry as to its meaning What is the use of reasoning when reasoning is sinful? You are told so-and-so, and you are to believe so-and-so, or to take the choice of eternal damnation, and so the matter ends. It is just the same with regard to Roman Catholic practices; if the Church says it is right to evade the rules of an institution, or to violate the laws of the State, it is your Roman Catholic duty to obey, and so the matter ends. Roman Catholic sisters and Roman Catholic children are therefore irresponsible beings, who have to do what they are told.

I shall show first that the system of Roman Catholic teaching in Ireland, and especially in convent schools, is godless even for Roman Catholic children, because it does not teach them any religion.

There are two kinds of godless schools, and it is difficult to say which is more dangerous to the rising generation. There are schools in which no religion is taught, and there are schools in which religion is taught, but in which certain practices are either taught by word of mouth or by example (the most powerful of all teaching), which are contrary to Christian morals. I propose to show that both these kinds of teaching are usual in schools under Roman Catholic control.

When the national schools were first put under the charge of sisters this practical deceit was quite a common occurrence. On several occasions the Inspectors, who are supposed to make "surprise visits," came unexpectedly into convent schools, and found statues of the Blessed Virgin and the saints exhibited openly for the devotion of the children. They were, of course very slow to expostulate. Expostulation might mean prompt dismissal from their situations, through the influence of the priests; but eventually they had to speak, and the sisters obeyed the rules in fear of a withdrawal of the grant which they receive, but not without many lamentations over the "persecution" to which they were subjected.

It would require more space than can be given to

this subject at present to enter into the character of the religious teaching given in the sisters' schools in Ireland, and the parochial schools, whether under sisters or lay teachers in America. But I say at once and boldly, that it is not Christian teaching. Protestants, who would shrink with horror from the very idea of making the Bible a forbidden book to their own children, are quite easy in their minds when their children are deprived of this grace, as they are when placed for education in convent schools or colleges. The command to "Search the Scriptures" is as universal as the command to "hear the Church," of which the Roman Catholic makes such capital. But St. Paul tells us that if even an angel came from heaven to preach another gospel than that which he had preached he was not to get a hearing. If we are to take the Bible at all as a rule of life and as a creed, we must take it as it is, and not select some parts for belief and calmly lay others aside.

Yet this is what the Roman Catholic Church does. She takes a plain sentence such as the command to "hear the Church"; she says she is the Church, and you have got to hear her or be damned; but she fights very shy of the command to "Search the Scriptures," which is quite as plain as the other. Now if children are not allowed, not to say if they are restrained, from obeying a plain command of Christ Himself, the religion which teaches them to do this is not a Christian religion, no matter what name it may call itself, and children who are taught in this fashion are not receiving a Christian education.

It may be said that I have written too much and too strongly on the subject of the Bible in schools, but I know both sides of this question from practical experience. I know what it is to be of the household of faith, where the Bible was the household book and guide, and to be of the household where the Bible was, for all practical purposes, a dead letter. It is no answer to the argument against the constant reading of the Bible, that some of those who read the Bible do not live up to its precepts. The question for us is simply this: Are we to deprive our children of free access to the Bible? How many conversions late in life are known to have been caused mainly, if not altogether, by the recollection of the Bible readings of early years; and does not the inspired Apostle himself congratulate Timothy on having been familiar with Holy Scripture from a child?

A knowledge of the Bible may not prevent those who have had that advantage in early life from being ensnared by Rome in later years, but when this happens it will be found, as a general rule, that the person so ensnared was ignorant of the true teaching of the Church of Rome, or had not received an intelligent Bible teaching. The Roman Church is wiser than the children of light. She takes good care that her catechisms shall be taught to children at the most impressionable age, and what is then learned is seldom forgotten, and is rarely questioned in later life. The system of deliberate deceit which is taught to children in convent schools, and to boys in Roman Catholic colleges, is a crying evil, and it is one which is absolutely inseparable from Roman Catholic education.

There has been a great deal of misrepresentation on this subject, and a great deal of useless debate. No one need expect any Romanist to admit that such a doctrine as that the end justifies the means is taught by his Church. In fact, Romanists will not admit anything adverse to their Church, and they are quite keen enough to know what is considered so. Nor will you find in any theological book in plain words that the end justifies the means. Rome, above all things, avoids plain speaking; but if it can be shown that certain acts are allowed and applauded, when these acts are for the advancement of the Church, though they are contrary to truth or justice, then the fact is proved past dispute that Rome allows that an evil action may be done, if the object to be attained is what she is pleased to call a good one. Facts are of more importance than the way in which the permission to do them is expressed. We have shown that in the Irish national schools there is a constant system of evasion of rules, which must weaken the respect of the child for authority. All this is justified by those who do it on the pretext that they are allowed by the Church to do these things, and that the Church is above the law of the land, which they are only bound to obey when the Church approves of it.

I do not think that anything can more seriously deteriorate the moral character of a child, than seeing deceit practised habitually by those to whom the child should look for the highest example of truth. Every Protestant mother who sends a child to a convent school for education, whether as a boarder or as a day scholar, places her child in danger of becoming a deliberate deceiver. Remember, once again, that the danger is all the greater because the sisters have not an idea that they are doing wrong or teaching deceit. They are only acting on the great principle of their Church, that there is no salvation out of that Church. They say, " The parents of this child are ignorant of the true religion; if they knew it they would wish their child to be taught it. When the parents die they will thank us for saving the soul of their child; besides, as the parents knew that we could not teach the child any other religion than the Roman Catholic when they placed her with us, we are not doing anything wrong."

In most cases the sisters do not reason at all; they simply act on the principle that the Roman Catholic religion being the only one in which the soul can be saved, they are fulfilling a sacred duty by teaching the child as much as they can of that religion. Even if not one word is said to the child, she is surrounded by influences which all tend in the one direction. All the attractiveness of Rome is ever before her, without a word of warning or explanation. The child soon learns to hide from her parents anything which might in the least alarm them as to what she sees or hears at the convent school, for it attracts and pleases her, and she fears that if the truth were known that she would be removed. A little hint can be given to her to that effect by the sisters, or by some of the Roman Catholic children, who are very sharp when Protestant children are in question; and then comes the first want of confidence between mother and child, and the way is paved for the eternal ruin of the little one.

As for the intellectual training given to children in convent schools, it is so inferior that Roman Catholic parents would much prefer to send their children to Protestant schools if they dared. The sisters may be good teachers of music and languages, of fancy work which is pronounced "so beautiful," and which is generally so utterly useless in the after life of those who spend so much time learning it, but a solid English education is rarely given.

Take, for example, the teaching of history. It should

be remembered that there are subjects which sisters cannot teach honestly or consistently with their religious belief. A child educated in a convent school will not be taught the Bible, except in little historical extracts. Not only this, but it will be taught the Ten Commandments in an abridged form, in which all reference to image worship is carefully omitted. No child will be allowed to know that Rome has seen fit to remove from the writings of the Fathers passages which tell against her modern creed. But this is not all. Even history as it is will not be taught, but altered to suit the claims of this "infallible" Church. Truly those Protestants who send their children to receive such an education have a grave account to give to God of their stewardship.

I could fill not one, but several volumes if I quoted all the condemnations which Roman Catholic editors of papers, and other Romanists have pronounced on their own schools. Now and then the truth comes out, and when it does appear it is worth hearing. It is not long since the Roman Catholic *Freeman's Journal*, of New York, published a scathing article on the tricks which sisters play on the children in the matter of giving prizes. I have heard again and again the very same complaints made by parents and children. Prizes are given to those who pay best, and whose influence is of most value in the schools. What an example for children! As to the class-books used in Roman Catholic schools, we need not go beyond the condemnation of them pronounced in a very recent number of the same paper. In an article headed "A Convention of Catholic Teachers," the writer says:—

"The manufacture and sale of Catholic text-books,

since it has grown to an enormous business, has been almost as fruitful of scandalous jobs as has that of textbooks for the public schools. Parochial schools in different localities, and in charge of different teaching bodies, have long been open to bid for a supply of textbooks. A dozen rival publishers compete. One cuts out another by offering the lowest terms for the introduction of his series. For twelve successive years each publisher takes his turn in the cut-throat introduction rates, which are sometimes less than half the regular rates, and often below the cost of well-made books. Parents are surprised that their children have to change their books every year for others that seem about the same, but they do not understand that the teachers change in order to make the large profits on introduction prices."

The teachers who thus deliberately defraud the poor, are " sisters," " brothers," and " priests."

The millions of dollars thus unnecessarily extorted from the poor Roman Catholic parents of America are not the worst evils of this method. The continual change of text-books clouds and confuses the minds of the children, who are kept perpetually going over the same grounds of knowledge, by different and often opposite methods. No real training of the intellect can be secured in this way. But a deeper evil has grown out of this system. " So sharp," says this Roman Catholic newspaper, " has this competition become at times, and so careless have teachers grown over everything except the prices, that certain publishers have actually foisted off editions of school books purporting to be Catholic, but really printed from the discarded plates of venomous anti-catholic text-books, which the publishers bought cheap in the junk shops. Some of these publishers made a pretext of altering these plates, but others deemed it best not to go even to that poor expense."

If a Protestant paper had exposed the worthlessness of Roman Catholic education and books as this Roman Catholic paper has done, and the system of deceit and trickery which is here recorded, what an outcry there would have been. And it is probable that the trenchant article I have just quoted, true as it is, would never have been written if the editor of the paper in which it appeared had not some personal object to serve. Now and then the truth comes out as to the inside workings of the Roman Church, but whenever light is let in we may be sure that there is a motive for it, and that it is done by some one with whom it is not safe for the higher ecclesiastical powers to interfere. My Autobiography shows how badly I was treated by Roman Catholic publishers, and how they were perfectly safe in doing it, as they had the Archbishop of Dublin to protect them. And this is the system which the public is asked to support in place of the public schools, which are open to public inspection. No matter what Roman Catholic schools may teach, or how they may teach, no one dare interfere unless the bishop chooses to give him permission to do so; and he often finds very golden reasons for silence besides the general Roman Catholic indifference to education.

The following extracts from another Roman Catholic paper will prove the truth of what I have stated here, and will also show that the alleged harmony in the Roman Church is not so perfect as its advocates try to make the world suppose.

"O'Shea's books are literally taken from the Montreal (Lavelle) books. And the editor of the *Freeman's Journal* might have taken the trouble ot finding this out before taking a brief to defend them. It is very suspicious to see an editor palpably fighting for a class of publishers whose works are notoriously the dearest and the poorest in the market. Has the question of advertising anything to do with it? Most of the school books printed by Catholic publishers are made from old plates.

"As to the question of advertising, any journalistic expert will inform our Philadelphia correspondent that more advertising can be secured from non-Catholic publishing houses than from Catholic ones. And the resources of the non-Catholic houses are so great that they can well afford to advertise liberally at all times. If the *Freeman's Journal* allowed considerations oi advertising to influence its editorial opinions it would be foolish to antagonise the secular publishers of school books. It needs no elaborate argument to prove this.

"The field of the Catholic publisher of school books is very limited. Hitherto it was more limited. While the secular publisher has had the magnificent patronage of the public school boards to depend on, the Catholic publisher has had to compete with him in the quality of his text-books, and at the same time to look entirely to the parochial schools for support. It is only of late that the secular publishers, the 'syndicate' publishers who control the public school book trade, have considered it worth their while to turn their attention towards the Catholic schools. But it has become worth their while, and from the letters of protest we have received we judge that it has become very much worth their while."

Catholics, especially in England, are given on occasion to loud talking about "Catholic literature." Most assuredly if it were not for the efforts of a few perverts "Catholic literature," even such as it is, would not be known to the public. Now and then an article of average merit finds its way into a Roman Catholic magazine; but I shall let Romanists themselves tell the tale of the failure of their Church in this matter, as well as in education. With Lady G. Fullerton (a pervert) began and ended the last attempt at Roman Catholic works of fiction.

The one and openly avowed object of the Roman Catholic Church is to secure the absolute control of the education of the young. The question is one of such supreme importance that it is almost impossible to say too much on this subject. What do Romanists propose to teach the young? We have seen what they will not allow them to be taught. Let us say once more, the rising generation must not be taught the Bible, lest it should make them wise unto salvation according to Jesus Christ; lest the reading of it should show them the impossibility of salvation through the saints and angels. The young must learn the Ten Commandments according to the abridged editions of the "Church, and they must not know that one of the Ten Commandments given by God forbids the making of images or of any graven thing for purposes of worship. The rising generation, above all, must not be allowed to read history according to fact; they must learn it according to Rome, which is quite a different matter.

"The education of the people," exclaimed the Cardinal Archbishop of Malines recently, in the course of a public address, "is the field upon which will take place the mighty struggle between error and truth, between good and evil."

In Austria, after twenty years of a modified form of so-called "liberal education," the exigencies of parliamentarism have necessitated within the past few weeks a partial, if not complete, restoration of the supremacy of the Church in all matters pertaining to education. The leaders of the clerical faction, including Prince Aloys Liechtenstein and others, took advantage of the autonomous and home-rule aspirations of the various nationalist groups in the Austrian Parliament to purchase their support in all educational and ecclesiastical matters by promises of assistance in their struggle for national autonomy; and thus Count Taafe's Cabinet has been forced to yield, and to perpetuate a retrograde movement, which cannot fail to exercise a disastrous effect on the complicated fortunes of Austria. The new law revives all the former compulsory religious instruction, and provides that the same shall be imparted by priests, whose authority over the pupils shall be equal, if not superior, to that of the masters. School inspectors are no longer to be chosen from among the professors, but from among the clergy, who obtain almost the complete control over the public schools in villages and small towns. Moreover, communal schools are to be closed wherever the Church schools are deemed sufficient for the local needs. This of course involves the abolition of a number of national schools, and will result in the multiplication of those of a professional nature.

A writer in the New York *Times* says:—

"Within the past three months the synod of Catholic Archbishops and Bishops of the kingdom of Bavaria have drawn up and presented to the Royal Government a kind of ultimatum, embodying the following concessions, to which they claim that the Church is entitled under the terms of the Concordat of 1818. In the first place, they insist that all Government supervision of the religious and doctrinal instruction in educational institutions should at once cease; second, that the 'simultanschule,' or schools for children of non-Catholic parents in which all doctrinal instruction is avoided, should be immediately abolished; third, that Freemasons and 'enemies of Christianism,' *ergo* heretics, should be legally disqualified, and debarred from teaching in any public or private schools, colleges, or universities; fourth, that all normal and primary schools in the kingdom, and all public libraries, should be subjected to the absolute and exclusive control of the clergy; fifth, that the supervision and control of all doctrinal and theological instruction in the national universities be confided to the Catholic episcopacy; sixth, that the Government refuse any longer its official recognition of the sect known as 'Old Catholics;' and lastly, that the internal administration of the Church in Bavaria, as well as its teachings and doctrines, be entirely freed from all further interference, supervision, and control on the part of the Government.

"Now although Prime Minister Von Lutz failed at the time to return an altogether satisfactory response to these demands, yet it must be borne in mind that his hesitation and reluctance to comply therewith will be speedily overruled. For not only are his relations with the Prince Regent, who is an exceedingly devout Catholic, much strained, but moreover, he is confronted in Parliament by an overwhelming Ultramontane majority. Indeed, his continued presence at the head of the Administration, in view of the fact that his adherents form an insignificant minority in the Chamber, is not only entirely unconstitutional, but is a direct violation of the terms of the Magna Charta of the kingdom. Moreover, it is well to bear in mind the fact that of the 5,500,000 inhabitants of Bavaria at least 4,250,000 are bigoted Catholics. Under the circumstances, therefore, the prospects of the early realisation of the demands of the Bavarian bishops may be said to be assured."

I have drawn particular attention to the above-mentioned ultimatum of the Bavarian episcopacy for the reason that it displays, in all its brutal nudity, the goal and object which the Papacy is striving to attain in every country in the world. In some portions of Europe these demands are more diplomatically veiled than at Munich, but the ulterior aim is always the same.

And lest any doubt should remain as to the fact that they originate directly from the Vatican, and represent the views of the Papacy, it may be of advantage to add that Leo XIII., in a papal brief dated April 29th, 1889, and addressed to the Bavarian Primate Archbishop of Munich, explicitly indorses every one of the demands put forward by the prelates in question. Nay, the Pope even goes beyond them, and declares that the commands and instructions issued by the Pontiff or his representatives are entitled to the most unquestioning and blind obedience on the part of all Catholics, even in cases where they happen to have failed to receive the sanction of the Government of the land. The Pope further claims that the behests and commands of the Vatican, not only in spiritual but also in temporal matters, must be obeyed to the letter, even if they happen to be in contradiction to the laws of the land. "The Divine doctrine founded by our Saviour," says the Pontiff in his brief, "provides for the preference of the decisions of the Church, over and above the prescriptions of the civil power and law. If that were not the case the fundamental laws governing humanity would be exposed to disastrous modification by each individual man, monarch, or Government."

The Pontiff therefore explicitly exacts that the laws enacted by the Curia of Italian prelates at Rome should be preferred, by all good Catholics, to the laws of the land to which they may happen to belong. Patriotism and the duties of citizenship are expected to take a back seat wherever the Church is concerned.

There is a subject in connection with convents which I would have thankfully passed by if I had not felt it a sacred duty to write of it here. I am frequently asked if there is immorality in convents, and I know that I have suffered considerably in public estimation from certain persons by my denial. I must add, too, as a specimen of the usual uncharitable style of Roman Catholic papers, that a third—or I might say a twenty-third-rate Roman Catholic paper, which receives the approbation of the Romanist Bishop of London, Ont., far from appreciating my truthfulness in this matter, merely notices it with a sneer, saying that I would come to that later.

There is no such thing as honour, conscience, or refined feeling in the Roman Catholic Church. I should rather say there is no Christianity. There may be a veneer of something which will pass for it with the unthinking and the uneducated, two classes who are the chief support of Rome; but when the touchstone of the supposed interests of the Church is applied, coarseness and brutality reign supreme. As for myself, it has long ceased to be a matter of the slightest concern to me whether I have had blame or praise from any one. My mission is to speak truth as I know it, and that done, it matters little who blames or praises. The coarseness and rage with which Romanists attack every one who leaves their communion is one of the many proofs which exist of its utterly unchristian character. There is no grief for the supposed loss to the person's soul. All is simply rage because there is another evidence that Rome cannot keep her hold on every one who enters her pale.

There are, I regret to say, some Protestants who do not appreciate statements of fact as they should, and are disappointed when they do not find sensation. For such I do not write. I speak of facts as I know them. As for the facts of others I have had no opportunity of investigating them. I say nothing for or against them. There will be always some few persons who seem to be—if I may say so—born frauds, and Protestants should be on their guard against them. There are also persons who never have been Romanists, and who must necessarily take their facts second-hand. No doubt such persons are honest in their desire to spread the Light of Truth, but when there are two persons to give evidence, one who has been for many years a member of the Roman Church, as either a priest or a sister, most assuredly it is the part of wisdom to give the most credit to their statements. Further, there are, and always will be, adventurers whose sole object is to make a living out of disclosures. Such persons should not be accepted without very careful investigation. I have found a case of this kind lately.

A woman, who had been an inmate of a Roman Catholic refuge for fallen women in England, actually represented herself as the daughter of a distinguished Roman Catholic family, described her magnificent dresses, her jewels, her high life, and last, not least, declared that she had escaped from a convent in England. Her whole story from end to end was a lie. She was simply a very clever adventuress. When I read this woman's statements, having so many years' experience with sisters and nuns, I saw at once that she had never been a sister or an inmate of a convent, except as a fallen woman. But it was in vain that I pointed out this to those whom she had deceived, and I got very little thanks for speaking.

I had opportunity afterwards of ascertaining that everything which I suspected was exactly what had happened. The woman averted suspicion by her cautious way of writing of the sisters. All she wanted was the advantage of appearing before the public, at a time of great excitement, as a person of a distinguished family, who had made immense sacrifices for religion. Her persistent refusal to tell where she came from should at once have awakened the suspicion of those whom she so cleverly deceived. I dwell on her case because Protestants cannot overestimate the importance of ascertaining who such people are. The injury which they do to true religion is difficult to undo. I have given a full account in my Autobiography of how I was deceived myself by a Roman Catholic, who pretended she was a Protestant, and obtained entrance to and help from many convents, on the plea of wanting to change her religion.

Another and a very serious evil which arises from taking up persons of this class is that it is a great triumph to Rome. Rome will have more to say about one adventurer than about a hundred honest men or women who have left the Church. Such persons, too, cannot but feel deeply discouraged when they see adventurers preferred to them; and it is a still greater and more serious discouragement to those who are yet in the Church of Rome and wish to leave it. All this trouble could be saved so easily if Protestants would insist on knowing the previous history of those who come to them from the Church of Rome. There cannot be any reason for concealment. Any one who comes before the public has a right to satisfy the public as to his or her identity. Excuses are simply cloaks to shield fraud, and should never be accepted. No possible injury could be done to a sister or convert from the Church of Rome, or to her friends, by her name being known, or the name of the convent from which she came. The only case in which concealment might be necessary would be in the case of a person inquiring who had not decided to leave the Church of Rome. In such a case the greatest secrecy might be necessary; but this would be only a form of prudence, which is a very different thing from the secrecy of fraud.

It is indeed lamentable when the fact of being deceived by such persons leads to coldness or indifference towards sincere converts. For such as these Protestants cannot do too much. They have trials and sufferings which an adventuress never knows.

It is with great regret I am obliged to say that, although I have no personal knowledge of immorality in convents, I do not question for one moment the statements which have been made by others on this subject. It must be remembered that Rome does what she dares. It should never be forgotten that her principles never change, and that her practice is modified to suit all circumstances. In countries where Rome is safe from the open light of public opinion her dark deeds are done. It is terrible to have to say such things of a Church which calls herself Christian, but history, and history written by Romanists, gives but too positive proofs of her evil deeds.

With regard to Maria Monk's much-talked-of book, it was written many years since, when Romanism in Canada was free to do as Rome pleased. What Maria Monk has alleged against the sisters in Montreal is simply what Roman Catholic historians admit to have been a common practice in the Middle Ages, and even later. It will be remembered that Gerson, the great Roman Catholic divine and theologian of the fourteenth century, declared that concubinage was a necessary evil, as it might prevent greater evils. For full and reliable information on this and other subjects Mr. Lea's work "History of Sacerdotal Celibacy," is invaluable. The Franciscans had their "Marthas," and were condemned by a Council held in Magdeburg (1403) for their dissolute lives. So general was the evil that the Franciscans attacked the Carmelites for betraying women. It is not to be supposed that when such was the state of the priesthood women consecrated to God should escape pollution.

"There is no injustice," says Mr. Lea, "in holding the Church responsible for the lax morality of the laity. It had assumed the right to regulate the consciences of men, and to make them account for every action and even for every thought. When it promptly caused the burning of those who ventured on any dissidence in doctrinal opinion or in matters of pure speculation, it could not plead lack of authority to control them in practical virtue. Its machinery was all-pervading, and its power autocratic. It had taught that the priest was to be venerated as the representative of God, and that his commands were to be implicitly obeyed. It had armed him with the fearful weapon of the confessional, and by authorising him to grant absolution and to pronounce excommunication, it had delegated to him the keys of heaven and hell. By removing him from the jurisdiction of the secular courts, it had proclaimed him as superior to all temporal authority. Through ages of faith the populations had humbly received these teachings, and bowed to these assumptions, until they entered into the texture of the daily life of every man. While thus grasping supremacy, and using it to the utmost possibility of worldly advantage, the Church therefore could not absolve itself from the responsibilities inseparably connected with power; and chief among these responsibilities is to be numbered the moral training of the nations thus subjected to its will" (p. 355, 2nd ed.).

When the Church had unrestrained power in the world, and used it so persistently for evil, how much more power had it in the cloister, and how much easier was it to use it there for the worst purposes? The crime was not for a priest to be unchaste, but for him to marry. For centuries of the Church's history there is evidence which no sane man can deny, that the lives of the priests were a scandal to the whole world, and that the lives of the sisters were little better. In a Bull of Alexander IV. (1259) he declares that the people were corrupted by the priests, instead of being reformed by them. In 742 such was the corruption of nuns that enactments were made by Pope Zachary for their punishment, when found guilty of adultery with priests. In 1251 in England the Bishop of Lincoln made enactments to test the virtue of nuns, of such a degrading character that I cannot repeat them here. The licentiousness of nunneries must have been fearful to have compelled a bishop to use such drastic measures.

And it may here be observed, in connection with the license lately given to the Duke of Aosta, by the present Pope, to commit incest for the sum of fifty thousand dollars, that the writers of the political and other ballads of the day allude severely to the "making and unmaking of matrimony" for money, which seems to have been the unvarying custom of the Roman Church for centuries. In 1101 Paschal II. was obliged to send an epistle to the ecclesiastical authorities in Spain on the subject of the cohabitation of priests and nuns. In 1394 a petition was presented to the English Parliament for the reform of the Church, and especially for the reform of nuns. In 1536 an effort was actually made by a commission of Cardinals to abolish the whole monastic system, such was the scandalous state of convents and nunneries. A work was published called "The Consilium de emendanda ecclesia." One of the ecclesiastics concerned in this good work was subsequently raised to the papal throne as Paul IV. But instead of carrying out the work which he had inaugurated before his elevation he quietly placed this book on the Index. Perhaps there has seldom been a clearer evidence of the character and aim of "infallible" Popes.

One thing is certain, that while "heresy" was punished with death, torture, and all the penalties which the cruelty of the human heart could devise, there was but very slight punishment for the open sins of priests and nuns. I shall only say here that so serious was the corruption of the spouses of Christ at this period, that numberless cases are reported by Llorente, the Roman Catholic historian of the Inquisition. He says the children of nuns and priests were openly acknowledged by their parents, if not without shame, at least without serious reproof. In Provence the scandal was open and horrible. In England Dr. Geddes, a Roman Catholic priest, who wrote and published, at the commencement of the present century, a book advocating the celibacy of the clergy, was suspended for this, and for publishing a new translation of the Bible. With two more quotations from Mr. Lea's work I close this painful subject.

"When the Grand Duke Leopold of Tuscany undertook to reform the monasteries of his dominions, and to put an end, if possible, to the abuse of the confessional, it led to a long diplomatic correspondence with the papal curia as to the jurisdiction over such cases. A public document of the year 1763 had already stated that the special crime in question had become less frequent, and attributed this improvement to the exceeding laxity of morals everywhere present, for few confessors could be so foolish as to attempt seduction in the confessional, when there was so little risk in doing the same thing elsewhere. Specious as this reasoning might seem, the facts on which it was based were hardly borne out by the investigations of Leopold shortly after into the morals of the monastic establishments. Nothing more scandalous is to be found in the visitations of the religious houses of England, under Morton and Cromwell. The spiritual directors of the nunneries had converted them virtually into harems; and such of the sisters as were proof against seduction, armed with the powers of confession and absolution, suffered every species of persecution. It was rare for them to venture on complaint, but when they did so they received no attention from their ecclesiastical superiors, and only the protection of the grand-ducal authority at length emboldened them to reveal the truth. The prioress of S. Caterina di Pistoia declared that, with three or four exceptions, all the monks and confessors whom she had met in her long career were alike; that they treated the nuns as wives, and taught them that God had made man for woman and woman for man; and that the visitations of the bishops amounted to nought, even though they were aware of what occurred, for the mouths of the victims were sealed by the dread of excommunication threatened by their spiritual directors. When it is considered that the convents thus converted into dens of prostitution were the favourite schools to which the girls of the higher classes were sent for training and education, it can be readily imagined what were their moral influences, thence radiating throughout society at large; and we can appreciate the argument above referred to as to the ease with which the clergy could procure sexual indulgence without recourse to the confessional" (p. 586).

"Rome itself was no better than its dependent provinces, despite the high personal character of some of the pontiffs. When the too early death of Clement XIV., in 1774, cut short the hopes which had been excited by his enlightened rule, St. Alphonso Liguori addressed to the conclave assembled for the election of his successor a letter urging them to make such a choice as would afford reasonable prospect of accomplishing the much-needed reform. The saint did not hesitate to characterise the discipline of the secular clergy as most grievously lax, and to proclaim that a general reform of the ecclesiastical body was the only way to remove the fearful corruption of the morals of the laity. When we hear, about this time, of two Carmelite convents at Rome, one male and the other female, which had to be pulled down because underground passages had been established between them, by means of which the monks and nuns lived in indiscriminate licentiousness, and when we read the scandalous stories which were current in Roman society about prelates high in the Church, we can readily appreciate the denunciations of St. Alphonso. A curious glimpse at the interior of conventual life is furnished by a manual for Inquisitors, written about this period by an official of the Holy Office of Rome. In a chapter on nuns he describes the scandals which often cause them to fall within the jurisdiction of the Inquisition, and prescribes the course to be pursued with regard to the several offences. Among those who were forced to take the veil, despair frequently led to the denial of God, of heaven, and of hell; feminine enmity caused accusations of sorcery and witchcraft, which threw not only the nunneries, but whole cities, into confusion; vain-glory of sanctity suggested pretended revelations and visions; and these latter were also not infrequently caused by licentiousness; for in these utterances were sometimes taught doctrines utterly subversive of morality, of which godless confessors took advantage to teach their spiritual daughters that there was no sin in sexual intercourse. As in Spain, it was the practice of the Roman Inquisition to treat the offenders mildly, partly in consideration of the temptations to which they were exposed, and partly to avoid scandal." (pp. 587, 588.)

When such was the state of the "holy" Roman Catholic Church when she had full control, and had no Protestants to hinder her liberty of action, as she so often complains at the present day, why should narratives such as those of Maria Monk, and of Father Chiniquy, be questioned? They only say what Rome herself has said, over and over again for centuries, in those feeble efforts to purify the Church which were made from time to time, when the state of its morals was such as to threaten its final dissolution. The book of Maria Monk was written many years since, when Rome had uncontrolled power in Canada. Such outrages on humanity, as she describes, would be impossible at the present day, and therefore would not be attempted; but let Rome again attain the same power, and the same results will follow.

But Rome has not changed. The case of Bruno, so recently before the public, should convince any one who does not wish to be deceived, or who does not deceive himself deliberately, that Rome has not changed. She would be immoral now as openly as she was for centuries, yes, and as openly as she is to-day in Mexico, if she did not fear public opinion. It is quite clear that if Rome can control American Protestant organisations like the Knights of Labour, and interfere in the government of nations, she could also, if she wished to do so, control and reform the morals of her own priests. When the bishop of a large diocese in the United States gives to the public such a horrible account of the demoralisation of his priests, as that which I have already quoted from the pen of Bishop Hogan, what must there be under the surface which will never be known until the day of doom? When Cardinal Manning cannot keep all his priests from drink and immorality, what is the state of the Roman Church in England, with all its advantages? And yet she boasts that she, and she alone, is the "holy" Church; and in all ages and all times she has found men who are fools enough to take her at her own valuation.

The superhuman skill with which Rome hides the iniquities of her priesthood is a matter of admiration for all men. She would have been wrecked long since by the sheer weight of her own vileness, if that vileness had not been hidden by threats of present and future penalties, hurled at those who wished to speak publicly of her sins. Roman Catholic gentlemen in New York have been heard to relate tales of the vileness of the priests of their acquaintance which I could not record on these pages, and yet these gentlemen still remain in nominal communion with the Church of Rome. It suits their political interests to do so, and as for religion they have none. The rising generation of American Roman Catholic men are going in precisely the same path as the men of Italy, of France, of Spain, and of every country where the Roman Church has had unlimited power. They first learn to despise their ecclesiastics, who teach one thing and practise another. Then they learn to hate them, and revolt against all religious authority soon follows. Yet with these facts before their very eyes Protestants will do all they can to support a system with which those who know it best will have nothing to do. Was ever infatuation so fatal or so foolish?

I am well aware that it is not love for Rome which

makes the American millionaire fall at the feet of the Cardinal of Baltimore, and the Archbishop of New York. They curse the necessity which obliges them to pay homage to these men, and, let me add, they imagine the necessity. The Roman Church poses before an easily gulled public as the guardian of law and order. The Pope says, " I am the only person, and my religion is the only religion, which will keep the king on his throne, or enable the rich man to hold his wealth secure ; " and the king and the rich man, looking in these troubled times for a power which will protect them, turn to Rome, and Rome finds occasion to appear as if she, and she alone, could control the hungry multitude. "See," she cries, "how I have brought these troublesome Knights of Labour to my feet. You feared they would revolutionise labour, you feared they would wring from you some of that capital to which for the present I recognise your right, without making any curious inquiry as to how it has been accumulated. Trust to me, and I will protect you." But why does not the too confiding millionaire and the anxious statesman ask, Why have you not succeeded in your own country? Why has your power been overthrown wherever you had temporal rule? Why do you not control the assassination societies in your own Church? Why do you not pacify Ireland? No; the shallow politician, and the unscrupulous politician, and the selfish millionaire grasp at the present good, and care little for the future evil. "After me the deluge. If I can hold my own now let the future take care of itself." And how the future will take care of itself let the past history of the effects of Roman rule tell.

If there is no prostitution in convents to-day, let it be remembered that it is so because a strong public opinion will not allow it in countries where Rome has not yet all the power she so ardently desires. I know how a Romanist shrinks with horror from the very idea of the spouses of Christ being even named with outcasts, but sentiment will not alter fact. There is too much historical evidence that the spouses of Christ could fall, as well as others of their own sex. No matter what we may feel or how we may shrink with horror, the facts remain, and our true wisdom is to prevent the recurrence of evils which are so terrible. When Rome not only tolerated but encouraged the concubinage of priests rather than allow them to enter upon the sacred ties of marriage, what may she not have allowed in the cloister?

For myself, no one could have heard of such narratives as that of Maria Monk with greater horror than I did. No one could have expressed greater indignation, or a more burning desire of vengeance on those whom I supposed had lied deliberately. I lived many years of my life with sisters who were as good and as pure as women could be, as far as their moral character is concerned. Naturally I believed that all the spouses of Christ were alike. As for priests, I believed that they were as near angels as mortal men could be. I was as indignant as the most devoted Romanists if I heard the least aspersion on the character of a priest. I had under my very eyes a case of the most lamentable depravity on the part of a priest; but so imbued was I with the idea that it was not possible for a priest to sin, that I did not see what, if I had been less suspicious, I certainly should have seen. It was not till I found not only that priests could ruin girls, but that very little was thought of it when they did so, that my eyes were opened.

I saw enough to open my eyes to the possibility of evil in convent life if I had even the least suspicion that such a thing was possible. I believe that the shock which is given to sensitive and spiritual minds when they find that there is evil, or when anything comes before them which even hints at it, is one cause why evil is so easily perpetuated. The power of the confessional is another great protection to the evildoer. If any Roman Catholic sees, or knows, of evil done by a priest or a sister, they are in duty bound to speak of it in the confessional, and here at once all further mention of it will be forbidden. However priests may abuse each other in private, they are at least loyal in protecting each other's—shall I say characters, or sins, in public? If, for example, I had mentioned in the confessional, as I ought to have done, that I had seen a sister and a priest in an improper position in a certain Irish convent, I would have had a more miserable life than I had, which is saying a good deal. It would have been the part of common charity and common prudence to have warned the sisters that this priest was a drunkard, a class with whom no woman is ever safe, yet for many reasons he was the very last person whom I would have ever suspected of drink, though others knew his real character.

I remember the late Dr. Moriarty, when Bishop of Kerry, talking to me one day of the strange "fancies" which sisters sometimes took, and telling me that a sister in one of his convents told him every time he came that the priests and the Rev. Mother were too familiar. I felt annoyed at his telling me this, as all Roman Catholics feel when they hear anything against their Church, and not the less so because he always seemed to think it was a good joke. While I was in

Kenmare the superioress of a large French religious order in Texas came there several times to look for young girls to go out with her as sisters. The way I was sought and visited there I know was one cause of my many troubles, for it excited the jealousy of the sisters, and especially of those who were natives of Kenmare, who, with one exception, were of that low and ignorant class who cannot bear to see any one noticed except themselves, and who have not sufficient intellect—shall I say common sense?—to appreciate the possibility of another having what God has not given them. This superioress told me stories of drunken priests which horrified me, and of the trouble she had with priests and sisters. I could not disbelieve her, but it was the first revelation to me of what I learned later was but too common in religious houses or convents where the Church of Rome is free from Protestant observation.

Later I learned that the further Rome gets from an open Bible the greater danger there is. Texas is not far from Mexico. In the remote and western States of America, as in Mexico, priests will live lives which they dare not live in the States, where public sentiment is to some degree controlled by Protestant opinion.

CHAPTER XI.

"*BY THEIR FRUITS YE SHALL KNOW THEM.*"

"Every good tree bringeth forth good fruit; but a corrupt tree bringeth forth evil fruit."—MATT. vii. 17.

WE have shown in the last chapter, on the undeniable evidence of the Roman Catholic editor of the New York *Freeman's Journal*, that sisters, to get a little money, deliberately deprive their pupils of the educational advantages which they are in duty bound to give them. If such a charge had been made against convent schools by Protestants it would be indignantly denied, and would be attributed to Protestant malice and bigotry. But this is not all. The editor says that the Roman Catholic poor, who can so ill afford it, are deprived yearly of "millions of dollars." But yet even this is not all. The same paper has the most caustic and cutting attack on the morality of the sisters, in the matter of their distribution of prizes. Nor can this be considered as of small moment. Only those who have been familiar for many years with convent schools and their workings can form an idea of the terrible shock which is given to the moral perceptions of children by any failure of justice on the part of those whom they are taught to revere so highly.

Let it be remembered that the children are taught to look up to the sisters as something superhuman, that the eyes and ears of these little ones are sharp, and criticising, though unconsciously to themselves, and that a defect, much more a serious fault, in a sister, is to them a terrible crime, and makes an indelible impression. I can quite endorse the criticism of the editor of the *Freeman's Journal*, but if I had accused sisters of the gross injustice as well as of the deliberate fraud of which he accuses them, it would be at once denied, and attributed to every motive but the true one. Here is what this Roman Catholic gentleman says of the way in which sisters' schools are conducted. The article is headed "The Reverse of the Medal."

"The medal nuisance reigns merrily in these days. Medals may be good for boys. They are very bad for girls and worse for girls' mothers. The heartburnings, the envy, the anger, the rash judgment evoked by these little bits of gilded metal leave traces for many years. Schools are injured by the competition for medals, friends separated, and priests and religious accused of all sorts of meanness in the height of the medal season.

"If Mary Scholastica Jones is to have the medal for useless industry, a branch very much affected in some schools, Mary Angela Smith's mother puts on her war paint. The Joneses! Everybody knows how old Jones made his money. And there are things about the Joneses that she could tell. As for Sister Mary Paul, who was obliged, poor woman, to invent a new study in order to give a new medal, it's as clear as daylight that if her mother wasn't a fourth cousin of Mary Jones' stepmother that medal would never have gone where it went. It is hinted, too, that if the Joneses had not given an extra donation to the organ fund the medal for useless industry would have adorned the deserving neck of Mary Angela Smith.

"The recent tribulations of some good religious in a neighbouring town will illustrate the troubles of those who give medals. They were to have a drama played by the *élite* of their classes. Intense excitement. White frocks. Curtain ready to rise. Good sisters charmed with the rehearsal of the *Long Lost Child*, who was also to be the Violet in an afterpiece, sing a French song later on, and play the Boulanger March (six hands) at the end. Applause on the other side of the curtain. But where is the *Long Lost Child?* She appears with her mother, who announces that there shall be no *Long Lost Child* that night if her Jane is not to get a medal. Then follow three other mothers with three other children, who have just discovered that they are to have no medals. The drama cannot possibly go on without these three, because one is Queen Esther, the other is a Hebrew Shepherd, and the third a Gipsy Maiden; and besides, they are down for 'Silvery Waves' on the programme. The consequence is that the curtain stays down. There is no drama, and four mothers return swearing vengeance against the school, and filling the air with taunts and insinuations."

Now it is certain that the mothers in question were also educated at convent schools, and this is the fruit of such training.

A novel was published some years since, in which the absurdities and the frauds of convent education were thoroughly exposed; and any one who knows anything personally of convents knows that "Hogan M.P." was true to the life. I have myself seen the bitterest jealousy and heartburning which has followed a public exhibition in English and Irish convent schools, and in the "commencements" in the United States, so graphically described in the above extract. What do the children think of the conduct of sisters who can stoop, and do stoop, to the meanest devices to gain the good word of the rich?

I heard the following account from the very lips of the sister concerned. The "Ladies of the Sacred Heart" (a curious name for those who take for their patron the lowly heart of Jesus) concern themselves very little with the poor. Their work is all for the rich; and it simply deprives the respectable and struggling Roman Catholic girl of one chance of earning her living. Roman Catholic girls have no chance of earning their bread by teaching except in poor schools; and even in these they are anticipated by sisters. The extent to which the sisters deprive both the Protestant and Roman Catholic working classes of a means of living is a subject which has never received the consideration it deserves. The Ladies of the Sacred Heart, however, have generally a few poor children in a separate school, to make some little show of care for the poor. The lady of whom I have spoken had charge of these children. On one occasion the Rev. Mother's Feast day came round, and of course she ought to receive a costly present. This system of making presents to superiors is one which is obviously a source of such heartburnings that in my own case I positively forbade it. The custom, however, is general. It happened that the young ladies of this school had been so heavily taxed for gifts and donations, that they were known to be absolutely penniless. The sister who had to collect the money for the present was in a sad dilemma. Just as it is considered an act of "disloyalty to the Church" when a priest fails to subscribe to a testimonial to a bishop, for whom he may have no real regard, so it is considered "disrespect" for a sister to fail in the accustomed marks of attention to a superior.

The money had to be got somehow, so the sister went to the sister who told me the fact, and said she must get the money from the poor children. The sister to whom this command was given had been a member of the order for many years, and had made her final vows, but she had not lost all heart and conscience. She positively refused to do this act of injustice, and declared that the poor children needed the money far more than the Rev. Mother, or any one else in the order. As these same sisters have recently refused four hundred thousand dollars for a small plot of land near New York which they own, some idea of their enormous wealth may be formed. This seems to have been the last drop in the cup offered to this sister. She had again and again been required to do things which she felt were against her conscience, and unhappily, or happily for herself, she could not invariably practise the "blind obedience" which is required from religious. The end was that she left the order, and is now living at home, though she still belongs to the Roman Catholic Church.

There were annual examinations held while I was in Kenmare, at which a much-edified but very ignorant public were surprised by the ready way in which the children answered questions which were, apparently, put to them for the first time at these examinations. This farce was, and I suppose is still, solemnly played out. The questions were all carefully prepared some time before the examinations, and the answers were also written out. The teacher asked the questions extemporaneously, and the children answered the questions, which they had been taught with much pains and labour, to all appearance in the same extemporaneous manner. On one occasion I was sitting next to the late Dr. Morriarty, their bishop. I saw that he was impressed, and I asked him what he was thinking of. He replied, "I am marvelling at the memory of that girl who is asking the questions." I knew then that the bishop at least was not imposed upon.

One must have lived in a convent to know all the little and the great frauds practised therein in the name of religion; and the worst evil is that it is made a sin not to do this evil, or even to condemn it.

A young lady, belonging to the upper "four hundred," who had been for a short time at one of the convents of the Sacred Heart, told me the following story. Here, if anywhere, we might suppose that humility would reign supreme; but this is far from being the case. The young ladies who are educated in these convents are the daughters of very wealthy parents, and are treated accordingly, and distinctions are made which produce incessant jealousy. This young lady told me she got into considerable trouble, and was eventually removed, at the request of the nuns, for asking questions when she should have held her tongue. One of her questions was sufficiently amusing. She had been told that whenever she met a sister she should make a profound bow to her, and stand on one side until the sister passed. She asked why this was required, and was told it was not intended to pay any homage to the sister, but that it was a reverence to the guardian angel of the sister.

One of the strange anomalies of convent life is the

existence of a class called "lay" sisters. These sisters are treated as inferior beings, and yet, according to the teaching of the Roman Church, they are as much spouses of Christ as the choir sisters, and should hold just the same rank. I may add that I had such a strong feeling as to the incongruity of the lay sister element in convents, that I decided not to have lay sisters in my own institutions, and therefore we were all equal. In America the idea of a "lay" sister is quite contrary to the spirit of the Republic. The young lady I have just mentioned thought that the lay sister should be treated the same as the other sisters, and acted accordingly in perfect good faith. But she was told that this was not right, that, on the contrary, the lay sisters should step aside for her, and bow to her when she passed. The girl asked if the lay sister had not a guardian angel also, and with the result that for this and other inconvenient inquiries, she was sent home as one likely to corrupt the morals of her companions.

I have seen the lives of some of the best sisters in Kenmare made perfectly miserable by the petty jealousy of others who were their inferiors in virtue, and in education. As the superioress was an uneducated person, she was entirely at the mercy of the sisters who understood the national system of education, and every one had to suffer in consequence. Two or three sisters who had never left the village of Kenmare, and had all the conceit of a very limited education, of which they thought a great deal, because they knew nothing better, ruled the house, and the children of the convent schools were not slow to see the state of things and to comment on it. Since my arrival in America I have met some of the children of the schools, who told me they often felt inclined to rise in rebellion against the insolent treatment which Sister Agatha, a very gentle sister who conducted the higher classes, received from Sister Joseph. So great was the insolence of this sister to myself (I regret to use the word, but I do not know how I can describe her conduct by any other term), that on one occasion I was on the point of leaving the convent, and taking shelter with a Protestant gentleman from her violence, in which she was encouraged by Bishop Higgins. I was some years her senior, and that circumstance alone restrained her.

If those who imagine a convent to be a place of repose and sanctity spent even a few weeks in one, they would soon be undeceived. Jealousy of each other, jealousy of superiors, jealousy of confessors,—these and many other things, which are inseparable from human nature when placed in certain positions, are the miserable result of convent life all over the world.

Those who only see sisters in the parlour or in the street are easily and sadly deceived. Sisters are prudent enough to conceal their animosities, and to hide their griefs from the public. I know it is difficult for those who have had no experience of convent life to understand why sisters conceal their troubles. But how many a wife is there who bears wrongs and sufferings in silence for years? Her pride or her self-respect keep her from open complaint. It is just the same with sisters. They know too well the uselessness of complaint, and that although it cannot help them in any way, it will most assuredly make their sufferings far greater. I have seen a sister nearly faint after spending hours rubbing the hands of a priest, who fancied this treatment, and required this and other services from the sisters.

I have seen the sisters day after day occupied for a considerable time bathing a priest's feet in the convent parlour, after he had been digging in the garden for his amusement, and in his awkwardness had hurt himself slightly. The man was undoubtedly a little erratic in his behaviour, and his meanness in requiring such services from women was a curious contrast to his high professions of sanctity, and of respect for the religious life. He died a bishop, and I presume in the odour of sanctity. I believe that his persistent persecution of myself arose from his keen suspicion that I had the most utter contempt for his pretensions of sanctity, and for his conduct in such matters. As for the sisters, the way in which they knelt at his feet to perform this unnecessary service, which if he had had a spark of manhood he would never have required, was sufficient to show their character.

The superioress of the Texas convent told me that on one occasion she and the sisters had to cut down a priest who was trying to hang himself, a victim of drink; but she seemed to think drink too common an occurrence to trouble much about it. She told me also that she had to keep a sharp watch over the young sisters and the priests. It is impossible for Protestants to understand how it is that a Roman Catholic, knowing all these things, can yet remain a Roman Catholic. Yet it is so.

I shall never forget the first time I saw anything like open quarrelling in a convent. It was soon after I entered the convent in Newry. There was a Sister Joseph there, also an unfortunate name as far as my experience went, for the saint, after whom she was named, whatever else he might do for his clients, did not make them amiable. Miss O'Hagan, as I have said in my Autobiography, had just been made superior, to the intense annoyance of most of the older sisters. She was herself a good woman, anxious to do her duty according to her light; but it can be easily understood that being very much younger than the sisters subject to her, she was looked down upon by them. Sister Joseph, I must say, lost no opportunity of annoying her, and this in a way which could not be complained of as a direct disobedience or fault. I could hardly suppress my astonishment at seeing this sister, and indeed many others, going day after day to receive the Sacrament of the altar, and yet day after day quarrelling with each other and with their superior, in a way of which any ordinary Christian would have been ashamed.

The choir was a subject of perpetual and disgraceful quarrelling. Those who know anything of how quarrels abound in Church choirs, Protestant as well as Roman Catholic, may form some idea of the trouble in a convent, though all its members are supposed to live the lives of saints.

In convents where young ladies are educated, and especially in the Loretto convents, it is the custom for a sister to chose or be chosen by each pupil as her confidant. The misery and heartburning to which this foolish custom gives rise could be scarcely understood outside the walls of a convent. A book has been published lately in England by a gentleman who spent some time in a monastery in that country, and who left it in utter disgust with the puerilities with which the monks occupied themselves, though it does not appear as if he had left the Roman Church. In a review of this book in an "Anglican" paper the writer states that he is sure the "Cowley Fathers" live a very different life. I can assure him, or others interested in these matters, that bad as convent life is in the Church of Rome, it is peace itself compared with the life of Anglican sisters. The want of charity, the quarrelling, and the pettiness which reigns supreme in these institutions is below contempt.

It was the misfortune of a friend of mine to pass a day and night, or part of a night, in one of these Ritualistic institutions in New York, under circumstances which should have secured her every kindness, but only to meet with conduct of which a respectable heathen would not have been guilty. Scarcely had she arrived when she was told that one of the three sisters who formed the whole community (for these ladies are very seldom able to get or keep many members, no matter how great their wealth) was jealous, and in a temper, because she had not been consulted about the visitor. The "Lady" superior was absent, and the sister who took her place went to her room and locked herself up, and left the amiable number three to do as she pleased. The lady who had asked the hospitality of these "sisters" had been recommended to them by a bishop, and a near relative of this bishop made all the arrangements, and was to have called for the lady the next morning. She was treated from the first with the utmost rudeness. The "Lady" superior arrived in the night, and next morning at daybreak came to the room which the lady in question occupied, and ordered her out of the house, with an insolence of tone and manner which no lady would have used to a servant. Nor was there even the shadow of an excuse for her violence. Heaven help the poor penitents who are consigned to the care of such "sisters."

An enormous sum of money is now being expended

on building a larger institution for these three women, and with the assistance of plenty of servants they will manage to carry on some kind of reformatory work. My friend suggested that if they commenced reformatory work amongst themselves it would be no harm. No doubt there may be some Anglican convents where Roman Catholic practices are not closely copied, and where consequently there is more peace and charity. To me the awful part of all this is the high profession of religion made by those who are daily and hourly guilty of such sins against charity.

It seems to be forgotten, in estimating the work of the so-called religious orders in the Roman Catholic Church, that it is our duty to judge the work by its results. In doing this I shall confine myself exclusively to Roman Catholic statements; and it is indeed amazing that Roman Catholics do not see for themselves how utterly their Church has failed as an educator, or as an elevator of the people. Here is what the *North Western Chronicle*, the official organ of Bishop Ireland, of St. Paul's, Minnesota, has to say on this question. And yet this bishop has done his best to bring thousands of unfortunate Irish to his diocese to incur the same unhappy fate. But when I asked permission to do a work approved even by the Pope, to save these poor children, I only met an insulting refusal. It is absurd for bishops and priests to complain, as they do continually, when Protestants come forward and try to save the offspring of their unhappy followers, while they will not use the least efforts themselves to save them.

"From the number of destitute Catholic children," says this paper, "that we see immediately surrounding ourselves, whom we cannot send to charitable institutions because they have no means to keep them; from the number of Catholic children in non-Catholic institutions throughout the country; from the number we see at large, thrown on a cold, selfish, and heartless world to seek their daily bread; and from the newspaper reports of distress in towns and cities, we are forced to believe that at the present time in the United States there are more destitute Catholic children exposed to the certain corruption of faith and morals than there were Catholics in this country nearly a century ago, when the Holy Father, Pius VI., appointed Right Rev. John Carroll to watch over, direct, and govern the American Church. What a terrible thing it would be if the Pope had then left the Catholic people of this country exposed to the loss of faith! And are not the souls of so many children of the Church who to-day are positively exposed to corruption, as precious in the sight of God, and as deserving of care? That there are many thousands, through exposure and destitution, on the way to apostasy is too patent to be denied. Perhaps never before in any other country has there been such an exposure of the children of the Church to apostasy and immorality, as here at the present time.

"The officials of a Protestant Benevolent Association have informed us that in twenty-one years they have sent to the West over 30,000 children, of whom at least 20,000 were Catholics; and still the train goes regularly once a month with from 130 to 150 children for distribution. We know several other societies, five hundred and more Protestant societies, that have in the West established agencies to which they are continually sending Catholic children. It is sometimes said that these societies kidnap the little ones, but we can hardly credit such reports. They can find plenty in destitution without stealing any. If the Protestant societies do steal Catholic children it is very disreputable for them. Yet we think it is more disreputable for Catholics to let so many go unheeded, and then complain of the few that are stolen.

"Last December we visited two Protestant schools, not the so-called common schools, but Protestant free mission schools; nor do they belong to the society that took care of the twenty thousand and consigned them to Protestantism. In both these schools there are about 500 Catholic children. They have been run for over twenty years with the same class of pupils, who also attend Sabbath School on Sundays. . . . Twenty-two years ago two priests were passing along the sidewalk as the children were coming out, and one of the priests said to the other, 'What a pity it is that we have no place to send these children, where they could be brought up in their own religion.' And to this day we have no place to send them. It is an undeniable fact that a large percentage of the children provided for by Protestant Societies were once inmates of Catholic institutions.

"A few days since a gentleman told us that on the 15th of last May (1879) he was at Kankakee, Ill., and saw two cartloads of children arrive from New York. They were quickly distributed to farmers and others who had been forewarned of their coming. From the children's Celtic features, he judged the majority of them were Catholics. And he inquired, 'Is there no way of stopping their (the Protestants) infamous practice of stealing Catholic children?'"

What a disgraceful confession this is, above all, when

one thinks of the enormous sums of money in the hands of the Church of Rome.

The *Catholic Visitor*, Richmond, Virginia, a paper published under the Episcopal approbation of Bishop Keane, gives the following account of the state of the Holy Roman Catholic Church in his diocese. It is no wonder that infidelty is the result of Roman Catholic education, and that this bishop, when made head of the Roman Catholic University at Washington, was obliged to go to Europe for professors.

"The greatest enemies of the Catholic Church are Catholics. The genius of this great country will never perhaps admit of a persecution of the Church. Yet the persecution will and does take place. Who are the persecutors? They are bad Catholics. It is a grand thing to be blessed with the faith, but to practise its maxims is necessary. We must not close our eyes to the great fact that the worst enemies of our faith and native land are Irish. There is a class of grovelling politicians who float themselves upon their Irish and Catholic names, and yet are in their lives a contradiction to everything that is sacred and grand in the Irish character. These are to be found in almost every village and city of the country. The Irishman who ignores the sacred obligations of his Church denies his God, and becomes the greatest enemy of his race and creed. We are in this country losing more by the infidelity of Catholics than we are gaining. The Catholic who neglects to assist at Mass on Sundays, or to approach the sacraments as commanded, is a living scandal, especially to the little ones. As soon as one command of the Church is ignored grace is lost, and the end no man knows. We need practical Catholics to-day."

Another Roman Catholic writer says, in an article headed, "Drink, Destitution, and Apostasy":—

"An immense amount of the preaching and writing among us this last half century has been, and still is, on the necessity of the Catholic faith. There is also some exposition of the 'doings of the drink,' 'economically, socially, and morally,' as the standard report is. That is all very good. But what seems to be commonly overlooked by the preachers and the denouncers of the drink is that the drink's injury to the faith almost countervails the benefits of the preaching. And this not merely, not chiefly, because the drink, in its conspicuous effects upon certain of the faithful, brings discredit to the Catholic faith, where otherwise it would be considered and embraced, but because it casts it out of where it was infused by the Holy Ghost. For it makes Catholic parents to leave their children destitute, and so they get reared, hundreds and thousands of them, in non-Catholic institutions, and in homes not only indifferent, but bitterly hateful toward the Church. Only for the drink, the few Catholic children that would be left orphans would find an abundance of happy Catholic homes qualified and glad to receive them."

As to the State of New York, where the wealth of the Church of Rome is almost unlimited, and where the archbishop makes and unmakes the chief magistrates at his sole will and pleasure, it is simply a disgrace to humanity. It is only necessary to read the records of the police courts to see the names, nationality, and religion of the criminals.

Philadelphia also supplies her share of Roman Catholic criminals.

The last report of the Presbyterian Hospital in New York shows that Irish and Roman Catholics are a very large majority of the cases treated; and yet these Protestant institutions, and all connected with them, are the subject of constant abuse by priests, while they grossly neglect their own people. I am acquainted with a hospital in Washington built right opposite a Roman Catholic Church, which the priest will not take the trouble to cross the road to visit, and where a Protestant gentleman reads prayers and Scripture every Sunday for the inmates. I could mention a hospital in New York similarly situated, where the inmates, Roman Catholic and Protestant, have to look to a Protestant minister for spiritual care, unless the priest is sent for specially.

The London (England) *Tablet* is full of complaints of the neglect of English Romanists to care for their Churches and their poor, and of loud and noisy lamentations at the zeal shown by Protestants in looking after those who are going on the downward path to ruin, uncared for by the Church of Rome, until it is discovered that Protestants are providing for them, when there is an outcry against proselytism, and a call for money, which seems to be the panacea for all the ills of Rome. Yet none of it is used effectively to lessen the torrent of evil. Priests die almost millionaires, but leave their churches in debt and their money to their relatives. A niece of a recently deceased priest was the happy recipient of $50,000, and other members of his family shared in proportion. The New York *Mail and Express* gives the following statistics:—

" The amounts appropriated to Catholic benevolent and charitable institutions since 1869 foots up in the aggregate nearly $20,000,000, the sums in individual instances being as high as $2,000,000, while a number of grants for several hundred thousand dollars are registered. Considering that the Roman Catholics are believed to pay only about one-tenth of the taxes, one would say that they had their full share of corn from the public crib. It is true that some of the Protestant denominations have received similar grants at times, but the amounts are quite inconsiderable, and the great bulk of Protestants are opposed to the principle."

The *Mail and Express* also states that $4,200,000 of New York city property is under control of Roman Catholics, who pay simply a nominal tax while agreeing to use the grounds and buildings for charitable purposes.

But if the Roman Church is so holy, and is doing her duty to her spiritual children, why should this state of demoralisation exist, which gives Protestants the opportunity to proselytise? The truth is, that Rome, weighted down with her own infallibility, cannot purge herself from evil. She can only utter querulous cries of complaint against those who are trying to save her lost sheep.

In England, in America, in Europe, it is still the same. The Rev. T. Regan writes to the London *Tablet*:—

"ST. CHARLES, OGLE STREET, *October 16th*, 1888.

"MY DEAR EVERARD GREEN,—You will be sorry to hear that the resources of this mission have diminished to such an extent as to threaten it with absolute extinction, unless timely help be forthcoming. I am up to the neck in debt, in spite of the cheese-paring economy which I am constantly practising."

The Rev. Charles Boardman writes :—

"Promising candidates for the priesthood are yearly rejected, because there is no one to supply them with intellectual food. Mass is said in outhouses for want of a few hundred pounds to raise a respectable building for the Lord of Hosts. And this in wealthy England.

"Well, perhaps the reader will ask if he reads so much of my letter, what do you want? I want more generosity on the part of the well-to-do. I want them, as the saying is, to come out strong. I want them to assist, and to assist with a strong lever, those whose shoulders are overburdened. I am not living in a college myself, so I can speak dispassionately. I am living in a small country mission, where I have learnt that God helps those who help themselves; but I have been in colleges, and have seen what I have here portrayed. I fear we are losing souls from a famine of intellectual Catholic food.

"I am, sir, your obedient servant,
"CHARLES BOARDMAN, D.D.

"LONGRIDGE, *October 25th,* 1886."

Bishop Cosgrove, of Davenport, Iowa, speaking of Catholic papers, says :—

"We find that about one Catholic in forty is a subscriber to one of them. We find the combined circulation of all the Catholic papers of the country to be less than that of some single issues of the *Police Gazette;* we find it less by thousands than that of the journal published by another single establishment, the Methodist Book Concern. Protestant exchanges charge that our people are ignorant, that they lack intelligence, and usually they have decidedly the best of the argument, for the facts are very stern and hard to face."

This indictment of Romanists for not supporting their own journals is significant.

The complaints of Roman Catholic papers—English, Irish, and American—of the utter incapacity of the Jesuits, the brothers, and the sisters, who teach the rising generation of Roman Catholics, are worth studying. And yet we are told incessantly that if the "Church" had only all the power she wants the world at large would be converted. Is it unjust to ask first for a little fruit from all the power which that Church possesses at present? The following, all from Roman Catholic papers, show the present state of Roman Catholic education.—

The New York *Tablet* says :—

"Sisters have not had the training indispensable for the efficient and honest carrying out of their duties. A religious vocation is not a certificate to instruct others, either unto righteousness or learning. When a complaint of this incompetency was made to a parish priest without obtaining a hearing, and when the matter was referred to higher authority, we were informed that the authority of the parish priest is complete and exclusive.

"We have no means of testing the truth of these averments, but our informant, while petulant and irritated, is reliable and conscientious. We draw the attention of pastors and superiors to his statements. He also draws attention to the fact, which is not disputed, that since the religious in France have been required to submit to the examination to which secular teachers are subjected, the schools conducted by the religious have greatly increased in value, and risen in the esteem of the Catholic people.

"We propose to say a few plain truths about our Catholic academies.

"The complaint is oftenest made by Catholic parents that they cannot send their children to Catholic schools because the latter must be prepared to make their own way in life, and the public schools are better conducted for qualifying them for it. This is not absolutely and universally true. But it is true in many cases. What is the reason? Or are there more reasons than one?

"Perhaps there is an atom of truth in the following letter, of which we print only the pertinent paragraph.

"'Will you undertake to defend schools whose teachers never pass an examination before assuming the functions of the teacher, and who a day before, being clothed in the gowns of religious, of 'sisters' of one community or another, are themselves pupils, and not scholars in any sense? Is it not a cruel imposition upon our working Catholic people that incompetency is thrust upon their children in the name of God, and that they are thus robbed, in a great measure, of the attainments and the training with which their Protestant companions set out in life? Is it not notorious that the discipline of Catholic schools is so lax that boys and girls come out of them utterly incapable of self-control?'

"These are serious questions, and they imply grave accusations. We do not propose to defend anything merely because it is Catholic, but we do propose to censure without reserve or fear anything avowedly Catholic which ought to be censured. Our correspondent claims in the body of his letter, which is not all in a spirit to justify its publication, that the teachers in some Catholic schools are notoriously incompetent."

Even religious instruction is neglected, as the following letter, published in the *North Western Chronicle*, shows :—

"SIR,—How very sad and even humiliating it is to look around, and within a very small radius, and see the number of young people, young men especially, who ought to be Catholics, and are never seen at church any more. Who is to blame, they or the parents? Have they got instruction enough to make them firm in their belief in the Catholic Church? Or have they been sent to catechism a few times, and perhaps to a priest who could hardly speak a word of English, and then expected to be good Catholics? They may continue going there while under their parents' control; but have their parents any reason for expecting they will continue in it once they get away from home, and if they do not, I repeat, whose fault is it? They got no instructions to make them believe in the right Church. Here is a ripe field for any Protestant. If Catholics would only take as much interest in their religion as Protestants do, there would not be so many going from the Church. Surely Protestant lay people are missionaries as well as their ministers, and sometimes a great deal more zealous. Anything relating to Church matters interests them at once, and they always keep up such an interest in conducting their Sunday School, while, alas! how true it is that the Catholics not only will not take hold and do nothing themselves, but will not even co-operate with the priest in anything for the promotion of their holy religion."

The Italian Romanists of New York, we are told, will not support their Churches, and their priests have to look to the Irish to do this for them. The editor of a New York paper had an article recently about an Italian priest who he says "died for his flock." He writes;—

"Father Kirner died for his flock, and yet at his Month's Mind there were many Irish faces, but scarcely an Italian one. At the great function of St. Anthony's the other Sunday there was hardly an Italian face visible, though St. Anthony's is understood to be an Italian stronghold."

The editor of another paper says :—

"Italians are never counted on to support their own Churches, or their own priests, in this country. They give nothing for marriages, christenings, or other ceremonies that in the churches of every other denomination call for acknowledgment. Their churches are built by the people of other nationalities, Irish most often, and maintained by them, and the Italian priests cannot look for sustenance to their Italian congregations. In fact, the pennies put into the poor box are often surrendered to the same Italian who, next moment, will revile the Church because it does not think it incumbent on it to give him a salary when out of work, or return him to Italy with the price of a vineyard in his pockets."

So much for Italian devotion to the Church of Rome. As for the statement that Father Kirner died a "martyr," it is on a level with the boasts about poor Father Damien. The latter went to the Roman Catholic lepers, who had been utterly neglected in a station where there were many missionaries to care for the leper Protestants. And yet from the way in which he has been mentioned it would be supposed that no one had ever attended to the leper settlement until he went there. Instead of boasting, the Church of Rome should be ashamed of her previous neglect of her own people—a neglect which was only remedied when Protestant attention was called to it. Father Kirner's case would be better described as suicide. He was warned again and again of the risk he ran in being his own architect, and when his Church fell the authorities were about to take action to protect the lives which his folly or ignorance had endangered; and yet he is called a "martyr."

If it had been said that he had caused the death of many of his flock it would have been the truth. It was well known in New York at the time that he would have been prosecuted before the fatal result, if it had not been for the power which the Roman Church has there, which makes it dangerous to cross a priest in anything, unless the ecclesiastical authorities are against him. No doubt in time to come Father Kirner will be quoted as actually having died for his flock, and perhaps he will be canonised, so easy is it for Rome to deceive the world

"Inspector Martin," says a writer in the *New York World*, "who was dismissed for negligence, states that he warned Father Kirner, but he knew that Father Kirner had influence enough to get the permit (to endanger the lives of the builders, and his own). It is hinted that it is easier to get such permits one way than another."

Surely the sacrifice of so many valuable lives should deprive Father Kirner of the title of "martyr," unless he has earned it by causing the martyrdom of honest labourers, whose interests he should have been the first to protect. The inspector is made the victim to public opinion, but if the priest had lived no one would have dared to blame him; and the inspector knew well what the consequences would have been if he had interfered with the priest. Such is the result of the power of the Church when unrestrained.

As for the Italians, their religious instruction is utterly neglected in Italy. Strange that the Pope, who claims that he can govern the world, is so careless about his own flock. If "an enemy" had written this what an outcry there would have been.

A New York Roman Catholic writer was very angry, when the truth was published in the Roman Catholic papers about the state of Italy. He says:—

"Was there then any need of bringing before the public the following indictment against the Italian clergy for criminal dereliction of duty, in order to explain the religious ignorance of some of the Italians in New York? The duty of even rudimentary instruction and training in the principles and practices of the Christian religion has been grossly neglected by large numbers of parish priests; the state of ignorance among this people cannot otherwise be accounted for.

"There are thousands of Italians in this city who do not know the Apostles' Creed. Multitudes of men and women of this people do not know the elementary truths of religion such as the Trinity, the Incarnation, and the Redemption.

"Mr. Lynch takes it for granted that the clergy have fixed revenues. It is hard to see how the poverty of the people can explain their ignorance. The apathy of the clergy in instructing the people is sometimes explained by the fact that they have fixed revenues, independent of the people, and fixity of tenure for life. They would be more energetic in imparting religious knowledge if they drew their income from the people, and their positions or promotions depended on their exertions.

"What, then, has been their religious life at home? Some peculiar kind of spiritual condition, fed on the luxuries of religion without its substantials. Devotions, pilgrimages, shrines, miraculous pictures and images—indulgences they have been accustomed to, together with, in all too many cases, an almost total ignorance of the great truths which can alone make such aids to religion profitable."

In other words, the religious life of these Italians, in their own country, was rank superstition, and their priests and bishops are responsible for it.

By all means, then, if an American or Irish priest, or Mr. Lynch himself, cannot go and instruct those who are yet across the water and are apt to remain, let a pious Methodist preacher and his wife be sent to Naples at once to instruct them. For Methodism is assuredly preferable to this "kind of spiritual condition, fed on the luxuries of religion without its substantials." The benighted people will at least be taught that in God there are Three Divine Persons, and that One of them became man to redeem us. They will also learn the Apostles' Creed, and no longer receive the sacraments invalidly, as they seem to be doing now, because they "are not well instructed enough to receive them."

The New York *Freeman's Journal* is very angry at Father Lynch for exposing the state of the holy Roman Catholic priesthood. It says:—

"Certainly Mr. Lynch must have told some home truths when he could excite all this indignation."

The London (England) *Tablet* has the following very logical statement about the condition of the Roman Catholic world before the Reformation; but what has it to say to the above (Roman Catholic) account of the state of the Pope's own clergy at the present day?

"It is quite true that there was still much irregularity and wickedness at the opening of the sixteenth century; otherwise the so-called reformation movement, begun in violation of self-imposed vows in robbery, sacrilege, and violence, could not have had so many ready and willing adherents. But judging by the principles and the practice of those old religious orders, by what they did and what they attempted to do, it is fair to conclude that the world has those orders to thank, that in spite of the weakness of poor human nature the 'Reformers,' after all, were not able to accomplish as much harm as they might have done otherwise."

The Roman Catholic *Tablet* prints the following criticism, from one of its correspondents, on Roman Catholic schools, lay or religious. And it is just because conscientious parents know well that their children will never get a thorough education under Roman Catholic teachers that they even dare episcopal wrath, and send them to the public schools.

"Most persons find that at this age (fifteen or sixteen) their boys have acquired a smattering of classics, a superficial knowledge of mathematics, and a vast fund of conceit, none of which is of the slightest use to them in starting life. I have asked the question of a great many masters, and certainly of a greater number of parents, and all agree that the majority of their boys leave college before they are sixteen ; and I think, therefore, that I am quite right in assuming that the heads of most of our colleges are officially aware that the boys will have to go into business, and will be withdrawn from college life before they reach this age. Yet, sir, knowing this, not one of the great colleges, such as Ushaw, Stonyhurst, Beaumont, Oscott, or others has a system of education calculated to prepare a boy for a commercial career.

"It passes my understanding how the Jesuits, for instance, who have beautiful colleges, complete with every comfort, equipped with all that the love of our holy religion, the love of science, the cultivation and knowledge of art and music can produce, deliberately pursue a system of teaching of which three-fourths of their scholars never remain long enough to obtain the full benefit. They learn Latin and Greek, but within six months of their leaving college they have completely forgotten them. Had they learnt French, German, book-keeping by double entry, shorthand, and a good deal of arithmetic, they would at once, upon entering an office, be found most useful to their employers, and rapidly obtain a position of trust. Did not the report of the London Chamber of Commerce, which was published and commented upon lately, fully point out how it was that young clerks of German, Dutch, and other nationalities, receive comparatively large salaries, and occupy all over the United Kingdom positions of responsibility in commercial houses, while young Englishmen, for want of familiarity with modern languages, and ignorance of moneys, weights, manners, and customs of foreign trading, have either to be content with subordinate positions, or have to emigrate to the colonies."

The Richmond *Catholic Visitor* says :—

"It is really a measure of disgrace to the Catholics of this city that they show so little interest in societies connected with their Church, but especially one of the nature of the Catholic Union. Just view what has been done for the Young Men's Christian Association, and no doubt among the contributors are many Catholics, who do absolutely nothing for the societies connected with their own Church. It is a shame, and it is as little as such can do to encourage this society by an occasional visit to the rooms, especially on literary evenings."

The Catholic *Citizen* says :—

"There is a great similarity in the Catholic type in all our cities. The education of the young has been such that a cheap 'hop' is their greatest attraction, and their nearest approach to the 'literary' is a taste for variety amateur theatricals. As for the older heads, they are often too modest to be worth mentioning. 'Put money in thy purse,' and evince no public spirit, are among their rules of conduct."

No wonder that educated converts complain thus of Roman Catholic ignorance.

"It is a pitiable fact that we have no Catholic historical associations, and that the works of our Catholic ancestors which as such belong to us, are published by Protestant societies—the Surtees Society, and the Camden Society, for example; and it is still more pitiable that in the list of members of these societies scarcely a Catholic name is to be met with. It would really be interesting to know in how many Catholic colleges and seminaries, not to speak of the libraries of either clergy, convents, or laity, the works of Catholic historians are to be found."

The following statistics are gathered from the census. In proportion to every 10,000 inhabitants in the United States :—

	Illiterates.	Paupers.	Criminals.
By public schools of State of Massachusetts	71	69	11
By public schools of 21 States	350	170	75
By Roman Catholic schools	1,400	410	160

In the state of New York the Roman Catholic parochial school system turns out three and a half times as many paupers as the public school system. No wonder that Macaulay says of Ultramontane education, that under its power the loveliest and most fertile provinces of Europe have been sunk in poverty, political servitude, and intellectual torpor.

The *Catholic Review* of April 1871 thus explains the reasons why this Church does not provide even the simplest elements of education :—

"We do not indeed prize as highly as some of our countrymen appear to do, the ability to read, write, and cipher. Some men are born to be leaders, and the rest are born to be led."

This is certainly true. The only pity is that so many Protestants try to support the pretensions of Rome. A recent public speaker, Chancellor Henry R. Pierson, of Albany, delivered an address at the commencement exercises of St. John Jesuit College, Fordham. He said, with a gush which has caused his speech to be copied into every Roman Catholic paper, and which will cause it to be republished and commented upon for years to come :—

" Though I am a Protestant, I can thank God that

there is a Catholic Church. You have nothing of which to be ashamed in the Catholic Church, and much of which you ought to be proud. I, a Protestant, tell you that you need to stick up boldly for your religion, and the people with whom you come in contact will like you all the more. That, in substance, is the feeling of every honest and candid Protestant."

Chancellor Pierson will no doubt be flattered very much by the Romanists, as "an honest and candid Protestant," and when there is a question of voting for any office which he may desire, he will be sure to have all their "honest" votes. But one cannot help wondering if the chancellor is honestly ignorant of Rome as she is, or if he is wilfully blind.

One would like to know what Chancellor Pierson thinks, not of the education of a few young men in a Jesuit College, but of the Roman Catholic population of the slums of New York, and indeed of its aldermen, and other Roman Catholic officials. Is he proud of them?

CHAPTER XII.

SOME ROMAN DIFFICULTIES WHICH PROTESTANTS SHOULD CONSIDER.

"Who comforteth us in all our tribulation, that we may be able to comfort them which are in any trouble."—2 Cor. i. 4.

THERE is at present a deep stirring of thought among Roman Catholic laymen, which is none the less earnest because, for obvious reasons, it cannot make itself heard in public. It should be distinctly remembered that public expression of opinion, unless it absolutely coincides, either from policy or from conviction, with the governing powers of the Roman Catholic Church, is absolutely prohibited.

Hence Protestants naturally think that a pale reflex of harmonious belief exists in the Roman Catholic Church, with a placid acquiescence in Papal infallibility. Never was there a more lamentable and disastrous conclusion. The Protestant who can speak his mind socially, politically, and morally, cannot realize how utterly impossible it is for a Roman Catholic, be he priest or layman, to say what he really thinks. A curious and very interesting evidence of this was given quite recently by Archbishop Walsh, in connection with the recent Papal pronouncement on Irish affairs.

He said that while Protestants were obliged to decide on such matters (he referred to the last Papal pronouncement) according to their conscience, Roman Catholics were bound to obey the voice of God as made known by the Pope, and were not allowed the exercise of a private conscience. "Happy Protestants," a Roman Catholic friend of the writer's exclaimed with some emphasis; "they are allowed to have a conscience, and informed that it is their duty to use it, whereas we Catholics are denied a conscience practically, since we are not to use that which we possess." In fact, it is the plain teaching of the Roman Catholic Church that the conscience, once submitted to Rome, must remain for ever submitted. How deeply the Papal questions of the hour are trying men's souls will never be known until the Day of Account.

Ancient upheavals of thought in the Roman Catholic Church should at least satisfy the world that there never has been a dead level of belief or opinion in that Church. What anguish of heart and soul there must have been in the ages of Luther and of Savonarola; what heart agonies in the time when the "poor men of Lyons" and the Waldenses suffered "loss of all things," for what they believed to be a purer gospel teaching. We hear only of the great warriors, the giants of the battle, the leaders in the fight, men whose thoughts set the world on fire; we hear little and think little of the rank and file; and yet they also thought and suffered anguish in their desire to obtain an answer to the stupendous question—What is truth?

How could missions of reform have been accomplished, if there had not been vast multitudes of thinking men to follow the reformer and leader? One hand may light the beacon fire of truth; it needs many hands to feed the flame and keep it burning.

There is as deep an agitation in the Roman Church

to-day as there has ever been. The fire smoulders; when and where the flames will break forth God only knoweth. But for those who desire truth to prevail there is a terrible responsibility if they "break the bruised reed, or quench the smoking flax."

It is unhappily the case in America that there is a very strong feeling amongst some Protestants against any change of religious opinion; and this feeling naturally finds an outcome on individuals who change. It is also an unhappy fact, undeniably and infinitely harmful, that some of the priests who have abandoned the Roman Catholic Church are of immoral character and degraded habits. Men of honour and self-respect do not wish to be classed with such men, and would endure any sufferings sooner than have the name of being one with them even in sympathy. Hence an immense and crushing difficulty lies in the way of those who see many evils in the Roman Catholic Church. They are powerless to reform it from within, and equally powerless to reform it from without. Men do not ask the cause of this miserable degradation of so many priests. They do not inquire why they came to be outcasts; they only see a painful fact, and draw natural but false conclusions.

Any other body of men may effect a reform in the discipline of their Church, or may leave it without reproach, if they believe that their conscience prompts them to do so. But it is not so with the Roman Catholic, be he priest or layman, be he ever so honourable, be his career ever so blameless, be his convictions ever so strong. He is maligned, sneered at, and persecuted by the Church he was striving to reform, and for the prosperity of which he would have given his life blood; and he is sometimes discouraged by Protestants, who denounce this Church for refusing liberty of conscience to her children, and yet, such is human nature, discourage those who act on this principle.

Let us suppose the case of a pervert to the Roman Catholic faith, who entered the Church before the personal infallibility of the Pope was made an article of faith, as I did; let it also be remembered that if a Roman Catholic doubts the personal infallibility of the Pope he is as surely consigned to hell for ever as if he doubted the Trinity. A pervert, then, is received into the Roman Catholic Church; he is taught that it is *de fide* to believe in the infallibility of the Church. There is no mistake about the matter; it is plain. The Church is infallible; its living voice is heard through the Councils, and through them only. The idea harmonises with his previous thoughts, for such men have generally been recruited from the ranks of advanced Anglicans, who, looking for certainty of belief in the multiplied confusion of opinion, have flung themselves in despair into the arms of what they believed would prove a happy certainty.

There was a certain grandeur, a commanding dignity about the infallibility of the Church as a body. The decrees of dogma came from the united voices of great and reverend men inspired by the Holy Ghost, and saying with the Apostles, "It seems good to the Holy Ghost and to us." In every congregation of men there must be a governing body. The decrees of the Fathers of the undivided Church demanded the respect of Christendom, and the obedience of the early Church.

All this the pervert believed, but suddenly, and with little warning, came the decree of the Vatican Council, that the Pope should be declared personally infallible. Was it to be wondered at if men wept at this terrible change, wept as the men of Israel wept when the glory of the first temple was recalled by the pale reflex of it in the second?

As no other ceremony, or condition, or sacrament of the Church was changed, the great multitude of Roman Catholic people concerned themselves very little about the matter. They had always been told what they were to believe, and now they were told to believe something else, and they were too indifferent, or too ignorant, to inquire further. But there were men who felt, men who thought, men who wept tears of agony in silence; for who dare trust his fellow in a Church where the least utterance of opinion is followed by condign punishment?

A letter by Bishop Strossmayer, published in the *Kölnische Zeitung* soon after the Vatican Council, puts this fact very clearly:—

"The Vatican Council was wanting in that freedom which was necessary to make it a real Council, and to justify it in making decrees calculated to bind the consciences of the whole Catholic world. . . . Everything which could resemble a guarantee for the liberty of discussion was carefully excluded. . . . And as though all this did not suffice, there was added a public violation of the ancient Catholic principle: *Quod semper quod ubique quod ab omnibus.* The most hideous and naked exercise of Papal infallibility was necessary before that infallibility could be elevated into a dogma. If to all this be added that the Council was not regularly constituted; that the Italian bishops, prelates, and officials were in a monstrously predominating majority; that the Apostolic Vicars were dominated by the Propaganda in the most scandalous manner; that the whole apparatus of that political power which the Pope then exercised in Rome contributed to intimidate and repress all free utterances, you can easily conceive what sort of liberty, that essential attribute of all Councils, was displayed at Rome."

How many thousands, how many millions sank into the depths of despair in consequence of this decision can never be known this side of eternity. It is only now, when the personal power and personal claim of the Pope to exercise that power in politics is being enforced, that the multitude has begun to realize what was done in the Vatican Council. Thought is stirred, action is sure to follow.

No doubt Emerson's saying is true, "Tell the truth, and the world will come to see it at last." But the world is sometimes long in coming, and the prophets of truth are very apt to have a good deal more respect shown to their sepulchres than to themselves.

Yet it is strange why a man's change of religious opinion should not be respected, as much as his change of opinion in matters of science. Men of science are obliged from time to time, in consequence of further reflection or of further knowledge, to change, to modify, or perhaps to abandon completely, preconceived opinions which they once firmly held. Yet they are not reproached for this. Truth is unchangeable, else it would not be truth. But do we always see truth clearly, and may there not be causes quite outside of our own control, or conscience, which may cause us to see more or less clearly at different periods of life? Does not reason develop with exercise? Does not our power of intellectual exercise increase with practice? And though the Roman Catholic Church forbids its members the use of reason in matters of faith, and practically forbids the exercise of conscience, yet changes have been developing, either for good or evil, in the Roman Catholic Church ever since its foundation, which give evidence that some of its members have used their power of reasoning with unconscious disobedience.

Irish politicians, like many of their countrymen, often inherit their religion from their mothers and preserve it through their wives; and as its numerical strength is the great point made by Catholics when they wish to impress on their own minds, or on the minds of others, the great power of the Church in this country, the numerical strength of the Roman Catholics in America has told, and has told beyond all doubt, in politics. But what is the real—rather we should say what is the spiritual value of this preponderating influence? Does it lessen crime? Does it lessen suffering? Has it elevated the moral or intellectual condition of the masses in New York? He would be a bold man who dared to say, in the face of facts, that the Roman Catholic Church has been a powerful influence for good in that city. And yet was there ever a body so boastful of its own virtue? It is time that some one cried out and awakened the rulers of the Church of Rome from their dreams of self-complacent security. If the shepherd sleeps, what shall become of the hapless flock?

Building churches, building schools, establishing colleges, publishing panegyrics on ecclesiastics which should make any self-respecting man sink into the earth with shame, that he should be the subject of such gross flattery; is this a sign of real solid Divine life? A very amusing instance of this abject flattery of ecclesiastics occurred lately. A poem was written by a priest, in which Cardinal Gibbons was glorified in metre, and out of it, with the grossest adulation. Each verse had the refrain, "Loved Cardinal, Great Cardinal;" but the poet suddenly burst into French, and finished by declaring that the Holy Father had given the cardinal the *coup de grace*, when he elevated him to that dignity.

Look at New York; it should be pre-eminently a Romish city. The mass of the Roman Catholic population is Irish, or of direct Irish descent, and of the most faithful Catholic nation on earth; but who will dare to deny the miserably social and religious condition of the mass of the Irish population? Look at the exterior and social aspect. It is true that New York is crowded with costly churches, rich vestments, much singing and show, which attract the multitude even as the flame attracts the moth. But what solid foundation lies underneath? The churches are magnificent and costly, and heavily burdened with debt; but few are consecrated, though they have been built for many years. Is this creditable to ecclesiastical management, or to religion? The poor are heavily—I might almost say cruelly—taxed to pay the debts, or rather, the heavy mortgage on these churches, and with little hope of reprieve.

We have before us a report made by the Rev. Father Colton in regard to St. Stephen's Church, lately occupied by the Rev. Dr. McGlynn. He announces a strawberry festival, to last through a whole week, for the benefit of the church. He urges the congregation to send him in contributions for an immense bazaar, and makes the astounding announcement that although the debt of the Church amounts to $140,000, he is about to increase it by $60,000 more. It is said in the report that much sympathy is felt for Father Colton at being obliged to increase so much the heavy debt, but that he will obey the mandate of the Council of Baltimore to the very letter, by building schools. The old buildings now occupied by the primary schools are to be destroyed, and handsome new structures are to be erected in their place. The *Catholic Review*, Archbishop Corrigan's organ, sympathises with Father Colton, but it does not sympathise with the people who are again to be taxed so heavily.

We have already shown, on Roman Catholic authority, the kind of education which Roman Catholic children will get in return for all this expenditure. The subject is of such great importance, in view of the unceasing efforts which Rome is making to control education, that I give here additional evidence from Roman Catholic sources of the utter incapacity of Romish teachers. The New York *Tablet* says:—

"But the fact remains that our Catholic schools must equip their pupils for getting on in the world. In some of them, especially in some girls' academies, the course of study is framed upon the fundamental idea that there is no world, or that there is to be no laborious getting on in it for the fortunate inmates of such institutions.

"This spurious standard of education is imported from the decayed courts of the Continent, and from the despicable and depressing circles of 'gentility' in Ireland and England. It has no proper place in the United States. Every child, boy or girl, should be equipped to make a livelihood; and should be given the most practical as well as the most refined and learned education which the circumstances of his parents enable him or her to acquire. The twin notion that there is a class in this country of 'superior' persons, ought to be driven in disgrace from our Catholic schools. The other day, a young miss attending an academy in the interior of a certain State was asked if there were any day scholars at it. 'Oh no,' she answered, with polite disdain; 'except some little peasant children from the village.'"

The truth is, that sisters, from the very nature of their mode of life, are the very last persons who are fit to train youth. They may prepare children for the other world, according to Roman Catholic ideas of preparation, but they certainly have failed to prepare them for this world, according to the testimony of an immense number of Roman Catholic parents of all nationalities.

The amount of money obtained from the Roman Catholic poor will never be known in this world, and is very little suspected. A priest, at his own will and pleasure, announces that a certain sum of money will be required weekly or monthly from each person; and woe to the unhappy individual if the demand is not met promptly. We know churches where three different collections are demanded and obtained at each Mass on Sunday, from a patient, though often indignant people.

As in the case of Dr. McGlynn's successor, each new priest must do some new work to get credit for his zeal. But all this is done at the expense of the poor of his parish. The priests get all the honour, and the poor get all the burden.

The New York *Freeman's Journal*, which expended so much red-hot shot on Dr. McGlynn for the debt which he left on his church, is lost in admiration of Father Colton for his zeal in increasing and probably doubling it. Father Colton, it says, is "quite cheerful" about it; and he well may be, considering that not one penny of the expense will come out of his own pocket, and that he will get all sorts of ecclesiastical and episcopal honours and glory for collecting other people's money. The statement of the editor of the *Freeman's Journal* is amusing in more ways than one, and we give it here. He says :—

"St. Joseph is a rich and powerful friend, who has often proved himself a benefactor to others even in darker hours than now, frequently causing magnificent churches, convents, and other institutions to rise seemingly out of nothing, as in the case of the splendid building erected by the late Rev. Father Dromgoole in this city (known as the Mission of the Immaculate Virgin, but erected by the St. Joseph's Union through the medium of twenty-five cent subscriptions), at a cost of over $300,000, not including the property on Staten Island, which with other expenditures would bring the total cost up to about half a million of dollars. . . . Would it not be well to try some special devotion to St. Joseph with the above intention, such, for instance, as keeping a light burning constantly before his statue until the debt is paid ?"

Well, if burning candles to St. Joseph will pay the debt, by all means let them be burned. But we fear the poor Irish servant girls of the parish will have a good deal more to do with the payment than St Joseph, and that it will remain for another priest to increase their burdens.

And here it may be well to ask if St. Joseph can do

all these wonders, why do not Roman Catholics ask him to put down the liquor traffic, which is causing such ruin to souls? While I write this there are five men under sentence of death in New York alone, who can trace their ruin to drink.

There is an utter recklessness in the way in which buildings are demolished, which certainly could be very well made to serve the purposes for which the new ones are intended, and handsome new structures are erected without the slightest regard to cost, because they are built at the expense of a long-suffering people, and though the vast mass of these hapless Romanists are suffering untold misery, not always from their own fault, but too often from the neglect of those who should be their guides.

There is but little money to spare for helping the honest poor, because splendid schools, and lofty spires, and magnificent colleges are supposed to be the great needs of the nineteenth century, and the Irish bear the burden of all. It was lately announced in the *New York World* that St. Anthony's Church, which is situated in one of the poorest parts of New York, and was especially set apart for Italians, is chiefly supported by Irish Catholics, though the congregation and the pastor are all Italians. We may well ask what is to become of the Roman Catholic Church in America if the Irish people are alienated from it, as the Catholic people of Italy, and France, and Germany, have become? The Italians will neither build nor support their own churches, and it is left to the Irish to attend to their spiritual welfare.

Reports will be sent to Rome of the devotion and care of the Archbishop of New York for the Italians of his diocese; but will even one word be said of their real benefactors? Will they receive even a passing meed of praise? And in this connection I may ask, will one word be said or known in Rome of the thousands of Italians in New York who paid honour to Garibaldi's statue, and who never enter a church? Here is a people who, of all others, should be devoted to their Church, and yet who have either abandoned it altogether, or do not care enough for it to give a few cents for its support. And it is well known, also that it is the Irish chiefly, if not exclusively, who build and support the French and German churches.

Romish papers are absolutely under the control of the bishop of the diocese in which they are published, and they are guilty of sycophancy to an extent that is simply nauseating. In the Roman Catholic Church as, at present governed, everything centres round the bishop; and for all practical purposes he is his own Pope, and the Pope of the people. Hence the profound deference that is paid to him, and which he accepts as a religious duty from every individual in his diocese. He is the local head of the Church, and a number of small deities who have to be pleased are more dangerous to society than one great autocratic ruler. A Protestant bishop would simply be ashamed to accept the fulsome flatteries, which are not only acceptable, but which are—must be—offered, to secure the patronage of the Roman Catholic bishop. No more deadly injury could have been done to the Roman Catholic Church than the maintaining of this practice; and it will be kept up until some noble bishop rises in his might, and forbids and denounces it for ever.

One favourite way of laying on this flattery well and wisely is to write an article on the great increase of Catholicity in the diocese, and attribute it all to the master mind, and financial ability of the bishop. No doubt a good bishop can do a great deal, but even a bishop needs help, both in the shape of mind and money. In fact, the bishop needs a people to govern quite as much as a people need the bishop. To praise one to the exclusion of the other is unjust; and injustice advances no cause.

A moment's consideration will show how very false these boastings are. The numerical strength of the Roman Catholic Church has certainly increased enormously of late years, but how and where? It has increased in the large American cities in consequence of Irish, German, and Italian emigration. We will let the Germans and Italians pass; the whole world knows how very little Italians care for their Church. The Germans are undoubtedly a religious people. If they do not give liberally to the Church, they know how to assert themselves, and are doing so.

But the Irish Roman Catholic is the great support of the Roman Catholic Church in America, and let us see what is his social condition. A few millionaires, a host of politicians, and a vast population of shiftless, thriftless, ill-cared-for people. Better, a thousand times better, that these people should be back in the bogs of Connemara, with their pure, fresh air, and their pure, fresh life, than in the crime-haunted liquor saloons of New York and Boston. Millions of Irish Romanists have fled to America; and when one thinks of their misreable state in this country, it is hard to feel that the head of their Church, whom they support so loyally, has not one word to say to stop this bleeding of the nation, this destroying of a people who have loved him, one might dare to say, not wisely, but too well.

They have increased and multiplied in the land of

their adoption, but what has become of the descendants of the first Irish emigrants? Are they now the stay and support of the Roman Catholic Church? Far from it.

In all Southern States, in every town, you find names which are unquestionably Irish. "The voice is the voice of Jacob," but they do not represent the Church to which, by their nationality, you would suppose they naturally belonged. Roman Catholic people have increased and multiplied in America, but they have not multiplied as Romanists, and no one knows that better than the ecclesiastics of their Church.

Of course the number of Romanists and Roman Catholic institutions has increased immensely in the last few years; but certainly thousands upon thousands of them have lost their faith, and either have no religion, or have joined other religious bodies, because of the gross neglect of those who should have been their shepherds, but are now their task-masters.

Once the principle is admitted that the Pope has a Divine and infallible right to decide on questions of morals, no man can deny his right to decide questions of politics, since many political questions obviously involve questions of morals; and if this is not apparent at the first glance, it is not difficult, with a little casuistry, to make it apparent.

But if it is admitted that the Pope's decrees on such questions are infallible, there is a corollary to the proposition which is the key to the whole question. The Pope being infallible, he has the right to decide when a question of politics is also a question of morals. In plain words, according to the teaching and authority of the Roman Catholic Church, as at present organised, any infallible Pope—and we know that they are all said to have been infallible—can decide infallibly when a question of politics is a question of morals, and no Roman Catholic dare gainsay him, under pain of eternal damnation.

Let us suppose, for example, there was a question of the election of a President of the United States, or of a mayor of New York. The Roman Catholic might be infallibly deprived of his liberty to vote. The Pope might make it a question of morals for whom he should give his vote. If, for example, Monseigneur Preston nominated for mayor his friend Joseph J. O'Donohue, in whose favour he has already issued a political announcement, and let us suppose, merely by way of example, that Henry George would make a better chief magistrate, since the nominee of a body of ecclesiastics would not be altogether a free agent, yet Roman Catholics would be compelled to vote for O'Donohue, though they might be certain that the other candidate would prove more efficient.

One cause, and I believe the principal cause, of the failure of the Roman Catholic Church to maintain a continued hold of the love and devotion of the people of any country has been the complete isolation of the interests of the laity.

The Roman Catholic papers, as we have shown, are full of complaints of the indifference of the laity to the interests of their Church. If these papers are to be taken as true witnesses in their own case, this indifference exists to an extraordinary extent, even in the United States, and it is not a "note" of ecclesiastical advancement.

The Pope has shown by acts, if not always in words, that he claims a Divine authority to rule and direct the temporal as well as the spiritual affairs of the whole world. He is the final court of appeal, not merely in dogma but in diplomacy. Now what is true of the general public, and the influence of the Pope on national politics, is true of the power and influence of every bishop and priest in local politics. As members of an infallible body they are practically, though not in theory, infallible; as members of the most powerful combination on earth, their power to control the laity is unlimited. If the commands of the Pope must be obeyed by all nations and rulers at the risk of eternal loss, the commands of the priests are practically, if not equally binding, or, for all practical purposes, quite as effectually binding. Hence if the Pope can change the policy or purpose of a king or emperor, the bishop can change the policy and purposes of the mayor or alderman.

The Roman Catholic laity have come to know this very well, hence their marked unwillingness to interfere in any affair whatever, which is in any way under ecclesiastical control. Nor are they willing to place themselves in any position where they may be made to feel the weight of the ecclesiastical arm. A priest, consciously or unconsciously, uses his spiritual powers to attain his temporal ends; if he did not he would be more than human.

Now, notwithstanding all the efforts which are made by Papal ecclesiastics to prevent the true state of Catholic affairs from being known, facts will sometimes be told, even through the Protestant press of New York, though it is more under Roman Catholic influence, probably from political motives, than is generally supposed.

The Polish National Alliance is a political as well as a benevolent organisation. It has a large membership.

The Polish priests have been recently denouncing this alliance in Chicago; they proclaim it to be more political than benevolent. The members of the Alliance are numerous and active; and have sent a petition to Rome, in which they say:—

"The priests want to control the private as well as the religious affairs of their parishioners, and render them virtually slaves to do their bidding, and failing in this, the priests have maligned members of the Alliance, and sought to create prejudice against them. The petitioners represent that they are true Catholics, do not belong to any socialistic, nihilistic, or anarchistic organisation, and in everything have deported themselves as true sons of the Church."

This incident is worth noting, and shows why the Roman Catholic laity are unwilling to act with the Church. They find that they are only allowed to be a Greek chorus to the bishops. They are to obey the Pope, to accept all decisions, even when they are against their own interests and judgment, sometimes, it is to be feared, when they are against their own conscience. Is it a wonder that the Roman Catholic laity speak with anxiety for the future of their Church; and that the Roman Catholic journals have lately published very strong appeals to the laity to support their Church actively?

A southern gentleman, the editor of an influential paper, whose opinion would command extraordinary respect if I could give his name, said to me not long since:—

"We (the laity) have given up all interest in Church affairs. We do whatever we believe to be necessary to save our souls, and we attend to our own business. Several times when we have tried to interest the bishop in plans which we believed would greatly benefit the Church and advance the interest of religion, we found our suggestions were not taken in good part, and were, in fact, considered as impertinent intrusion, and we heard so much of humility and obedience that we determined for the future to withdraw altogether from Church affairs. The Roman Catholic Church in the South," he continued, "is dying of dry rot. We have indifferent bishops, who are scarcely ever seen by their people, and who do not care in the least to consider any plan which they have not suggested themselves, and who only express an interest in the laity when they want to get money."

It was well known in the South that the Roman Catholic laity there did not want Cardinal Gibbons to organise an immigration scheme; its immediate object and its probable result are too plain. The Cardinal likes to come before the world as a man of affairs, and there is no reason why he should not do so; but the consequences are of immense importance. His presence on public occasions, and the singular respect which is paid him, are all used to make the Pope and Propaganda believe that he has all America at his feet. Americans believe that from political reasons their Presidents must honour Roman Catholic public functions with their presence, and that they must ask men like Cardinal Gibbons to public ceremonies. But in Rome all this is taken to mean that in a very short time America will become Roman Catholic; and that as her prelates are treated with such distinction there, they will soon be able to govern the country at the pleasure of the Vatican. But with all this effort to spread the Romish faith in the Southern States, what is the truth as to its real position there? Even Roman Catholic authorities declare that it is falling away. We know from the lips of a Jesuit Father how true such statements are. Roman Catholic schools for higher education have only two or three pupils where they used to have a hundred, though the names of these institutions still remain on the Roman Catholic directory as prosperous. Sisters cannot find vocations among the few Southern Catholics, and their sisterhoods are dying out. With regard to the coloured people the *Catholic Review* says:—

"Since the war thousands of negroes, so we have been reliably told, have fallen away from the truth, and to-day Methodists and Baptists have strong footholds among the blacks, where formerly they were unknown. To-day the faithful among the coloured people frequent the parochial churches, while, parodoxically as it seems, their children have separate schools and institutions."

The fact is, that Romanists have very little interest in each other. In Protestant Churches each member, if there is any life in the Church, looks on every stranger as an individual who might be won to Christ, and knows no way of winning him so good as that of Christian courtesy. The very nature and aim of the Roman Church produces a precisely opposite course. It is to the priest's sacerdotal influence everything is to be attributed; hence the people as individuals are of very little account.

At High Mass on Sundays halls and doorways are often so crowded as to make it appear as if the congregation was immense, when the half of the seat accommodation is unoccupied, being left for those who have rented the pews. No doubt they have a right to the pews, but we are not here speaking of rights or wrongs, but of Christian charity.

The tenement-house evil is the evil of New York. What is the Roman Catholic Church doing with all its wealth to remedy this evil? "The policeman's club," says a recent writer, "keeps order, and the courts shove men and women into prisons and children into institutions."

New York and Naples afford abundant evidence of the utter failure of Rome to Christianise the masses. When will the world realize that the Gospel, and the Gospel alone, can touch, purify, and elevate the human heart? In these two cities, where Rome has had almost supreme power, the result, as far as civilisation and decency are concerned, has been the same. Naples has been the reproach of Christendom during centuries of Rome rule, in consequence of the dirt and degradation of its people, and this with every advantage of climate, and of the religion professed by the people.

The children of the poor in Naples were left to swarm in the gutters, to be fed as best they might, and to learn to worship or curse the Madonna, as their inclination led. They blessed her, and burnt tapers in her honour if she complied with their requests. They abused, and threatened their puny wrath on her, if she did not answer their prayers. I speak of what I know, for I have turned with horror from the travesty of religion, which the Church of Rome not only permits, but encourages, amongst these unhappy people. I have visited the Roman Catholic Churches in Naples, and turned away horrified with the mockery of religion I beheld--immense figures, named at pleasure after some saint, dressed in gaudy rags, and worshipped. I have already given extracts from the article written by Mr. Lynch, which tells of the neglect of Italian priests to teach their people even the commonest rudiments of religion. And yet the Pope asks permission to teach and rule the world at large. Surely he should at least begin his rule at home, and give some proof of his ability to Christianise his own flock before he offers his services to others.

And what of New York, where certainly the Roman Church has all the power and all the wealth which the world can give? Archbishop Corrigan has only to ask and to have all that he pleases for the temporal or the spiritual advantage of his people. And yet who fills the police courts, the gaols, the workhouses, the lunatic asylums? Who are the most corrupt of officials, and who does the Church delight to honour? Is it not the very men who are a disgrace to their religion, and to their nationality? We are constantly informed in the public press that the prayers of sisters are offered for the acquittal of men who have been notorious criminals, because they have given large donations to the Church. And this is the morality which we are asked to admire, and which we are told is the religion of Christ. I have kept a list of those men for whom the Church has such a tender interest, and for whose acquittal she has prayed. It shows that Rome has not changed, and that to give money to the Church is the test of holiness, rather than the giving of a good life to God.

CHAPTER XIII.

PROTESTANT SUPPORT OF ROMAN CATHOLIC FAILURES

"Come out of her, my people, that ye be not partakers of her sins, and that ye receive not of her plagues."—REV. xviii. 4.

ONE of the strangest mysteries of the day is that the Roman Catholic Church should be supported, as it is, by Protestants. The political support of the Roman Catholic Church in America is, however, quite comprehensible. There the Irish vote counts for so much that no politican can afford to risk it. And whatever Irishmen may say or write about their religion, their nationality is their real religion, and any man who stands to the "National" cause will have their support. Besides, the great majority of active politicians in America are Irish and Roman Catholic. They are not always a credit to their religion or to their nationality, but they have power; and that is all that is needed to enable them to control the destinies of their adopted country.

The power of the liquor saloon in politics is supreme in America, and the liquor saloon is controlled by the Irish, and the Irish are controlled by the priests. A man aspiring to the highest offices in New York, who has the support of the liquor saloon business, is sure of success. The "boss of the ward" and the proprietor of the largest liquor saloon in the ward, are one and the same person, and a power which makes itself felt.

The "boss" can do a good many things not apparently connected with politics. He can send the children of the unfortunate parents who have been ruined in his liquor saloon by drink to some Catholic reformatory, out of which they emerge in a few years' time to walk in the footsteps of their fathers, to shout for Ireland, to uphold the holy Catholic Church in every way possible, except by giving a good example. But what do I say? The kind of example which we Protestants consider good, is not the kind which passes as such in the estimation of the rulers of their Church. It matters very little how immoral the life of a Roman Catholic may be if he has "kept to his Church." It matters not how honestly he may have lived, if he has not paid all his dues to the Church, and if he has shown the least sympathy with Protestants, as the following will show :—

(*By telegraph to the "Herald."*)

"BOSTON, *March* 10th, 1889."

"Mrs. Mary O'Neil, an elderly communicant of Father Brosnahan's Church in Waltham, was buried to-day without a Church funeral, because the preparation of the body, and the arrangements for the funeral, had been committed to a Protestant undertaker."

And this is no uncommon occurrence. Even to have the services of a Protestant undertaker deprives a Roman Catholic of Christian burial, as effectually as if he have listened to a lecture by Dr. McGlynn before the Church of Rome had deprived him of the right to minister at her altars.

There is also one point on which a great deal depends.

No matter what a priest may do or say, there must be silence as regards his faults. The priest has the singular privilege of having his character protected by the Church, not that the Church cares very much about the matter as far as the priest is personally concerned; if she did, she would have better men to minister at her altars to-day, but she must look well before the world. The evil is there, and she knows it, and the cause of it. She cannot remove the cause by any attempt to reform the priest, as the circumstances would be sure to become known to the public; and, weighted down as she is by her own infallibility, she cannot admit that wrong has been done.

The editor of *Le National*, published in Plattsburg, New York, August 20th, 1888, says:—

"It is a fundamental principle of ecclesiastical law that the clergy ought not to be arraigned before the incompetent tribunal of public opinion."

It does not surely need much discernment or knowledge of human nature, to see what power this gives the higher clergy in dealing with the lower clergy. The bishop claims the Divine right to be judge in his own cause, and the world at large is required to submit in silent acquiescence.

Rome cries out in undignified rage because she is not allowed to burn her modern Bruno, and her modern Joan of Arc, and calls on the world to sympathise with her because her own nation has made a grand and dignified protest against ecclesiastical tyranny. If Rome was not prepared to re-enact such scenes, why does she complain? Why does she ask for secular power, but to enable her to repeat her persecuting history? Rome has had a splendid opportunity for repentance, repentance which would have strengthened her hands. Even suppose that she condemned Bruno as an infidel, could she not still continue her condemnation, while expressing her regret for the inhumanity of his punishment? The Inquisition has failed to Christianise, or even to Romanise the world, though Rome slew and spared not. Why will she not now try a different way of doing the work of Him whom she claims as her Master?

Karl Blind, writing in the *Nineteenth Century*, says :—

"What were Bruno's sufferings in the darkness of the dungeon in which the Inquisition kept him? What ferocious attempts were made to bend and break the energy of the highly-cultured unfrocked friar, whose mind was nourished with the love of antiquity? If, as a prisoner, he had a moment of faltering, the answer has been given in the words, 'How can you expect that torture, even though applied for hours, should, prevail against a whole life of study and inquiry?'"

Campanella, who, after Bruno, was kept in prison for twenty-seven years, said of his own sufferings : "The last time I was tortured it was for forty hours. I was fettered with cords which cut to the very bones ; I was hung up with hands tied back, a most sharp piece of wood being used, which cut out large parts of my flesh, and produced a vast loss of blood."

Perhaps some day, when the archives of the Vatican become fully accessible, we shall learn a little more of Bruno's last years of torment. On being informed of his doom he, in the face of a horrible death, heroically said to his inhuman judges : "Perhaps you pronounce your sentence with greater fear than that with which I receive it." Among those who formed the tribunal was Cardinal Bellarmine, the same who later on forced Galilei to an apparent recantation, and Cardinal Sanseverina, who had called the massacre of the night of St. Bartholomew "a splendid day, most pleasant to Catholics." The sentence against Bruno was, as usual, to be carried out "without the spilling of blood." In the bandit language of the Inquisition, as Herman Brunnhofer expresses it, this signified burning at the stake. Before the victim of priestcraft was sacrificed his tongue was torn with pincers. But it still speaks to posterity in powerful accents.

More and more it is seen that a great deal of that which in this country Darwin, Huxley, Tyndall, Lyell, Lubbock, and others have by their masterly and successful researches made the common intellectual property of all educated people, had been divined in some measure by the prescient genius of Bruno. Unaided by exact science, he anticipated, in a general way, the scientific results of ages to come. The struggle against obscurantism has still to be carried on. While I am writing this numerous voices of the Ultramontane press come in from abroad, which speak in tones of inquisitorial fury of the " Bruno scandal," and urging a crusade for the restoration of the temporal power of the Papacy. Some of these papers go the length of justifying the burning of the Italian thinker by "the necessity of guarding the Church against dangerous heresies."

The *Salzburger Chronik* says:—

"He that will not listen and obey, must be made to feel. In order to save the good, the evil must be annihilated. This doctrine is the very basis of the penal law and of the Divine command, which punish murder, and which therefore must all the more punish the murder of souls. This is in accordance with human conscience and with justice."

Bruno himself foresaw an age of enlightenment, a coming century of progress, when the powers of darkness would sink down to the nether world, and the hearts of men be filled with truth and justice. To this prediction refers the proud inscription on his monument:—"To Giordano Bruno this memorial has been raised by the century prophesied by him on the very spot where his pile burned." It may be open to doubt whether this nineteenth century has fulfilled yet all that which Bruno foretold. But whether Galilei's often-quoted word was spoken or not on the famous occasion when the Papal Church fancied it could stop the rotation of the world by bringing him down on his knees, the truth of his saying in more than one sense becomes ever apparent :—

"*Eppur si muove.*"   "And yet it moves."

And here it may be said that the present demoralisation of the Roman Catholic Church in America is deep and grievous, to every one who has even the least respect for truth and virtue. The tremendous power which has fallen into the hands of an ignorant class of men has had the usual consequences. An educated priesthood may be a dangerous priesthood, but an uneducated priesthood is capable of acts of tyranny which are only equalled in their exercise of irresponsible power by the Herods and Caligulas of old. It is the old story of man dressed in a little brief authority; and when the man so dressed is ignorant, uneducated, and either a bigot, or what O'Connell well described as a pious fool, the consequences are deplorable, and in the Roman Catholic Church they are irreparable.

What a miserable condition of things was revealed by the McGlynn affair. Many Protestants have sided with Archbishop Corrigan from political motives, and from the delusion so common in America, that the Roman Catholic Church is the protector of property and the guardian of law and order. Even Chicago will not open the eyes of those who are wilfully blind. I have carefully preserved all the documents connected with the McGlynn case, but they would require more space than can be given to the subject in the present work. Some of the points, however, are too important to be passed over altogether. Protestants who do not care, like Gallio, about these things, were loud in their condemnation of McGlynn, and yet his best friends were and are Roman Catholics.

It was made to appear as if he was forsaken by every one except a few women. Yet some of the best men in his late parish have defied all ecclesiastical censures, and held to him through all opposition. It should make Protestants pause, and ask, " Are these things so ? " when they see such an influential movement in the very heart of the Roman Church. But that Church works well and wisely for herself. She has the absolute control of the press in America, with some few exceptions, and can act accordingly. Paragraphs are carefully prepared for the benefit of the public, which insinuate that the doctor's cause is failing, that he himself is failing. It would be amusing, if the subject was not so serious, to note the way in which efforts are made from time to time to depreciate his work, and to leave the impression on the minds of the public that it is a thing of the past, and that the movement which he has inaugurated will soon die out.

It will never die out. I know, from my own personal

knowledge, that Dr. McGlynn has the sincere sympathy, and I believe the financial help, of some of the best priests in Archbishop Corrigan's diocese, and that the opinion of many of the best members of the priesthood in New York is that he was shamefully treated, and yet such paragraphs as the following are going the rounds of the press :—

(Special despatch to the Boston "Sunday Herald.")
"New York, *August* 25*th*, 1888.

"Dr. McGlynn, the eloquent head of the Anti-Poverty Society, is threateningly ill. His health seems generally shattered, and his friends fear that some fatal disease will be developed by his bad mental and physical condition. He is now undertaking to open a vigorous campaign for the so-called Labour Party, and it was on Sunday last that he made his first speech. The famous series of Sunday evening meetings in the Academy of Music, which for awhile had drawn so many people ready to pay for admission that the spacious house would not hold half of them, fell off in popularity greatly before they were suspended in May."

Later still the following appeared :—

"There is no question that the Roman Catholic Church has devoted all its influence in New York to a quiet but very effective destruction of Father McGlynn's popularity. Archbishop Corrigan early and openly directed all priests to refuse absolution to persons who attended the anti-poverty meetings. Three priests, sympathetic with his movement, have been removed to out-of-town charges. The wonderful power of the Roman Catholic clergy over its people has been exemplified, and Father McGlynn is wrecked in every way.

It is said that he will now take a trip to Europe in the hope of recuperating his health."

While there are so many Roman Catholic reporters on the New York press, it is very easy to send such special despatches all over the country. As a matter of fact, it would have been no wonder if Dr. McGlynn was taken sick; but to the grief of his enemies he is more vigorous than ever, and more successful as a lecturer.

The ink had scarcely been dry on the excommunication which Archbishop Corrigan forced from Rome, ere Dr. McGlynn's house was, I had almost said, broken into by a belligerent priest; and if there was no other act of tyranny and injustice to complain of in the New York diocese, this should have merited the scorn and contempt of honest men. Some good, however, generally comes out of evil; and the good in this case has been to show the world, if the world is wise enough to see what is plainly before it, that there was a good deal more of personal animosity in the case, than love of God or zeal for religion. It should be noted that not long before this occurred Archbishop Corrigan had made use of the popularity of Dr. McGlynn to obtain an appointment for General Newton, and had sent the former to Washington for that purpose, another evidence, if evidence was needed, that the Church of Rome rules Washington. There were great jubilations in the Roman Catholic papers over this appointment, and General Newton was held up to public admiration as another man of scientific attainments, who was an honour to the Church. In his case, however, and in many others, the appointments have been a failure, and the General has disappeared from office, and no longer receives the praise of the Roman Church, for reasons best known to the parties concerned.

The way in which Dr. McGlynn was treated by his brother priests, or at least a considerable number of them, is instructive. Like carrion crows they fell upon the man whom they believed practically dead, and tore him to pieces, as only ecclesiastics can rend each other. Certainly he had a few faithful friends, and all honour to them. It is the fierce and successful policy of Rome to crush utterly, when she cannot burn alive. Happily for Dr. McGlynn it was not possible to burn him as Bruno was burned; it was only possible to break his heart. His popularity had been a sore thorn in the side of those priests who had failed to win the love of their own people. Then there was the usual cry of loyalty to "the Church," in the person of Archbishop Corrigan; and great was the zeal to prove the devotion of these priests to the higher power, all of course from the most sublime motives. It was a state of things which would have rejoiced the Inquisitors of the Middle Ages. The two great pillars of the Church in New York are Monsignor Preston, and Vicar-General D———. The latter gentleman was sent to evict Dr. McGlynn. He did so. He went to Dr. McGlynn's house, and demanded admission. He did more; he went to Dr. McGlynn's room, and took possession. It was in vain that the other priests offered to give him any room he pleased in the house, so as to allow the doctor time to remove his books and clothing. No, the cup was to be made as bitter as possible. The doctor was to be made feel the full weight of episcopal displeasure, and his priest persecutors were to show their "loyalty" to the Church, in the person of their archbishop, by heaping indignities on their brother priest. All that I now write was the theme of discussion in the public press of New York for months.

A servant girl in Dr. McGlynn's house, not understanding this form of Christianity, and thinking that even if he had done wrong, he should at least be treated with ordinary courtesy,—for even the criminal has some pity shown to him by his executioners,—expostulated with Vicar-General D—— a man from whom, if she had known him better, she need not have expected even ordinary good manners under any circumstances. His only reply was to divest himself of all the garments which he could remove with the commonest decency, and then fling himself on Dr. McGlynn's bed. A Roman Catholic paper now before me describes Vicar-General D —— as "a man of brutal manners." There was a priest, also a doctor of divinity, who was sincerely attached to Dr. McGlynn, and he wrote a letter to the press, in which he used some very plain language about this matter. He had let his affection and his sense of justice outrun his discretion. But he was made to suffer. No priest, or for that matter no Roman Catholic, is allowed to write or say anything publicly about his ecclesiastical superiors, except his language is couched in the terms of the highest eulogy. He may write and publish verses of which a third-form boy would be ashamed. He may use French to complete the praise of those who live on praise, and make the subject of his adulation and himself ridiculous, as the ecclesiastic did, who said that Archbishop Gibbons had received his *coup de grace* from the Pope, when he was made a cardinal. But to say one word that even might bear the faintest semblance of blame, that is not permitted. So Father Curran had to be made an example of, and duly punished.

There was very strong feeling among Roman

Catholics in New York, as to the gross injustice with which Dr. McGlynn had been treated. There were a great many priests who sympathised with him, and a great many who hated their ecclesiastical superior, and on that account were prepared to give very substantial tokens of their sympathy to the suspended priest. News of this was going to Rome, and there were public rumours that all was not serene in the diocese. Something had to be done for the archbishop by his sympathisers, and something was done. But it only made matters worse in the eyes of all sensible and thinking people.

It told in Rome, however, and that was all that could be desired. Of what avail was it for the *New York Herald* to advise the Pope to make Archbishop Corrigan a Cardinal, and to declare openly and without contradiction that the same paper had been chiefly instrumental in obtaining that much-coveted distinction for the late Cardinal. A document, which would be signed unanimously by the priests of the diocese, was necessary, for it was rumoured in Rome that there were a good many of the best and most popular priests in that city who were not well affected to the archbishop's rule.

A carefully-worded document was prepared, the object of which was to show that the priests of New York were one and all agreed that Dr. McGlynn had deserved his excommunication, and that one and all were in full agreement with their archbishop. But as the question is a grave one, I shall give the evidence, as it was published in a Roman Catholic paper. I must premise that I have in my possession a mass of documents which show that the state of things which exists in New York has its counterpart in every diocese in America, and yet the Church of Rome talks of its unity, and the world believes her.

I heard a student of the archbishop's seminary declare that he believed that such a system of tyranny never before existed, as that which was then the normal state of the diocese; that the students were afraid to open their lips to each other except on the most commonplace subjects, and even then with due caution, through dread of the system of espionage. A priest, the rector of a very large parish in Jersey, called his bishop a "little puppy" again and again in my hearing, and informed me that he was so called generally by the priests of his diocese. What a state of things in a Church, which those who know nothing of her inner life imagine to be so perfect.

The Roman Catholic paper to which I have referred (the *Catholic News*) had the following account of the McGlynn business:—

" Holy week of 1887 is come and gone, and we are safe in saying that never in the history of the Church in New York was there a sadder one, or one less calculated to inspire devotion. The Catholics of this city tried to forget the burning question that for months has agitated all Christendom, and to follow in spirit the 'Man of Calvary;' but in sorrow it must be said, that not since October last has there been so exciting a week, such a casting of fuel into a furious fire. To the credit of the parishioners of St. Stephen's, it must be said that they restrained themselves admirably, bearing in patience and quiet, and with all the equanimity they could command, the insulting innuendoes against their pastor, and the unjust discipline of his friends. Doctor Curran, the faithful disciple, was not forgotten at the

Hoboken Monastery, for great crowds went to see him, and to all he spoke freely of why he was there. It seems that the first report of his transfer to Ellenville was untrue, for a later report, coming also from the cathedral, said that he was removed on account of his devotion to Dr. McGlynn. This denotes two things very clearly.

"First, that any of the clergy sympathising with Dr. McGlynn are marked men, and sure of official displeasure. Second, that we cannot always depend on the utterances of certain people, that they are unreliable. As Dr. Curran's interview with one of the daily papers is of much interest we give it in full.

"'I am not doing penance, for I do not consider that I have done wrong. This retreat means nothing more than a voluntary retreat. My time is my own. I shall use it for study and reading and for religious exercises. I said Mass this morning in one of the little chapels, and I am sure there is nothing in this little stay here the least bit disagreeable. It is a punishment certainly. I am sent here to give me a chance to reflect on my conduct, and I have always tried to be a good priest and to do my duty. I willingly obeyed the order to come here, but it is a question whether the archbishop can be justified in ordering me here. The question is one that has a broader application in the case of Dr. McGlynn, and how it will be settled I don't know. I was sent to St. Patrick's in Mulberry Street, and I was happy there, and tried to do my duty. Father Kearney, and all the clergy there were, I thought, very kind to me.

"'One evening, it was March 25th, Father Kearney met me in the hall and said the archbishop wanted to see me. "Very well," I said, and I told him I would go up to the archbishop's house that evening, and I did. The archbishop came down and greeted me pleasantly, and surprised me by saying that he heard that I did not get along well with Father Kearney. "That is a revelation to me," I replied. "He says you are away from the house too much to attend to your duties," said the archbishop. "That is a lie," I said, with just as much emphasis as I say it now. Father Kearney had never said a word to me about his dissatisfaction. I could think of only one thing that could justify Father Kearney in his assertion. He has a rule which I think is not in use in other churches, that the outside doors shall be fastened at 10.30 every night. He has an immense key which locks the door, then a great bolt is pushed, and to cap it all, a great chain is drawn across and hooked. When I was in nights and heard that bolt and chain grate and rattle I felt as if I were in the tombs. I admitted that I had subjected myself to the accusation of being out after the doors were locked, but I am a secular priest, not a monk, and am considerably over twenty-one years of age, and know of no rule that would require me to be in every night at 10.30.

"'Well, the archbishop thought that so long as they were the rules I should have obeyed them. The archbishop said it would not be pleasant for me to go back to St. Patrick's, anyway. He also referred to my appearing at Jones' Woods on St. Patrick's day. He told me to go up to Ellenville for a while, and I suppose it was a sort of punishment to be sent up to the country, but I had a very pleasant time.'

"Where the good doctor will be sent next, or if the 'ten days' will be extended, we cannot at this time of writing conjecture."

A reporter of a Brooklyn paper called on Father Malone, a distinguished priest of the diocese of Brooklyn, who had just returned from New York, where he heard of Dr. Curran's punishment, and the venerable priest was not slow to express his views. He was present at Dr. McGlynn's great speech, and when the reporter asked him if he had been warned against supporting him, he replied, "Oh, that is nonsense." Then after a pause, in which his face showed agitation, he exclaimed, "Are we in Russia? Can't a man attend a meeting without being sized and 'disciplined'? If this were the first day of April instead of the second I should say this whole affair was an 'April fool.' I have never agreed with Archbishop Corrigan's methods, but I cannot understand him now. His behaviour is tyrannically inhuman, and totally without reason or excuse. What has young Father Curran done that he should be put on a diet of bread and water? Father Curran had been with Dr. McGlynn for eleven years. He had seen him for hours at his private devotions, and knew many of the secrets of his godly life. Why should he forsake him now? If I found a poor friend in the gutter and did not help him, would I be acting like a Christian? And now this young man, for simply attending this lecture by his old friend and co-labourer in God's work, is 'disciplined.' It is a crime. Father Curran came from my parish. I baptized him, and know that he is an intelligent, honest priest of the Church.

"It is the work of a madman," he said. "Archbishop Corrigan is so excited that he is no longer to be reasoned with. Nothing but the power at Rome can touch him. There are a hundred thousand Catholics in New York who hate the little archbishop. His usefulness is practically gone. The very idea of attacking

Dr. McGlynn's position in 1882, for lending his voice to the famishing people of Ireland. In this whole matter the archbishop has been wrong as wrong can be. I think it will end in his removal. The priests ought to have the courage to take sides on this question, and send to Rome their opinions for or against the archbishop's position. But they lack independence."

"Do you think Dr. Mc. Glynn should go to Rome?"

"Why, no; why should he? He is not accused of any fault as a priest. He is not accountable to Rome for his opinions on political economy. He believes in a tax on land; but what reason is there in that to subject him to a call to Rome? Dr. McGlynn has been faithful to his Church, his God, and his country. He will, if need be, suffer unto death. If he yielded to the efforts to establish one-man power in New York, how do you think we could answer such antagonists as Dr. Fulton? He must stand as the champion of the Church. The placing of Father Donnelly, a man of brutal manners, in his place at St. Stephen's was a sad mistake; but it may have been for the best in one sense, as it crystallised the sentiment in the parish quickly. I understand that this latest action of the archbishop has caused the greatest excitement yet known in Dr. McGlynn's old parish, and that even those who place pence on the plate are to be boycotted. It is a sad state of affairs."

Quite recently two of the clergymen of New York proposed that a paper or testimonial should be got up testifying to the loyalty of the clergy of the archdiocese to its spiritual head. It was to have been presented to the archbishop on his return from Bermuda. For this purpose a meeting was called at the house of a sympathising priest, but no one responded to the call save the two promoters of the scheme. It failed, only, it appears, to be revived in another form. Here is what the *Daily Herald* has to say on the matter:—

"A reporter was assured recently that Dr. McGlynn's opponents were carrying out a scheme to make it appear that the deposed pastor of St. Stephen's had no sympathisers. An interview with a liberal-minded Catholic layman, who is known to almost every priest in New York, revealed the fact that a document was really in circulation among the clergy calling for their indorsement of Archbishop Corrigan.

"'It is an attempt,' said this gentleman, 'to coerce the priests whose comfort and freedom are largely at the mercy of the archbishop. It was a friend of mine who notified the *Herald* of this dodge on Thursday.'

"'Is it really the suggestion of the archbishop?' asked the reporter.

"'I will not be positive of that,' was the reply. 'But here are the names of the priests who are engineering the affair, Monsignor Preston, of St. Ann's; Father Lynch, of the Church of Transfiguration, in Mott Street; Father Kearney, of St. Patrick's Cathedral, in Mulberry Street; Father McGean, of St. Peter's, in Barclay Street; and Dr. Brann, of St. Elizabeth's, Washington Heights. Monsignor Preston's hostility to Dr. McGlynn is well known. Father Lynch is also very hostile. He was once an assistant to Dr. McGlynn at St. Stephen's, and Dr. McGlynn had good reason to cause his removal. Father Lynch then went to Father Preston's Church, where you may be sure his dislike to Dr. McGlynn was not suffered to diminish. He is one of the most active circulators of the coercion document.'

"'Have you a copy of that paper Mr. O'Donoghue?'

(The reporter had asked permission of the gentleman to let him call him Mr. O'Donoghue.)

"'No; I do not think there are more than three in existence. When one of the emissaries brings a copy to a priest for his signature, if he finds it necessary to leave it for a time, he exacts a promise from the bull-dozed one that he shall not give it away, divulge its contents, or make a copy of it. I have seen it, however, and it is to this effect :—

"'"That the priests of this archdiocese desire to assure His Grace that they heartily approve of his conduct in the troubles now existing in the diocese. Especially do they approve of your conduct toward Edward McGlynn, whose disobedience to your authority has been a source of great scandal not only to us but to the clergy and to the laity."

"'The document then goes on to say that Dr. McGlynn's disobedience has been aggravated by his subsequent conduct toward even the holy Father, and that his motives have been dictated by a spirit of vanity and vindictiveness, and not by a regard for law and religion. It has this quotation from Proverbs:—

"'"He that soweth iniquity shall reap vanity, and the rod of his anger shall fail."

"'Observe,' continued Mr. O'Donoghue, 'that this document, in referring to the recent pastor of St. Stephens, drops all title, and merely calls him "Edward McGlynn." There are numbers of poor priests who have signed this under protest, feeling that if they did not they would be marked men. As a Catholic, I must say that this is a scheme unworthy of Catholic gentlemen, whether they be priests or laymen.'

"The reporter then went and interviewed several

clergymen. One said, 'I am not in full sympathy with Dr. McGlynn, but why should I be compelled to attribute vanity and vindictiveness to Dr. McGlynn, whose whole life has been that of an honourable and an upright man, and an exemplary priest?'

"A third: 'It was sprung upon me suddenly, and I was asked which side I was on. I signed it under protest.'

"A fourth: 'It is bull-dozing pure and simple. The paper is going to Rome to create a false impression, and eventually all our names are to be published. I feel I have done something I shall regret. A man never knows when it may come his turn to suffer next.'

"Many other priests spoke in a similar strain."

The Rev. Dr. Curran wrote the following manly letter in reply to the inquisition made on him to sign the address, praising the archbishop and condemning Dr. McGlynn:—

"REV. AND DEAR SIRS,—I have received from you a circular letter requesting my signature to a printed address to our archbishop. I cannot conscientiously comply with your request.

"I regret that you and other priests of this diocese find it necessary to express in a public document your loyalty to authority. I should feel guilty of a calumny if I should sign the paper sent to me, containing, as it does, these words: 'We desire on this occasion to record our emphatic disapproval and reprobation of the act of disobedience and disloyalty to your authority of which a certain member of our body has made himself guilty, an act of disloyalty aggravated by his subsequent course.' It is not disloyalty to act according to submitted principles of Catholic theology. These principles teach us that every Catholic is free to adhere to an opinion until it shall have been condemned by the one legitimate authority.

"You speak of a certain member of our body as 'disobedient and disloyal.' I know of none such. The priest to whom I am told you refer in your address has declared again and again that if the doctrine, for refusing to abandon which he is still suspended from his pastoral office, should be condemned by the only authority we all recognise in such matters, he would, as a Catholic, repudiate it. And I know with certainty, that that authority, so far from condemning, has never even examined the doctrine. I am entirely at a loss to know what 'aggravation' of his alleged disloyalty you are able to find in what you call his 'subsequent course.' Is it not true, on the contrary, that Dr. McGlynn has maintained a discreet silence, broken only by a statement made necessary to supplement the incomplete presentation of his case in an authoritative document? Moreover, I shall feel guilty of a pharisaic hypocrisy, if, after seeming, by my signature, to approve that portion of your address which I have just said I could not sign without feeling guilty of calumny, I should join with you in saying: 'We have been patiently hoping and praying that our dear brother would change his mind and return to his Father's house.' It would seem to me mockery to call one 'my dear brother' at a moment when I knew I was calumniating him; and while pharisaically praying for the return of the 'dear brother' to his Father's house, I should be conscious that I was calumniating him by implying that he had ever abandoned his Father's house. This calumny would be all the more unpardonable since the 'dear brother' has several times publicly asseverated, with the greatest emphasis and solemnity, that he never has and never will abandon what you must mean by his Father's house, the holy Catholic Church."

I regret that it is not possible to give the entire history of Dr. McGlynn's case in the present work. It is one of the greatest importance in all its bearings. It is a proof, if proof were needed, that Rome has not ceased to persecute, and that she is limited in the expression of her displeasure only by the exigencies of the present times, which do not allow of the public execution of heretics, or of those who from any cause have offended her.

The spirit of vengeance, and of what can only be called petty spite, on the part of Dr. McGlynn's brother clergy, shows how little mercy they would have for each other, if power was placed in their hands to act as they pleased. It shows that there is very little of the spirit of Christ left in the Church of Rome, and that the persecuting spirit of ages supposed to be past, needs only opportunity to revive.

CHAPTER XIV.

*THE EFFECTS OF ROMAN CATHOLIC TEACHING—
ROMAN CATHOLIC UNIVERSITIES AND HIGHER
EDUCATION.*

"The fear of the Lord is the beginning of wisdom."—PROV. ix. 10.

SOME remarkable admissions which have been published, on the subject of the effects of Roman Catholic teaching, in the *Tablet*, the leading organ of English Roman Catholic opinion, are, in view of present discussions, well worth consideration.

The Roman Catholic religion has had every advantage in England. It has been fashionable. It has had political prestige. The fashionable perverts to this faith, if they have not increased in numbers, have not decreased in power. The Roman Catholic episcopacy are not slow to see all that can be made of social position; and as, by means of their influential friends, they can gain access to families which they might not otherwise have entered easily, they know well how social position affects the prosperity of Romanism. And in the meantime, what of the English perverts, and the Roman Catholic Church in England? What of the vast multitude of the English people? Are they being won over to the Roman faith? What of the English priests and the English missions? Are the distinguished perverts caring for them?

If the accounts published in recent copies of the

Tablet are true, a considerable number of these unfortunate priests are half starving. One priest writes that he is living on porridge only, because if he did not do so he would not have the money to keep up his schools. Another priest says, "I beg for a few shillings or sixpences." Another writes a piteous appeal to a gentleman in London, which this gentleman publishes in the *Tablet*. He says that one of the largest Churches in London is so seriously embarrassed and in debt, that he fears it will be unable to meet its ordinary expenses. A priest has a sensational and pathetic advertisement, which commences thus: "HELP, HELP, MY CHURCH IS FALLING," and continues, " For the love of Mary, help me to rebuild her church at Lynn." It is to this that the Roman Catholic Church has come in England; and these almost despairing cries for help are repeated day after day in the English papers, and apparently there is none to heed them.

A remarkable appeal was made in these papers in the year 1888, which was curiously pathetic in its character. A priest wrote a letter, which was purported to be written by a gentleman who had just died, addressed to his wife. Its object was to draw the attention of this lady to the difference revealed to him in purgatory between the luxurious appointments of his own house, and the poverty and misery of the house of God. He describes in glowing language the feelings of shame and grief which he experienced at the contrast between the two. It certainly was a plain hint to her to do something for the Church.

In mediæval ages the priest would have had a vision, and would have informed the bereaved widow that her late husband had commanded her to make certain offerings for the release of his soul. I do not know whether this lady took the hint thus cleverly conveyed, but however this may be, it shows how little Roman Catholic teaching has been able to do in England, with all its advantages of a share in the public government, and with perfect liberty to teach as it will.

But it is not only as to the results of Roman Catholic teaching, as far as devotion to the Church is concerned, that we are enlightened by this writer, or rather by these writers; for the contributors to the *Tablet* are numerous, and among the most influential of English-speaking Roman Catholics. The whole question of education is discussed with a freedom which would be surprising, if we did not realize that English Roman Catholics have always found their opinions respected by the Court of Rome.

There is no other religious body which fears the least breath of criticism as they do, and this has been the cause of great trouble in England. The perverts, who form the only educated portion of the Roman flock, are very much alive to the advantages of higher education, and greatly desire it for their children. The priests, and in some cases even the convent priests, are of another opinion. At first a compromise was hoped for, when the experiment of establishing a Roman Catholic university was made in Ireland, and the name of Newman was used to charm. It was supposed that the Irish people would be won over by the compliment of this selection of their own country as the location of the university, which was to be so famous, just as the astute Bishop of Richmond hopes to captivate the people of America by the selection of Washington for the American Roman Catholic university.

It was confidently expected that the name of Newman would have secured the interest and patronage of English Roman Catholics, and that the chronic feud between English and Irish Roman Catholics would have died a natural death. But, alas for human hopes and plans! Even Newman's name did not heal internal dissensions and jealousies, which seem to exist with special intensity between those who love their faith so much, and their religious brethren so little. The Irish Roman Catholic university proved a miserable failure, although money was poured out on it like water.

The next effort and the next failure was in connection with the plan to establish a Roman Catholic university in London. Again money was poured forth like water. All that ecclesiastical power could do was done, only to add another failure to the list. It was next proposed to have a Roman Catholic college in Oxford, and this plan might have been carried out if it had not struck terror into the hearts of the higher clergy, who opposed it resolutely, fearing lest the close communication which must necessarily arise between the Roman Catholic and the Protestant students would result in loss of faith to the former. Those who wished for higher education for their children were obliged to yield, but they were not satisfied, nor were they silenced.

The London University has been the literary refuge of the hapless Roman Catholic youth, who knew that his own colleges could give him no diploma which the world would recognise or respect. It was a poor substitute for a greatly desired good; and now the Roman Catholic papers are full of the complaints of heads of families who have discovered that this supposed good is not only useless, but that it is even injurious. A gentleman writing in the *Tablet*, and signing himself Bernard Whelan, says:—

"There should be no attempt to pass students at the

London University. The whole system is one for the manufacture of probable prigs. As the years go on we want reasons, and we have none. With intelligent beings surely reason is the dominant faculty. Why should it not be cultivated as much as the memory or the imagination even from childhood?"

Why the reasoning powers are not sufficiently cultivated in the Roman Catholic Church is told very plainly in the same paper.

Attempts are made from time to time by English Roman Catholics to promote the circulation of Roman Catholic literature, but these attempts have always ended in a miserable failure. A "Catholic Truth Society" (so-called) was established in England some time since, and is only kept alive by spasmodic efforts. In reporting a meeting of this society the editor of the *Tablet* laments the good old time when ignorance was bliss, and there was no need for teaching the people anything. Now they will argue, and must have a reason for what they believe. The editor says: "A generation ago, when children had thoroughly learned the truths of the catechism, and had happened to be placed in a settled home life, there was less reason to fear." To fear what? Plainly that the poor Roman Catholic would learn to know or read anything beyond his catechism. Colonel R. Chichester, an ardent and educated Roman Catholic, is so little satisfied with the Roman Catholic school system in England that he says: "It is the duty of parents to find out the educational power of each school. Every boy and girl should be obliged to pass an annual examination at the hands of a State official."

After all, Roman Catholics themselves are the best

evidence of the failure of their own system of priestly interference in the affairs of life.

What has been the result of the establishment of Roman Catholic universities? Such establishments have simply been utter failures, socially, religiously, and financially. This is a bold assertion, but I give proof of it from Catholic sources, and from personal knowledge.

And first we may consider the condition of the Roman Catholic University of Dublin. A more miserable fiasco is hardly on record. It may be said that the exceptional conditions of that country made failure inevitable. But there is one point on which success is always sure for any Catholic undertaking, engineered by a few Catholic bishops, and that is financial success. Success in that direction has been more easily obtained in America than in Ireland. Urgent as were the demands of the Irish priests under episcopal compulsion, the funds so obtained for the Catholic university in Dublin fell very far short of the desires of its promoters. In America the case has been different. While hundreds of thousands of hapless children and long-suffering girls are left to the tender mercies of public officials and institutions, hundreds of thousands of dollars are poured forth like water to build and endow an institution, on which some, even of the Roman Catholic episcopacy, look with no favourable eye.

An article on the Irish Catholic university appeared in the *Dublin Review*, for October 1887. This quarterly, poor as it is in literary merit, is the only serial of the kind to which British Catholics can lay claim. Let us look, then, at the Irish Catholic university, and see what has been said of it by Catholics, and what has been the result of all this lavish expenditure, principally of the money of the poor. If the Irish Catholic university proved a disastrous failure, what hope is there for the success of an American Catholic university, which has only the one additional advantage of being able to secure enormous sums of money, but which wants the many special advantages of the Dublin institution. The article referred to in the *Dublin Review* opens thus :—

"The project of a Catholic university for Ireland, started by the Synod of Thurles in 1850, has had such scanty measure of success, while on the other hand, centres of the higher instruction, such as Cardiff, Bangor, Liverpool, etc., based on the principle that very probably there is no God, have prospered as soon as founded, as if they met a clear want of the time, that there is abundant reason why a Catholic should examine the matter very earnestly and very closely."

The writer of this article in the *Dublin Review*, who is well known, and who describes himself correctly as "one of the old staff," declares what the object of the Dublin Catholic University was :—

"It is no use," he says, "indulging in generalities and fine words. What practical result did the Thurles Synod and their lay supporters look for ? By establishing a Catholic seat of learning they hoped ultimately to secure this ; that if an Irishman in any part of Ireland, or of the world for that matter, wished to know what were the latest theories and the most important books on early Roman history, or on Turanian philology or Assyrian cuneiform inscriptions, or quaternions, or the doctrine of probability, or the correlation of forces, or the Elizabethan dramatists ; in short, upon any one whatsoever of the subjects of higher or more difficult inquiry with which the human mind is at present engaged, he should be sure of finding some learned scholar or savant in Dublin capable of giving him all the information he required, and of showing him all the books, apparatus, specimens, experiments, etc., necessary to guide his judgment."

This, then, was the object to be attained, possibly because no other object was attainable. The Dublin Catholic university was not to be a university of students; it was to be a university of professors, a sort of living encyclopædia of general information. Anything more absurd could scarcely be imagined. Anything more certain to fail could scarcely be devised. But no matter, the bishops willed it; and as they obtained the Pope's approval no one dared say a word against it. If the laity objected, so much the worse for the laity. It is their duty to give their money, promptly and humbly, but not their advice. The bishops do not certainly claim personally infallibility, but they claim obedience to their mandates all the same; and the unhappy man who dares to even discuss them is denounced as "disobedient to the Church," which practically and very effectively places him under a ban spiritual and temporal; and he consequently soon finds out that the game is not worth the candle. If he is honest and outspoken he may burn his fingers once or twice, but he eventually subsides. And if he is poor—and ecclesiastical support is necessary for his advancement in life, as it very often is in America as well as in Ireland—he shuts his teeth hard, and pays the tax of submission necessary for success.

This is not a fancy picture. It might be drawn a good deal stronger from personal knowledge. The cry of the victim is not heard, or if heard is not heeded as long as he submits, and his grievance is not made in public.

It does not seem to have occurred to these learned bishops that the staff of professors required for this "Inquire Within" institution could not always be found. They hoped indeed that sooner or later there would be no lack of students; but the students were not forthcoming, either sooner or later, and once again the Catholic bishops proved by a public failure their utter inability to manage affairs. Once again they attributed failure to every cause except their own incapacity. How then could they be mistaken? And indeed he would be a bold man who dared to say that they failed, even if he clothed the stern assertion in the most flattering attire, and hinted rather than spoke out. For do not these bishops denounce and discipline their Galileis? And then when Galilei is found, either in past or present ages, to have been unjustly denounced and cruelly disciplined for knowing more than his masters knew, they retire gracefully, and even with new laurels, because they only imprisoned and boycotted where they might have excommunicated. And even if the poor Galilei turns out to have been condemned wrongfully, he should have had more patience, and submission, and loyalty to his Church—*i.e.*, to some obtuse ecclesiastic—and not have spoken till he had permission; and then there will be gentle insinuations that the ecclesiastical superior knew these scientific truths as well as the irrepressible Galilei, but was waiting the proper time to disclose his knowledge.

This, then, says "one of the staff," was the object of the Irish Catholic university. This, then, was the object, not to provide lectures and opportunities of distinction for clever young men, but to found a seat of learning. To open the walks of the higher education to the Irish youth was also an object, but it was secondary. So a university was established purely, if not exclusively, at the expense of the Irish peasantry, to support a staff of English professors.

A very gentlemanly class of professors was provided, but it does not appear to have occurred to the governing body of Irish bishops that they could not live for ever, that a university could only be kept up by obtaining recruits for its professional chairs from the ranks of its students, and that the professors, whether present or to come, could not be permanently supported by the poorest people on earth, even if the support was demanded and enforced by episcopal authority.

There is one marked difference, however, between the Irish Catholic university and the American Catholic university. The gifted and youthful prelate who has obtained the rectorship of the Catholic university at Washington has stated plainly that it is intended principally, if not exclusively, for priests.

The Dublin Catholic university was exclusively for the laity. The reason of the difference is obvious. There is no Maynooth in America with its great prestige. The establishment of an American Maynooth, which is the secret object of the Catholic university in Washington, would certainly be an immense support to the Roman Catholic Church in America. And let it be said that the Roman Catholic bishops in America have a much larger range of experience than Paul Cullen or Cardinal McCabe possessed.

The friction of a new country has not been lost on them. They will have their Maynooth, but it will be a nineteenth century Maynooth, with a good show of liberality, but not one whit more liberal in its views or useful in its literary character than the old Maynooth of Ireland.

But it will be a Maynooth well-endowed by the millions of the millionaire, although already the promoters have begun to ask for the pence of the poor. Later, indeed, the poor will be compelled to take more than their share of the burden. But the American Catholic working man is not so docile, or so easily controlled as the Irishman, and there may be difficulties in obtaining funds for this new institution which did not exist in Ireland, and which the founders are too sanguine to anticipate. And has not Archbishop Corrigan already arranged for a private Maynooth, for which he demands another four hundred thousand dollars? Certainly the future priests of America will be well provided for. It is said that there was some jealousy as to the location of the university. How easily such affairs are arranged in the Roman Catholic Church, where a bishop has only to speak in order to obtain all his desires.

But there is an inner side to this history of failure. The Irish Catholic university was opened on Whit-Sunday, June 4th, 1854, by the solemn installation of Cardinal, then Dr. Newman, as rector. Nothing could have been grander than the commencement, and nothing less anticipated by the promoters than the disastrous finale. The only wonder is that a man of Dr. Newman's acute perceptions should not have anticipated what he soon realized, that the whole affair was bound to collapse.

When Newman consented, the question of rectorship was easily settled. He was then at the very zenith of his intellectual power and fame. If a one-man university could be a success, the one man to make it such had certainly been found. What need to say more? The name of Newman is of world-wide fame. Nor was there any serious difficulty about the selection of professors, except, indeed, the one of nationality. A few Oxford men of more or less intellectual calibre had quite lately been perverted, and were consequently left destitute, or nearly so. It was certainly an anomalous arrangement that an Irish Catholic university should be governed by an English rector, and taught by English professors. But what will you have? Are not Irish affairs always anomalous? None of these men were particularly brilliant, but they were English, and for that reason they were specially acceptable to the pro-English Cardinal Cullen. Then it was a grand boast for the world at large to say, "Here are gentlemen who have left your English Protestant colleges, with all their prestige. We will show that we are not behindhand in establishing such institutions."

There is one subject, and a very important one, on which we are no longer left in doubt regarding the new American Roman Catholic university. For the present it is only to "teach" theology. To ordinary beings this seems somewhat absurd; but the Roman Catholic Church in some of its late decrees is nothing if not contradictory; and thinking men, hearing of new dogmatic moral and theological controversies, ask themselves, some in fear and some in grievous distress, "What next?" In the meantime what is the object? What work is to be done in this university, where "teaching" will be conspicuous by its absence? A great many compliments are paid to the Bishop of Peoria for having "broken the ground," and now we shall say a word of the inner workings of the institution. He certainly broke ground, and he did a great deal more, by inducing his niece, Miss Caldwell, to devote to it the trifling sum of $300,000. The new episcopal rector of this university tells about the money he has got, with great *empressement* and gratulation. He has on hand $700,000, he is "sure" (happy man!) of $100,000 more.

The divinity building, which cost $175,000, is "ready to be paid for." By this we presume that the learned prelate has the money in hand. The grammatical construction of the sentence is poor for the head of a university. There is to be a "really splendid chapel," and we know what a "really splendid chapel" means in the Roman Catholic sense of the term. It means that gold, and silver, and silk, and ornaments, and costly carvings, and paintings, and statues procured from foreign countries, and which a king might envy, are to be placed in it, and paid for, generally, by the poor, and all for the honour and glory of Him who said, "Foxes have holes, and the birds of the air have nests; but the Son of man hath not where to lay His head."

The divinity department, we are told, is a "success." Eight divinity chairs for professors, who are only to teach theology, and presumably for students who are to learn nothing else, are already provided for.

There seems to be only one little difficulty, only one drawback, and that is, how to secure a supply of students. But the new rector is sanguine, as well he may be with all this money in hand, and a joyful assurance of millions more. He says he will begin with ecclesiastical students, and that arrangements are to be made to "stimulate" a supply of such students. To the ordinary mind it is quite as difficult to understand how students can be "stimulated," as it is to understand the use of a university which is not to teach anything but theology. It may be well, however, to say that the student "stimulation" scheme consists of the endowment of divinity scholarships "in perpetuity;" and the rector is quite sanguine that he will get the institution filled, "or nearly so," as the respective clergy of the country will have to secure for their respective dioceses scholarships enough "partially, if not fully," to fill the institution. Yet the "promising young students," who are to come when duly "stimulated," are told that they must pay all the same, the enormous endowments notwithstanding. As a passing trifle, scarcely worth noticing, the rector says he will require about $100,000 more for a divinity library, and to commence the "beautification" of the grounds.

How enormous must be the wealth of the Roman Catholic Church in America we have further evidence of in this remarkable statement. He says, for example, that ten days' work in the city of Philadelphia by himself and the archbishop of that city, secured $96,000, and he did not go beyond the limit of two parishes. The reader can see that, as he says, "the real resources of the country are as yet untouched." But Bishop Keane is well aware, for no shrewder bishop lives, that his non-teaching and money-requiring institution is not popular with all his brother bishops. And with becoming candour, and knowing their dislike to the establishment of a university at Washington, he says:—

"It is late in the day either to make or answer objections to the university. The two main difficulties have been the feasibility of raising the necessary funds, and the choice of the city of Washington as the site. We think that the first objection is amply met in this article. As to the second, an opportune and competent witness is at hand."

And then he brings for his second competent witness as to the desirableness of Washington, the late President of Cornell University. It is very remarkable how Roman Catholic prelates, and even Popes, defer to Protestant opinion when it suits their purpose. But it is whispered—indeed, it is an open secret—that it is not altogether unnecessary for Bishop Keane to fall back on the support of Protestant opinion, as to the desirableness of Washington as a locality for the university. A note of disunion has even reached the Pope, and it will be a curious investigation for the historian of the future to ascertain from secret despatches just how their "Graces" of New York and Baltimore, and their "lordships" of Peoria and Richmond, managed to reconcile their differences, and to satisfy their respective ambitions.

The *Catholic Mirror*, of Baltimore, which is the quasi-organ of Cardinal Gibbons and Bishop Keane, in a report of an audience granted to the heads of the Roman Catholic colleges and seminaries, March 21st, 1888, says that "the Catholic university of America was specially uppermost in the thoughts of the Holy Father." It is quite wonderful how some writers and some bishops know exactly what the Pope thinks, and what he ought to say. "He spoke," says the editor, "with emotion" (as indeed he well might, knowing the serious differences among the American Roman Catholic hierarchy), about the university at Washington. "It is my desire," he said, "that all the bishops should work together with unity and amity. It would greatly grieve me if there should be any want of agreement in regard to it."

The editor of the *Catholic Mirror* says:—

" These are rousing words from the Vicar of Christ, and they must scatter any lurking evidence of a hesitating doubt." " Leo XIII.," he continues boldly, " shall not be disappointed." Which means that Cardinal Gibbons and Bishop Keane are determined to have their own way. So far so good; but here is the reverse of the medal. The New York *Freeman's Journal* is the paper which Archbishop Corrigan delights to honour, and it reciprocates his good will by constantly expressing admiration of himself and his works. Its late editor was a power in the Church, principally on account of his fine gifts of sarcasm, and utter indifference to the feelings of ecclesiastics. They were, in fact, terribly afraid of him, and respected him accordingly.

Here is what Archbishop Corrigan's organ in New York has to say of the Catholic university in Washington, on which such enormous sums of money have been and will be expended: " The Catholic university," says the *Freeman's Journal*, " will in a short time perhaps realize the hopes of its projectors." Why Washington was chosen as the site remains a mystery, and why the particular place in which the corner stone was laid should have been marked out for the great future edifice is a greater mystery. A more eligible site could easily have been found.

But this is of no moment to a Roman Catholic bishop, who has this infinite consolation in his difficulties, that he has only to will and to have. One bishop wills to have the university at Washington. And although there is one already established there by the Jesuits, on a scale of splendour which is envied by our first American public schools—what matter? A bishop desires it; an obedient clergy and laity have but to submit.

But another theological university is desired at New York. If Archbishop Corrigan is disappointed, it only remains for him to have a university of his own, and he has sent out his orders for its establishment. It will cost, to begin with, $400,000. But what will you have, when a prelate has only to speak in order to be obeyed, when he has no care for results, and when he can throw the blame of failure on others, and take all the credit of success to himself, though all the share he has in making the success is to issue an order for money on a patient people?

We are told that in four years' time this university in Washington will open its doors to lay students. The New York *Freeman's Journal*, indeed, says that "it is more difficult to get men than to build colleges." We believe this significant assertion; and with the example of the Dublin Catholic university before the projectors, we might suppose that it would be taken into account. But no. The young rector calculates that there will be assembled at the national capital a large body of lay students, enjoying the advantages of "the highest education which can be offered by the scientists of the nineteenth century." The lawyer, the physician, the politician, the merchant, the journalist, the man of elegant leisure is expected there, and is expected to learn how to hold his own among the men of these critical times. He says the divinity department will need a "grand total" of $1,000,000; the other departments will require a similar amount each.

A letter has been published lately in the Dublin *Freeman's Journal*, which is a very different paper from the New York paper of the same name. The letter is written by Mr. Charles Dawson, an eminent Irish Catholic gentleman, and the subject is the bribe which England always offers to Irish Catholic bishops, in the shape of endowment for their dying Catholic university. Of this university he declares that "notwithstanding all papal benedictions and commands, the Irish people would have nothing to do with it;" and he adds:—

"The upper class of Irish Catholics never gave the university a helping hand. It matters little to them that it was established by Pius IX. These Catholics studiously absented themselves at the laying of the foundation stone, at which twenty-four bishops attended; they fled from its walls to those of Trinity and the godless colleges. These are the persons who are so anxious for the interference of the Holy See in Irish affairs."

The men who were educated in this Irish Roman Catholic university are Nationalists, like Dillon, Kenny, and Cox.

The moral of all this is simple. Roman Catholics will give their money to endow Roman Catholic universities and schools,—there are political reasons for doing so,—but they will be very slow to go to them themselves, or to send their children as students. The prestige of a Protestant institution will always tell.

Here is another and equally important and recent evidence on the same subject. Mr. Arthur Cleary, also a distinguished Irish Catholic gentleman, at a public meeting has declared that when he was auditor of the Dublin Catholic Historical Society, he went to ask the late Judge O'Brien, a Catholic, to attend at the opening meeting, and he absolutely refused to do so, or to have anything to do with the Irish Catholic university. Later he was sent on an expedition by Cardinal McCabe to ask the English Government to interfere with the Italian Government to obtain some favour for ecclesiastics. He went from one Catholic to another to get up petitions, and eventually had to fall back on Protestants for assistance.

In the June number of the New York *Catholic World*, Bishop Keane had one of his many articles on his favourite subject; and what does he prove? Simply that the Catholic universities of France have been total failures. They had money, they had bishops, they had the influence of the Holy Father; but Catholic students would have nothing to do with them. We doubt if the young rector would have brought this subject forward if he had not had a purpose of his own in doing so. He wants to show that too many universities may be established at the same time, though he admits that they were required by the immense population of France. One of these universities, he says, is "languishing to death," and those of Paris and Lyons are kept up only by heroic efforts. The whole article is amusing when read between the lines. In order to conciliate the other bishops, he says: "The extent of our country" (America) "will assuredly call for several Catholic universities eventually, but that the success of one" (his own) "must be made sure before starting others." It would appear indeed, from this article, that ecclesiastical students were the only persons to be found in the one French university which has proved anything like a success.

One word more, and it is a word of very great impotance to the American people. The rector says he expects eventually to have Catholic laymen in his university— men who are to be lawyers, physicians, politicians, journalists, and " men of elegant leisure," who are to learn how to " hold their own among the men of these critical times."

Now it would not be fair to judge of the institutions and mental calibre of an enslaved race immediately after it had obtained freedom. But the Roman Catholic Church in America has had freedom, and enormous wealth, and every advantage for at least a quarter of a century, and what has been the result?

Look at New York, the stronghold of Roman Catholicism in America, where the public press is manned by Catholic journalists, where many politicians, bankers, and tradesmen are of the same religion. What is to be said of the politicians who have been educated by the Catholic Church? What is to be said of the lawyers? What is to be said of the journalists who defend or write for its cause? What are the names and religion of the men who have plundered and robbed their country and the poor, some of whom are in gaol, and some of whom have fled to Canada, and who will help the Jesuit cause there? By whom were they educated? Do the people of America wish to have Washington turned into another New York, where the votes of the country are openly bought and sold in the liquor saloons, where vice, and vanity, and degradation reign supreme in the very class from which those students came who are to teach the country?

Wherever the carcase is there will the eagles be gathered together. The man came with the need, and the man was Mr. P—— F—— I believe that it is of the greatest moment that the power of the Church of

Rome in politics should be clearly understood, and the cause and effect of that power; and certainly Mr. P—— F—— has nothing, from a Romanist's standpoint, of which he need be ashamed. He has simply acted as a "good Catholic," and why should he not have his reward? The history of his case is very instructive, and it is also amusing. Indeed, it was made the subject of a ballad, which the comic press of New York was afraid to publish, but which nevertheless was privately circulated in that city, to the intense enjoyment of a select circle. We give it at the end of this chapter.

Mr. P—— F——'s career is very well known in the United States; and if his antecedents were somewhat anti-clerical, what matter? All is forgotten and forgiven, and he is a man *honoris causa*, whom the great Archbishop of New York delights to honour. Why should he not, since Mr. F—— came to his rescue when he was in the direst strait of his life? Mr. F—— was, as I have already stated, for some years the editor of the *I—— W——*, a paper openly published in the interests of dynamite, yet strangely, it did not fall under ecclesiastical censure until Mr. F——, in an unhappy moment, so far forgot himself as a "good Catholic," as to write a pungent article on the style of living which the late Archbishop of New York affected, and which he sternly denounced. It was a matter easily passed over if he collected enormous sums of money for dynamite, though he made no secret of the manner in which it was to be used; but when he dared to touch the "Lord's anointed" it was quite another affair.

To propose the murder of an Irish landlord, or to blow up a public building with hundreds of innocent people in it, was a trifle not worth noticing, but to hint, no matter how delicately, that the Church of

Rome might prosper better if it looked a little more to the poor, and a little less to the rich; if it used its enormous wealth to teach the ignorant, to prevent sin rather than erect costly cathedrals, and enable its ministers to live delicately, was considered by the Roman Catholic Church a crime which could not be tolerated for a moment. So Mr. P—— F—— was denounced, with the usual result. The circulation of his paper fell at once, and he was nearly ruined—another evidence both of the power of the Roman Church, and of the way in which it exercises its power. But Mr. F—— saw his opportunity to regain what he had lost, and he was not the man to lose so splendid a chance. Dr. McGlynn was denounced; and it is so easy and so pleasant to be on the side of power, and it is also, in the Roman Church, so virtuous. Why should he not gain the appreciation of those who hold the keys of the kingdom of heaven, and the keys of the kingdom of earth also? Why not secure both worlds, when it can be done with so little trouble? Sometimes these men forget that Rome can be ungrateful if they are not sufficiently subservient, or if they do not submit to the commands of superiors at any sacrifice of feeling or principle. Witness the case of Herr Windhorst. Even if the subject is a momentary digression from the present one, it may be well to call the attention of the reader to the facts of his case, as it has an important bearing on the question which we are considering.

We cannot by any possibility imagine St. Peter writing to Rome to dictate a special line of politics to his followers, or St. Paul sending Timothy to obtain a higher military appointment for the faithful centurion. When the Papacy was a temporal power it was necessarily involved in temporal affairs, but when Providence changed its condition,—and if we believe in Providence we must recognise its restraints as well as its action,—then a happier state of existence was opened to the rulers of the Church. Happy indeed would it have been if this condition had been accepted. As individuals, Romanists should have been left to their individual inclinations in public affairs, while their Church, as a body, could have held a strict neutrality of action.

The sight of a coalition between Bismarck and Leo XIII. might make apostles weep. Most assuredly it has tried the faith not only of German Catholics, but of their Gallic neighbours. The object of this singular episode is not difficult to discern. It is a positive interference in politics, and one that can be sharply criticised, because the motive is so apparent. There is no doubt that the Papal homage recently paid to Bismarck, though with an utter disregard of the wishes and the national aspirations of the Romanists of Germany, is the beginning of an end, the results of which no man can foresee.

The tone of the Papal correspondence concerning German political affairs should be observed carefully. Italians, as diplomatists, have no equals, and cardinals have a record for diplomacy not easily surpassed. In the Jacobini letters care is taken not to give any command from the Pope, and it is stated several times that the object of Papal interference is to promote peace, and to avert a continental war. But the real object comes out at the end of the cardinal's second letter:—

"The Holy See," he writes, "in the advice it gave regarding the Septennate, wishes to bring about a new opportunity of making itself agreeable to the German

Kaiser and Prince Bismarck. Apart from this the Holy See, from the standpoint of its own interests, which are identical with the interests of Catholics, cannot allow an occasion to pass for favourably disposing the powerful German empire to the end of improving its position."

It will be noted that it is said many times that the Pope merely expresses his "wishes." But royal wishes are commands, and here is precisely where the political injustice comes in. Italian cardinals are as Roman as the Celt is Irish. Their intense and galling bitterness against the court of Victor Emanuel should be known to be understood. Hence no means will be left unused to regain the lost temporal possessions of the Papacy. There are men in the Curia who would agree with Mr. Preston of New York, in making individual souls or feelings of no account, men who to attain their end would crush the hearts and the souls of thousands. But while might may be victorious for a time, it is not always so, and acts of injustice recoil with terrible force on the perpetrators.

The case between Bismarck and the Vatican is contemporary history, which may have results as important as were the differences between Leo X. and the electors of Saxony. How bitter was the quarrel, how keen the open threats, how sharp the denouncements! The German Catholics, a strong and resolute body, as events have shown, were urged in every term of entreaty and affection to stand true to their faith and the chair of Peter. Herr Windhorst was their leader. He whose lifted hands were blessed and praised by the Pope, was appointed to deliver his people from Bismarck, and in good truth he did deliver them.

This marvellous man is honoured even by his enemies. One who has seen him for the first time rising to speak after Bismarck, smiles at the idea of such an insignificant person following the man of blood and iron.' But Windhorst, if small in person, is great in speech. A few plain statements of facts, a few statistics, followed by keen cutting sarcasm, and you listen and forget all save his eloquence and the subject. When the Kulturkampf raged in its fury Windhorst was at the very height of his power, and even the heart of Bismarck yielded for a moment to his impassioned appeals for liberty of conscience for his fellow-Catholics. And now, when Windhorst's head is white with the snows of over seventy winters, when he has spent his life and his energies in defence of what he considered the religious liberties of his fellow-Catholics, he reaps his reward.

Bismarck, who has oppressed the Church of Rome, is now honoured and courted by the head of that Church, and Windhorst received, with scant courtesy, an advice, amounting to an order, to change his whole policy, and submit to the dictates of the man whom he has so long considered not only his personal enemy, but the enemy of the ecclesiastical superior who has uttered this strange mandate. Herr Windhorst may well ask, Is life worth living?

But German Catholics are made of sterner mould than those of other nationalities, and how the battle between Bismarck and the Pope and the German people will end God alone knows. One thing is certain; it will lessen the faith of French Catholics quite as much as it will lessen their respect for Germans.

The interference of the advisers of Leo XIII. between the English Government and the Irish bishops was a mere passing breeze in comparison with the storm which this affair has occasioned. The Irish bishops were not slow to use very plain language to His Holiness. The Irish people took the very simple and effective line of stopping the supplies. But there is very little credit due to the Irish people for this independence. They had the full and earnest support of the Irish hierarchy, with four well-marked exceptions. If the Irish bishops and the Irish people had taken opposite sides in their views of their duty of submission to the Papal decisions on the Parnellite question, the result would have been very different. In Germany there is no question of religion; it is a question of politics pure and simple. Herr Windhorst may be a Catholic first and a German after, but he is a German, and he is bound by every tie of religion and of honour to vote and to use his influence in favour of the policy which he considered to be for the general good. If there had been any question of religion or morals the case would have been different. It is policy pure and simple. But there is more. Political—shall I say?— feeling, or animosity, runs high in the German Senate. Windhorst has been the opponent of Bismarck, and now indeed he is called on not merely to submit to a policy which he condemns, but to submit himself absolutely to his ancient enemy.

All the world knows that the man of blood and iron is like all such men of imperious will, and not over scrupulous as to the means by which he attains his ends in the Reichstag, or elsewhere. He will accept as his ally his arch-enemy the Pope, and he would be more than human if he did not rejoice in the discomfiture of Windhorst; but it is quite another question how far he will respect those who have inaugurated this policy. There has been no concern expressed for the coercion and degradation inflicted on the faithful Roman Catholic Germans and their champions.

To return to Mr. F——. There is another noteworthy matter in his career, while he was editor of the *I—— W——* and preaching dynamite with very great success, as a money-making institution. Mr. McMaster was then editor of the *F—— J——*. If report does not belie both parties, Mr. F—— is credited with having spent a day following Mr. McMaster round New York from one liquor store to another, and publishing afterwards the result of his investigations. Mr. McMaster died the honoured death of all good Catholics, and Mr. F——, by the grace of the archbishop, is now the honoured editor and proprietor of the same *F—— J——*. But there is more yet. Mr. F—— is credited with some political transactions in the interest of the Church, and in his own interests. The editor of the *Boston American* is my authority for the following:—

"At a great Irish-American jubilee in New York last December to celebrate the Republican victory, it was openly declared that the victors owed their success to P— F—— and his crowd. No one mentioned the notorious fact, though it was well known at that time that A—— S—— had made a deliberate sale to Blaine, Elkins & Co. His followers were to call themselves 'Irish-American Protectionists.'"

It will be remembered that A—— S——, with the connivance of E— and F——, sold the Clan-na-Gael to the Republican party, the price being a certain amount of cash, and several fat offices, including a consulship for E——, and a cabinet position for S——. The following are a few of the florid expressions of the enthusiastic gentlemen who either spoke at the meeting or forwarded their sentiments in writing. Herbert Radclyffe, secretary of the Home Market Club, Boston, said :—

"The Home Market Club sends cordial greetings to those true sons of Ireland and America who turned their backs upon false leaders, and followed you, the *Irish World*, and other noble patriots, in the glorious path of Americanism, and all that it stands for."

Congressman R. T. Davis, of Fall River, said :—

"Irish-Americans who have broken party shackles, and voted to protect American industries, have proved their loyalty to the land which shelters them. You are the leader of this movement, and entitled to the gratitude of the American people."

Hon. George F. Hoar said :—

"Heartiest congratulations to the noble Irish-American protectionists."

Senator Palmer of Michigan said :—

"All hail to the loyal Irish-Americans whose love for their native land intensifies their devotion to the land of their adoption."

James G. Blaine said :—

"The Irish-American protectionists were a very potential element in securing the election of President Harrison."

But Mr. Ford was not always as affectionate to Mr. Blaine as he is now, and he found it as convenient to change his political opinions as he did to change his religious views. A Roman Catholic writer says:—

"Patrick Ford was here, there, and everywhere during the week, running around excitedly, pausing every now and then to make sure that the Irish vote didn't jump out of his pocket and escape, until he got into the presence of 'the greatest living American,' Pat Ford excepted.

"'You are welcome home,' said Pat Ford to Blaine. The man from Maine has a good memory, and remembered that not many years ago this same Mr. Ford, in his paper, the *Irish World*, called him a 'demagogue,' when he presided at an Irish-American banquet. Patrick Ford then said:—

"'Mr. Blaine is reported as having presidential aspirations. As Blaine is a thorough demagogue, he thinks perhaps that he may succeed in winning some Irish-American votes by figuring as one of the orators at a St. Patrick's night banquet. He forgets that his presence at such a meeting after what he has done is an insult to every intelligent Irishman present.'

"Blaine must have thought Ford an arrant hypocrite when he called to mind what that gentleman said of him on another occasion. Said Ford in his *Irish World*:—

"'Does James G. Blaine for a moment suppose that American citizens, with Irish blood in their veins, will ever forget that when he was Secretary of State, he allowed American citizens residing in Ireland to be arrested and imprisoned on mere suspicion, without his calling the British Government to account for this violation of international law, as he was in duty bound to do?

"But Ford himself seems to forget it, although he never thought he would, when he denounced Blaine for leaving Irish-American citizens at the mercy of the British Government.

"It is notoriously true that Patrick Ford has not the general good will of Irishmen. He belongs to the rationalist body in New York, and has never been identified with any Irish movement that had not the success of the *Irish World* in view. He has not the confidence of American working men, and the so-called labour demonstration in New York city was a meeting of the Ford family, nothing more, and no representative of organised labour was on the platform. Labour men who were invited ignored the invitation, and stayed away. The reviewing stand was filled with *Irish World* employées and with Fords. When an acquaintance of one of the latter called out, 'He's there, Ford,' about one-quarter of the crowd turned round and said in unison, 'Who called me?' In the throng that gathered in front of the platform there was not a single banner of a trade's organisation. Not even a delegation from a union appeared, nor even a 'strikers' labour organisation appeared upon the scene. Instead, there was the same old-fashioned Republican crowd, who always cheer the bloody shirt and the protectionist chestnut around election times. This gathering was swollen by the crowds of pedestrians who usually frequent the thoroughfares near the square at that hour of night, and who were no doubt attracted by the novelty of the scene."

The New York *Catholic News* says:—

"McMaster's death was in my opinion hastened by the responsibility of managing a paper into which he had all his life been putting money, without getting it out again. The mental state of an honourable man who always paid his bills, and when subscribers were not careful to pay theirs to him, may be easily conceived by any Catholic editor who does the same thing; and it was a strange thing that some of the old friends of the *Freeman's Journal* in New York, who knew of Mr. McMaster's difficulty, showed no particular concern about it."

When the conduct of superiors becomes the subject of street ballads we are within measurable distance of a revolution, and this has been the case in New York. It must be remembered that all Dr. McGlynn's followers were Roman Catholics, and most of them, like himself, still belong to that Church, while they freely denounce the evils which they are powerless to remedy.

"Ten dollars and ten days" became a standing joke in New York after the archbishop had sentenced Dr. Curran to ten days' imprisonment in a monastery, for his temerity in speaking the truth about the way in which Dr. McGlynn was treated. But it is significant that the sentence of excommunication, far from having the effect which was anticipated by those who procured it, was made the subject of a most ridiculous street ballad. This ballad was headed "Corrigan's Curse," and was published in Henry George's paper, the *Standard*, besides being circulated in ballad form all over the country. We only give a specimen verse here, though it is important that the manner in which the excommunication was received amongst the Roman Catholics of America should be known everywhere. It was headed—

("With apologies to the 'King of the Cannibal Islands.'") Take notice, friends of Dr. McGlynn, WE've excommunicated him.

"*Ipso facto et nominatim.* That's Latin for 'let him down aisy.'

" Ye'll understand we might do worse, but the law says a dollar for iv'ry curse,
Too much of a hole in an archbishop's purse; so we let the man down aisy.

CHORUS.—For Justice Duffy might do worse than fine us a dollar for iv'ry curse
'Twould make a hole in the Corrigan purse, so we'll let the man down aisy.

" So me and old Eyetalian Sim, we've excommunicated him,
Ipso facto et nominatim. (The Latin'll send ye crazy.)
And that's to make ye understand that this is now a Christian land,
And divil a Yank can raise his hand widout OUR high permission;
'Twas Simmyony made the plan, that wonderful great Eye-ta-li-an;
'Tis notice sarved on iv'ry man, yez all have changed condition."

(CHORUS AS ABOVE.)

But if some of his clergy failed the archbishop in his hour of need, it was not so with politicians.

The New York *Freeman's Journal* says :—

" A correspondent asks for a definition of genius and friendship. Nothing is harder than to adequately define words which mean so much. While apologising for inability to do it, permit us to offer Cardinal Newman's admirable definition of the word friend :—

" ' But give me for my friend one who will unite heart and hand with me, who will throw himself into my cause and interest, who will take part when I am attacked, who will be sure beforehand that I am in the right, and if he is critical, as he may have cause to be, toward a being of sin and imperfection, will be so from very love and loyalty, and a wish that others should love me as heartily as he."

"A circular was sent last evening to the *Herald* which purports to be the text of an amended declaration of loyalty to Archbishop Corrigan. It is introduced in very vigorous language, and is described as a 'New Coercion Bill.' The amendment is said to be the omission of Dr. McGlynn's name from the original document, although the reference to the former pastor of St. Stephen's indicates him as plainly as if his name were mentioned. This new circular is said to have been sent out on Tuesday or Wednesday of last week, accompanied by a letter from Father Lynch as 'secretary.' Father Lynch, according to the correspondent who sends the document to the *Herald*, disclosed its real purpose by a frank statement to several of the clergy, that 'it was for use at Rome against the efforts of Cardinal Gibbons and Bishop Keane.'

"The following is the document:—

"'Most Reverend Archbishop, we, the priests of the archdiocese of New York, come before you to express our sincere attachment to you, and our unfeigned and cheerful loyalty to your authority. We recognise in you our ecclesiastical superior, who, being in full communion with the head of the Catholic Church, the successor of St. Peter, lawfully rule, teach, and judge this portion of the flock of Christ, the archdiocese of New York.

"'Conformably to the exhortation of St. Paul, we look up to you as our prelate, who speaks to us the Word of God, whose faith we follow. And pondering the grave injunction of the same Apostle, "Obey your prelates, and be subject to them; for they watch as having to render an account of your souls, that they may do this with joy and not with grief; for this is not expedient for you" (Heb. xiii. 17). We desire also on this occasion to record our emphatic disapproval and reprobation of the act of disobedience and disloyalty to your authority of which a certain member of our body has made himself guilty, an act of disloyalty aggravated by his subsequent course. We have been patiently hoping and praying that our dear brother would change his mind and return to his Father's house; but observing that our charitable silence is construed into acquiescence in and approval of disobedience, and that it causes some surprise both here and abroad, learning, moreover, that it is publicly asserted that he is believed to uphold the cause of the clergy, in general we feel it our duty to make this solemn declaration to you, that the clergy of the archdiocese of New York utterly condemn all disobedience to lawfully constituted authority, especially to the authority of the Church, and can have no sympathy with the efforts of those who in any way set that authority aside. Our motto shall always be: "An obedient man shall speak of victory" (Prov. xxi. 28)'"

It may be well here to give the history of some more of the men whom the Roman Catholic Church delights to honour, as it has honoured the dynamiter Ford.

The *Chicago Herald*, a Democratic paper, says:—

"It would seem, from the present view of Dr. Cronin's assassination, that all the Clan-na-Gael professionals, the mysterious individuals, the Number Ones, the dynamiters, the treasurers, without a treasury, the blunderers, without a pause, are citizens of the United States only so far as their votes are needed for the

Republican party. If we catch an Irish patriot who is too near the assassination, do we not catch a Jim Blaine Republican?

"Egan was made minister to Chili by the Secretary of State; Austin E. Ford, a nephew of the editor of the *Irish American*, is a candidate for Surveyor of the Port of New York, his principal backers being Patrick Ford and James G. Blaine; John F. Finnerty, of Chicago, is stated to be Mr. Blaine's candidate for Sub-treasurer at that city; the man Maloney, arrested and released in New York as an accessory to Cronin's murder, is a Blaine candidate for a Custom House position. These are all Clan-na-Gael professional patriots.

" But chief of them all is Mr. Alexander Sullivan, who it was currently stated at the time was to enter the Cabinet as the representative of the Irish-American vote, in the event of Mr. Blaine's election in 1884."

The *Boston Advertiser* says :—

"This man Sullivan, who as head of the Clan-na-Gael secret society is under arrest for complicity in the murder of Cronin, is a man whose name has been foremost for some years among the gentry who have figured as chief recipients of the money wrung from sympathetic Irishmen to help the Irish cause. . . . He is forty-eight years old, son of an English sergeant stationed in Canada. . . . In 1869 he was made Collector of Internal Revenue in New Mexico, and in a few months a shortage in his accounts caused his removal. While there he shot and wounded Judge Hough, but soon after leaving his first place became, through the influence of S. B. Elkins (Mr. Blaine's chief lieutenant), postmaster."

"Thence," says the *Advertiser*, "he fled to Chicago, became Secretary of the Board of Works, a bankrupt, then the slayer of one Hanford, for whose murder on the second trial he escaped conviction, 'by the secret use of his influence in the Irish organisation.'

"In 1884 Sullivan was at the head of the so-called Irish movement in aid of Blaine, from which much was expected, and practically nothing came. He was in the employ of the Republican managers, who were deceived by his statements, and the supposed influence that he had with the Irish. He was handsomely paid during the campaign, and an expensive headquarters was run by him in New York city. He charged for speeches never delivered, and promised thousands of votes which were afterwards cast for Cleveland."

But there is other and even more direct testimony regarding the character of this English, Irish-American, Roman Catholic patriot, and coadjutor of Mr. Blaine and Mr. Egan. In a letter from certain prominent members of the Irish-American Club to the *New York World*, it is asked, "Does not he" (Michael Davitt) "know that Sullivan was adjudged bankrupt in court, yet when afterwards elected President of the League spent $100,000 in speculation?" The *St. Louis Republic's* Washington correspondent, in a despatch to that journal, says:—

"Now that the coroner's jury has declared that the Clan-na-Gael is not in harmony with and is injurious to American institutions, and that Alexander Sullivan is behind the bars accused of being the leading spirit in the conspiracy for murder, Mr. Blaine is far from happy. It discredits entirely Blaine's Irish Roman Catholic supporters before the country, in fact, before the world. Egan has been rewarded with an important diplomatic position, although he is even now high up in the councils of the Clan-na-Gael, if not actually one of the famous, or rather infamous, 'triangle.' It also was brought out during the investigation, and no doubt will be brought out plainer during Sullivan's trial, that Sullivan and Ford speculated with the funds of organisation contributed by patriotic Irish people for what they considered to be patriotic purposes. It was shown also that Sullivan and Egan, as commanders of the Clan-na-Gael, sent men to Great Britain to blow up buildings with dynamite, and murder not only men but women and children.

"Can anybody imagine any other single Secretary of State, from the first of them to Mr. Bayard inclusive, having such friends and allies as the Egans, Fords, and Sullivans? Is it possible to think of Jefferson, Randolph Pickering, Marshall, Madison, Monroe, Adams, Clay, Livingstone, Webster, Buchanan, Calhoun, Everett, Marcy, Cass, Black, Seward, Fish, Frelinghuysen, sleeping in the same political bed with such a crew? It is not Mr. Blaine, not Mr. Harrison only, who suffers, or who suffers most from such associations or connections near or remote with it. It is the good fame of the country that suffers most of all. It is the country that is dishonoured, shamed all the world over by the selection of plotters and dynamiters to places of honour at home and abroad, and who are selected solely because they are able or pretend to be able, to control the vote of a secret society, whose purposes are abhorrent to civilisation, and dangerous to the institutions of the country."

It is well for Americans, it is well for all English-speaking people to know what is the true character of the men who govern America. They are good Roman Catholics certainly. They will never be excommunicated like McGlynn, or refused Christian burial like John McGlynn, yet do not think they deserve endorsement as good Christians.

But there is yet another, and if possible, more serious evil connected with the political power of the Pope. It is the utter demoralisation of the masses of the people. The politicians of America must cater to the liquor saloon interests—in fact, as I have said elsewhere, the liquor saloon-keeper is the boss of the ward, and is respected accordingly; but what shall be said when priests who should say with their Master, " My kingdom is not of this world," use the means which others do, and degrade themselves and their office accordingly?

The liquor saloon-keeper is, with rare exceptions, " a Catholic and an Irishman." He has all the superstition of his race and of his religion. The victims of his saloons die beautiful and holy deaths, attended to the scaffold by Sisters of Mercy and priests, after they have repented more or less in gaol for brutal murders. To have saved them from so terrible a fate, and from the need of such a late repentance, would seem to some of us to have been a greater mercy. Then the power of the liquor-saloon keeper is invoked to help their unfortunate and destitute children; but would it not have been better to have tried the power of the Church to keep the husband and father from drink and crime? Then the sisters, already well paid by Government (the politicians see to this), go to beg in the same liquor saloons which ruined the father, taking with them these little orphan children, who, later in life, will remember how they were brought to these places by sisters, and received liberal support from the generous dram-seller. Besides this, they collect ceaselessly from the poorest of the poor, always more ready than the rich to help them, and yet they are not satisfied.

A few priests have dared to speak out on this subject, and to denounce the liquor saloons, but they generally suffer for their zeal. The liquor saloons not only provide for the Church, but they also supply priests to the Church. The father of Archbishop Corrigan was a liquor saloon-keeper, who, if report does not belie him, dropped dead in his own store on Sunday after he had defied his priest, and insisted on his right to keep it open every day in the week.

Mr. Skinner, writing to the *American Citizen*, Boston, says :—

"The type of nobility and morality in the Romish Church of to-day is but little better than that of three hundred years ago.

"The following escapade of a prominent Irish Roman priest occurred in Raleigh N. C. early in May last, and was published at the time in the *New York Herald*. John J. Boyle, in charge of the Roman Catholic Church of the Sacred Heart, was arrested and committed on a charge of brutal assault upon an amiable, intelligent, and respectable young lady of fifteen. She was the daughter of an ex-mayor, a well-known Romanist.

"We could easily go on multiplying these cases of brutality and immorality into hundreds if necessary. These are the men who have been, and are still, before the masses of Europe and America as the spiritual teachers and moral educators of the people. These are the men whom the great mass of Roman Catholics reverence and fear as their spiritual fathers, and as having the power to grant absolution for sin for money. These are the kind of nobility that the Church of Rome has ever produced, some of whom have been its representative men. These are the men with whom corrupt and ambitious politicians fraternise, because in many instances they can control a large number of Romanist votes in the municipal and state elections. These are the men, including Alexander Sullivan, the murderer of the superintendent of schools, Hanford of Chicago, who manipulate and control, to an alarming extent, the associated press of this country, suppressing important facts and news items as they please, or whenever the interests of the Clan-na-Gael demand it. These are the men who, because they have been in many instances ward politicians, and recognised leaders in important political campaigns, claim that they should be sent to Congress or to State Senate, or as ministers to Chili or Mexico or some other country. These are the men who arrogate to themselves the right to supervise the education of our boys, who are to be the future citizens of America, and would, had they the power to do so, destroy our colleges, academies, and state institutions, and build upon their ruins a Roman hierarchy that would wither and blast every free institution of this Republic."

Even men like Ford may find that they have leaned on a broken reed, or we may rather say that they have served a serpent which will sting when they least expect it. The word gratitude is unknown to Rome. We have quoted the case of Windhorst. When Rome, to serve her own purposes, could throw aside a man like him who had served her so long and so faithfully, to please an enemy like Bismarck, what may others expect? The Pope would sacrifice a hectacomb of

Windhorsts without a moment's thought to gain a political object. The Church is the Baal to which every knee must bow; yet even those who have bowed the knee to her will often find that all their sacrifices have been in vain.

But the great and important fact remains, that Rome cares but little what weapons she uses to gain her end. Whatever Mr. Ford's political or moral character may have been, he is now the favoured journalist of the head of the Roman Catholic Church in America. He is penitent for his past offences against the Church, though he may not have recanted his dynamite sins. He came to the defence of his ecclesiastical superior by issuing a special edition of his paper to glorify him, and to denounce one of the best, most moral, and charitable priests who ever lived in the Roman Catholic Church in America, and he has (for the present at all events) his reward. Whether it will pay better to be the apostle of Archbishop Corrigan, than to be the apostle of dynamite, remains to be proved. The Archbishop of New York has the political patronage of that city at his disposal, and can reward in many ways.

The following is the ballad referred to in this chapter. Part of it was published in a New York paper at the time.

YE LAMENT OF YE PENITENT, F——D.

PATRICK knelt in the penitent's chair
(Many a better man has been there),
At one side his grace, and at one side a friar;
And they said, "Repent, and you may aspire
To anything short of the President's place,
For we rule this land through the Church and our race."

And Patrick he murmured soft and slow—
"My circulation is gone low, low."

"And in order to keep up the Church and our rule,
We intend to bring to the penitent's stool,
Without any other preamble or fuss,
Any bad politician who differs from Us.
It is ours to rule and theirs to obey,
And we've done for George and McGlynn from to-day."

    And Patrick he murmured soft and slow,
    "It is mine to obey when the way you show,
    My circulation, alas! is slow."

His grace he asked for his bell and his book,
And solemnly cursed, by hook and by crook,
Every man, and woman, and worthless child,
That would not obey his rule so mild.

"Alas!" murmured Patrick, "I had no sense
When I used to write against Peter's pence,
And tell the people who read my paper,
Even if cursed with bell, book, and taper,
To keep their money till Rome would learn
To feel the want of hard cash, and turn
From the rich and the great, to the poor and the lowly,
And make matters up, and live more holy.
  "Mea culpa," he softly said;
  "Mea culpa," he bowed his head,
And great tears ran down his furrowed cheek—
"Never again will I hard words speak,
If a bishop rides in a carriage and pair,
  Or takes the good things of life galore."

    And he paused, and he wept, and he softly said,
    "My circulation is nearly dead."

"Never again will I stop Peter's pence,
No matter how great is the Pope's offence;
Never again will I dynamite fling,
Though I thought it once a holy thing.
I confess I denounced the political ways
Of Mgr. P—t—n in my simple days.
Will this noble and kind and holy priest
Accept me a prodigal late at the feast,
Of political plenty spread at his board,
And let me share the good things he has stored?

For, alas! and alack a day he said,
"My circulation is nearly dead."

"I wrote—I know I was guilty then—
Of those holy, and saintly, and blessèd men,
The English landlords of ancient Erin,
Who wished the people were more God-fearin',
Who went to the Pope with hearts sincere,
And who had only one thought and only one fear.
Oh, blessed friar! O Lord and grace!
A blush comes over my agèd face
When I think how I questioned their motives pure,
In driving their tenants out from the door;
Sure, they only wanted to make them obey
Their gentle rule, and their fatherly sway.
Once, alas! from that green land I'd have had them swept,
With dynamite fires (for my sin how I've wept!),
But now I know, when they spoke to the Pope,
It was with the pure and holy hope
That they would reform the Irish race,
And bring them back (to pay rents) and grace.

"And as for the case of Dr. McGlynn,
I wanted to see which side would win
(And sure and certain that was no sin),
Ere I lent the aid of my dynamite paper
To spread the light of your holy taper.
But father, and grace," he said soft and low,
"Even you sometimes look how the wind will blow."

And he sobbed and he cried, and he softly said—
"My circulation is nearly dead."

CHAPTER XV.

THE CONFESSIONAL AND THE LIVES OF THE POPES.

AS Rome claims above all things to be a "holy" Church, we cannot be reproached for dwelling on this aspect of her case, above all, as on that alleged holiness she founds her principal claim to the obedience and respect of mankind. We propose to consider only two of what she claims to be the sources of her holiness and doctrine. In the first place, she lays great stress on the confessional as a source of holiness, and as a means of preserving it. She is certainly unfortunate in offering us this evidence, for the current history and statistics of the present day, as well as that of past ages, show that Rome, as a Church, has no right whatever to claim exceptional holiness, that is, if we judge her claim by the light of Gospel teaching.

I admit that Rome can claim, as no other Church can, the submission of her followers to all her commands, but it is easy to show that the commands of Rome are obedience to herself, which is a very different thing from obedience to the Gospel. In fact, the commands of that Church are unhappily too often opposed to the Gospel. We, then, are looking at things from very different standpoints. If the "holiness" of the Roman Church is to be judged by the obedience of Roman Catholics to her commands, we have no more to say.

But even in this case, how little the world at large is aware at what a cost of misery, and of unspoken, but none the less real rebellion, Rome maintains her exterior submission.

A distinguished Roman Catholic and Italian bishop published a pamphlet recently, in which he criticised the attitude of the Pope towards the Italian Government; but he did this with all the expressions of deference and abject submission which Rome exacts from her subjects. Still he criticised. But no matter how abject the flattery, or how humble the tone, it was an unpardonable and deadly sin. Now let this case be considered for a moment. Here is an educated and intelligent Roman Catholic bishop, a lover of his own country, a man who might even, according to the teaching of the Romish Church, be supposed to know, above all others, the needs of the country, a man who had its welfare at heart. And how the Italians love their native land we who have lived with them, and know them so well, can tell. Yet even he must not dare utter one word, or express even the most deferently framed opinion as to the best way to govern the land of his nativity and his affection. How monstrous! The organ of the Pope, the *Osservatore Romano*, announces that this bishop has "publicly confessed his sorrow for the views which he had advanced," and had announced " his complete submission to the will of the Pope," and thereby gained the honour of being once more a "holy" member of the holy Catholic Church. In the same way any one who was rash enough to pass even the least remark on the dispensation given by the Pope to Prince Amadeus to commit incest, should either make an abject apology for his fault, or cease to be considered a "holy" Catholic.

No doubt the Pope looks on this bishop as siding with his enemies, and with the usurpers of his throne. But even if Victor Emmanuel was a usurper he had the nation with him; and surely a nation has a right to choose its rulers.

I have this bishop's noble work before me while I write. It proves at least that there is some education amongst the Italian clergy, and some thought. He describes the state of the Roman Catholic press in Italy as miserable. A few journals edited by men who are too ignorant to know that the people have forsaken the Church of Rome, and will have none of it in temporal affairs, no matter what wailing there may be over their defection. Men who are too stupid or too much blinded by prejudice to realize facts that lie straight before them, are, alas! the guides of a minority, who, taking their literary and religious teaching from them, are their equals in ignorance and prejudice.

The temporal power of the Pope exists no longer save in Papal fond imaginings. The bishop speaks of the temporal power as "morto per sempre." He says it is so dead that no one thinks of speaking of it. And yet at this very moment the Pope would not hesitate to shed the blood of millions of Catholics, or to embroil the whole of Europe in civil war, if by so doing he could win back the crown of temporal sovereignty.

But we are more concerned at present with the fact that at this period of the world's history—and in face of all the boasted toleration of Rome, and its professions of allowing liberty of conscience—a Roman Catholic bishop is subject to the deepest humiliation, and is punished publicly, because he has dared to say that the temporal power of the Pope, being a thing of the past, should not be allowed to become a cause of trouble in the present. The bishop very carefully refrains from expressing an opinion as to the wisdom of the Papal claim for temporal power. This is noteworthy. As it is more than probable that belief in the temporal power will be made a dogma of the Church of Rome, which all Catholics must accept under pain of eternal damnation, he is wise. Whatever may be his private opinions, he is very careful indeed to state that he does not even wish to hint a word against the claims of Peter's successor to the sword of earthly power, as well as to the keys of heaven. But his argument is simply a common sense one. A certain state of things exists—there is no hope of change—should we not make the best of existing circumstances? And for saying this he must do abject penance. If he had lived in the days when the Pope had temporal power, how easy it would have been to have erected a scaffold before the Vatican Palace, and put an end to his troublesome theories by consigning him to the flames! Rome has an easy way of ending all controversy. Whether it is a Christian way or not is another matter.

This bishop might be a drunkard or live an immoral life, and no word would be said; such faults, which are only against the law of God, are easily passed over. But to express an opinion which differs from that held by the Pope is a sin which requires the severest punishment.

Now let us consider the moral result of all this, and we can better understand why nations have been demoralized, and have sunk so low in the social scale wherever Rome has had absolute power. Is it likely that this bishop would have ventured to express himself so openly if he had not formed very strong opinions on this subject? Would he have dared Papal displeasure—and he well knew what he dared—for a mere opinion that could be changed or modified at pleasure? What a terrible demoralization this man has suffered! We cannot for a moment suppose that his carefully formed opinions have changed, but all the same he is obliged to lie or to die, at least ecclesiastically. He is obliged to declare his regret for having said what he believes to be true. He is obliged to express his abject sorrow for having made a statement which he knows to be true. He must express himself and accept punishment as one who had committed a terrible crime. And why? Simply because he has said what thousands of his fellow-countrymen, and probably a vast majority of his fellow-ecclesiastics, know to be a fact—that there is not the least hope of restoring the temporal power. It is not a question of heresy, though he is treated as a heretic. He must submit to the Pope's political opinions, or be denounced as an unworthy child of the Church. At present the Roman Church would probably say that it was a "Protestant lie" if we said that Roman Catholics were obliged to believe in the temporal power of the Pope as an article of faith. But what are the facts? We have them here plainly before us. Any one who dares to say that there is no hope of the restoration of the Pope's temporal power, and that this being so it is a question of common sense to make the best of the situation, is treated as a rebel and is punished accordingly. It is no wonder that the Pope resented the erection of the Bruno statue so bitterly; it was a public declaration that whatever punishment he might inflict in the future on those who differed from him, he could not silence them by death or torture.

Now what must be the mental state of men, like the

Bishop of Verona? He knows perfectly well that the Pope is wrong, and that he is right. But you will say that he cannot be a good Catholic unless he believes the Pope to be always right in everything. This is the theory of obedience in the Roman Church. But how does it work? Is it not evident that it is perfectly impossible for a man to give up his carefully-formed opinions? He may be silent, but he cannot alter his judgment. Besides, this is not a question at present of infallibility, and here is a point to be noted. When I entered the Roman Church, the immense latitude which is allowed (on paper) by the Church in matters of opinion, was pointed out to me; and I was assured over and over again that the Church only asked submission of the mind and judgment on matters strictly defined to be of faith by the whole Church. But how very different is the real state of the case. Now the Church has abandoned her ancient faith in herself she is no longer infallible, her divinely given power is abandoned, and handed over to an individual. And see the disastrous result: every political opinion of a Pope is made a subject of infallible decisions, and woe to him who controverts them. Practically, the temporal power of the Pope is as much a doctrine of the Romish Church as the personal infallibility. In fact, we may say that the one is logically involved in the other. If the pope is infallible in all his pronouncements, why should not he be infallible in his political pronouncements? In fact, while the Roman Church denies that she interferes in politics, despite ample proof to the contrary, she nevertheless admits that when political questions come within the domain of morals, she has a divine right to make an infallible pronouncement. And note it well, she and not you, or even her most faithful bishops, is the judge of the circumstances in which her political decisions are infallible. Was there ever such a tremendous claim to power, so well concealed, and so surely acted upon?

Rome demoralizes her subjects by crushing every aspiration, and by involving the conscience in ceaseless difficulties and doubts. The divinely inspired voice of conscience speaks all the time by the will of God. A man may submit from fear to a decision which he knows to be wrong, but his conscience revolts all the same. He may resist God to obey man, but for a time at least, the power of God works against the power of man; and demoralization at last ensues when, the voice of God in the conscience being more or less deliberately disobeyed, the man ceases to respect himself. How can a man respect himself when he has violated his conscience? He falls lower and lower even in his own estimation. Some men fall into reckless, mental demoralization, and become eventually infidels; others fall into moral demoralization, and seek in the gratification of their passions a relief for the suppression of their reason.

The unhappy bishop having acknowledged in public that he has committed a sin, when he knows that he has merely expressed himself on political questions, must now express the same contrition, and do the same penance in the confessional, as if he had committed murder. If he had been a layman indeed he might have easily obtained permission from the Pope to have broken the law of God, but priest or layman he could never obtain permission to differ in politics from the infallible head of his Church. To such inconsistencies are men driven when they hand over their God-given reason to a mortal like themselves.

The confessional is indeed a system of sinning made easy. It is useless to deny in the face of recent events that Rome does not grant indulgences for a consideration. The facts of such grants are before the public. But it does not need much study to know that the confessional is a ready resource for the free commission of crime at pleasure. Roman Catholic moral theology is simply a sort of intellectual sleight of hand in which he who shows how the most sin can be committed with the least penalty, is the most successful student. I am aware that I am making a statement which, if it were incapable of proof, would be a very wicked one. I might give my personal experience, and I have a right to do so. I shall never forget the shock which I received when I was told by a priest the casuistry of the Church of Rome on the subject of—shall I say truth, or lying? I was assured by an eminent theologian that you could tell any lie you pleased, if you made a mental reservation to the contrary. For example, if you were asked if you had a book, or any thing else, you could reply boldly No, without telling a lie, because, though you had it, you had not got it for the person to whom you spoke.

But I give proof from the books used by the Roman Church for the instruction of her priests. Just as I have quoted from the officially approved catechism of the Church of Rome, on the question of the real teaching of that Church, and have begged those who may be in controversy with Rome to make their opponents keep to their own authorized statements, so now I say it is just, both to us and to Rome, that we should judge her system of moral theology by her books of moral theology.

It is the proud boast of Rome that she never changes.

That she does change her religious belief all history proves, but we take her at her word, and therefore we are justified in quoting from her books of moral theology, ancient and modern. The fact is, that she has been obliged to change her theology, and therefore to change the teaching in her catechisms, and public opinion has obliged her to modify some of the statements in her manuals of moral theology. For example, her famous "Dens Theology" has been practically withdrawn, because of its too explicit statements, and other manuals have been substituted which teach the very same doctrine in a more discreet form.

A religion which does not inculcate the great virtue of truth, is a poor sample of Christianity, and Rome has shamefully and persistently persevered in teaching moral theology in which the necessity for truthfulness is conspicuous by its absence. In "Dens Theology" it is plainly stated that the person who wishes to deceive another can do so without sinning, by mental reservation. If you are asked, "Have you seen Peter?" you can say you have not seen him, although you saw him a short time before, because you did not see him at the moment when you were asked. In fact, the whole system of Roman Catholic theology on the subject of truth gives the greatest latitude for lying, and carried out to its plain end would destroy all confidence between man and his fellows. As for equivocation it is explained, approved of, and allowed in the plainest terms, and you may safely equivocate even on oath. If, when you take an oath, you use an expression which bears two meanings, and you apply your own meaning to the expression, though you know that your questioner will apply a totally different one, you do not lie. In fact, the theology of the Roman Church amounts to this: You may lie at any time or place, above all you may lie under oath, if you do so in such a way as not to be found out.

I must confess that until I had studied "Dens Theology," which is the great text book and officially approved authority, of the Irish priesthood especially, I often wondered how it was that men about to be executed, who had most certainly committed murder, could die after denying with their last breath that they were guilty, while the priest who had heard their confession and knew their guilt, approved the act by his presence. But Roman Catholic theology teaches that a man may deny his guilt and not lie. For instance (this is the example given in "Dens Theology"), a man may deny that he has killed another by saying, "I have not killed him," if he understands secretly that he is not obliged to say to the questioner that he has done so. In plain English a man cannot lie to a priest without sin, because he is bound to tell the truth to the priest, but he may lie to anyone else, because he is not absolutely bound to tell the truth to any one else.

It would be waste of time to go further into the refinements of lying authorized by the Roman Church, but we must say a word of the teaching of the Jesuits on this subject, both because they are experts in the matter of skilful equivocation, and because their moral theology has the full approval of the Church of Rome.

The Provincial Letters of Pascal are too well known by name to need much explanation as to their object. As for the facts contained in them, as all the statements are taken from the highest authorities in the Jesuit Society, there can be no dispute as to their accuracy. One of the most extraordinary assertions of Jesuit casuistry is in regard to the necessity of loving God, or rather as to the needlessness of loving Him, for in fact, the teaching of Jesuit theologians amounts to this: that we need not love God if we avoid hating Him. As a matter of precaution it may be as well to love God, Suarez says, a "little previous to the hour of death." This easy theology of the Jesuits, has made them the favourite confessors of young men and women who wish to enjoy the pleasures of this life, and secure the joys of the next. Nor is this easy theology for the laity alone. A monk may, without sin, leave off his habit if he wishes to frequent immoral houses, to dance, or to steal. Indeed the study of the Jesuit theology of several hundred years ago is at once the best evidence of the necessity for the suppression of the society, as well as the best evidence of the utter demoralization of society when it was under the absolute control of the Roman Church. Priests and friars according to this theology are allowed to kill, not only an enemy, but even one whom they may have reason to suspect may attack their society, or speak what they consider evil of it.

But the great modern theologian of the Jesuit order is the Rev. Father Gury, a priest but lately deceased. His moral theology is open to all the world, and it would be impossible for any honest man or woman to read it without saying, "Here indeed is the mystery of iniquity." If ever a work was written to make sinning easy for the rich, and reparation by the poor unnecessary, this book bears off the palm of wickedness. All that is needed is to have a good "intention," and you are told with great care how you may make a bad action good and permissible by the most ingenious arrangement. And this is religion! This "sinning made easy" is the great grace which a Church professing to have been founded by a God who abhors sin offers to her followers.

There was a famous apparition some years since in France, about which there was considerable dispute amongst Romanists. The girl who claimed to have seen the apparition was called Mélanie. Whether she was deceived or a deceiver matters little to the point to which I wish to draw attention. In her letters she speaks again and again of the corruption and the evil and immoral lives of the Roman Catholic priests of France. In one of these letters she says, "France has been ruined because the clergy fear man more than God." Then she speaks of how she has been denounced by the priests because she has told the truth about their neglect of the poor, and their love of money. In another letter she says, "The sins of priests cry for vengeance, and vengeance is suspended over their heads." This is certainly very plain language. In fact, according to her account, the priests of France lived grossly immoral lives. In this same book there are some letters written by St. Francis of Paula who lived several centuries ago. He too speaks of and condemns the evil lives of the priests of his day. Indeed it is a noteworthy fact that, in every age of the Church, we find that those very men and women who were afterwards canonized by the Romish Church, denounced the priests of their times as the great cause of the evils of their day. It is remarkable, as an evidence of the fear of episcopal censure for saying anything which might be disparaging to the priesthood, that in several cases the words which denounce the priests and specify their crimes, are put in cabalistic language, while in other cases the places where the passages come in, wherein priests are censured, are put in a condensed form in brackets, though denunciations of princes and others are given in full.

A very remarkable work has been published recently in France, called "Necessary Reforms in the Church of France." It is published anonymously, but the authorship is well known. What a reflection it is on the holiness of the Romish Church that no priest or bishop, no matter how illustrious by his virtues, dare publish, over his own signature, one word of the most necessary criticism of the grossest evils. How this reminds us of the charges made in the inspired Scriptures against the Church of the Laodiceans which boasted that it had need of nothing, while it was miserable, and poor, and blind. Surely if ever a Church was blind, and wilfully blind, that Church is the Church of Rome. Like the fabled ostrich she hides her head in the mantle of her infallibility, and refuses to see until the judgments of God come upon her for her crimes.

The writer of this work uses very plain language. "We see every day," he cries out, "our people forsaking their churches and deserting our services, and we know not how to recall them. Impiety and indifference increase day by day. Let us tell the truth: the laity hate us." What a fearful avowal! "Our people," he continues, "wish for religion, but they do not wish for priests."

Could there be a greater evidence of the utter failure of the Roman Catholic Church to evangelize the world? France cries out for the bread of the Gospel, and the "Church" gives her the stones of forms and ceremonies. "Society hates us, it defies us, it declares that priests are hypocrites." It is tempting to multiply quotations from this work. But they are all in one strain: the writer has not dared to enter on the subject of the moral reform of the clergy, he keeps solely to the fact that the priests are tyrannized over by the bishops, and that the education which they receive is so defective that they cannot hold their own in any fairly educated society. All this is no doubt true, but he does not touch on equally important matters, because he dare not. His risk has been sufficiently great in speaking of the tyranny of bishops, and the ignorance of his fellow-priests. If he touched on their moral degradation as he has touched on their mental inferiority, he might be sure his anonymous cloak would soon be torn from his shoulders, and that he would suffer the penalty of his daring as long as his life should endure.

Here are some of the expressions which he uses in regard to the educational status of his fellow-priests. "Is it not too true that we are ignorant not only of science and profane studies, which indeed we have never learned, but even of theology, which we have only learned imperfectly? Do we not consider a man who has some knowledge of history, or who knows a little Greek, or even a little Latin, quite a marvel of learning? Is not this our own fault? We are far inferior to the laity even in the rudiments of learning. Yes, it is our own fault. I will dare to say more: it is the fault of our bishops. And those who study and have some knowledge—are they not made the subject of ridicule and contempt amongst their brethren?" Then he complains that there is no inspection, no examination of those appointed to professors' chairs. The nomination of the bishop is the all-sufficient test of fitness; the pupils, he says, become attached to the professors, and even if they were capable of judging of their capacity would be blinded by affection.

This too honest priest tells how a professor of English was appointed in a college, who did not understand one word of English. Have I not already said that the affairs of the English-speaking world are arranged in Rome by men who do not know one word of the English language—who are as ignorant of political economy as they are of history, and even of geography?

The writer of this remarkable work shows how the very enactments of the Council of Trent are set at naught by the bishops, who profess such veneration for the Church. Such is the tyranny of these same bishops towards their priests, that, he says, they ask themselves sometimes, Are they in Russia, or in Turkey? Jealousy reigns supreme: both on the part of bishops, who relegate any studious or earnest priests to remote places, where they may eat out their hearts in solitude; and on the part of the other clergy who make their inferiority felt by their exhibitions of petty spite. And this is a Roman Catholic account of the "Holy" Roman Catholic Church in France, whence we hear from time to time such grievous lamentations as to the defection of the laity from the Church. What wonder—when the laity have left the priests so far behind in education, and even in morals!

Rome is a wrecked and ruined Church, holding her position, such as it is, not by the upholding arms of faithful children, but by the sword of political powers, who hate her even while for political reasons they support her. Even Ireland, long faithful in spite of all rebuffs and slights, has at last woke up to the true state of the case; and has declared in plain terms that she will no longer submit to the political dictation of Rome.

The Rev. T. Connellan has given an account of the

demoralized state of the Irish priests which is horrible. This priest, who has recently left the Roman Catholic Church, says :—

"When I was a boy, engaged in birdnesting, or watching the speckled trout as they plunged in the crystal stream beside my home, I went daily to the same village school with two families, and every one in the locality regarded them as the offspring of two priests. They may not have been—I do not state they were—I merely state what was believed and publicly stated by those competent to judge ; believed, too, by a people who to this day would expose themselves to any risk in order to shield a priest or cloak his failings. Now this parish, I presume, was a type of a great many more. Indeed I am aware that a very much worse state of things prevailed in others. Several years ago a priest, who was my own contemporary in college, was stationed in a remote district where his nearest neighbour was a lady of some taste and refinement. I do not write these words to hold him up to odium, but for the purpose of exposing the system to which he fell a victim—a system introduced by a fanatic in the Middle Ages, and afterwards made a part of the Church's polity. Well, a great intimacy was apparent between this pastor and his favourite lamb. After some months the lamb was obliged to beat rather a hasty retreat to Dublin. Her flight was too late, however. An *accouchement* took place in a small town *en route*, and believing herself dying she revealed all to the parish priest of the place. The seal of confession did not prevent him—Roman theology specially provides for such cases—from making the fact known to the erring priest's bishop. Of course the modern

Abelard was put under ecclesiastical censure, but my readers will be happy to hear that he is now engaged in propagating Roman Catholicism under the Southern Cross. At the only Irish wedding at which I have ever been present the parish priest was drunk when performing the marriage ceremony. He had afterwards to retire to a bedroom, where his housekeeper, quite as drunk as he, kept him company. The family of the house charitably drew a veil over the scene by locking the door, and withdrawing the key. Indeed I might cover pages with facts like those first mentioned, but I have said enough for my purpose. Then the vices of gambling and drunkenness were almost universal among the Roman Catholic clergy of my acquaintance. Six tumblers of strong punch at a sitting was not considered much of a feat. 'Spoil five' and 'unlimited loo' were the favourite games. I have known them to be protracted until the rays of the morning sun had penetrated the room. Then those engaged went off to their several districts, some to celebrate Mass at station-houses and denounce such vices as drunkenness and gambling with an eloquence which drew ejaculations of horror from the old women present."

But when the head is corrupt what can be expected from the branches? Even Roman Catholic historians of the lives of the Popes cannot deny that many were corrupt, and but few good. And how corrupt the many were cannot be told in these pages, except in brief.

What shall be said of the Papacy from 1378 to 1417, during which period there were constantly two or three rival Popes? Can a ship with two or three captains even proceed on its course—to say nothing of its engaging an enemy? Of Pope Alexander VI., 1492, we read:—"The undisguised licentiousnesses displayed during the late pontificates were now carried to a monstrous excess: for the first time the bastards of a Pope being brought forward as his acknowledged children." The terrible Cæsar Borgia and the infamous beauty Lucretia Borgia, whom it is impossible to vindicate from murder and licentiousness, were of the number of the children of Alexander VI. It may here be noted that from 1417 the so-called Papal Succession ceased. Originally the Bishop of Rome was elected by the clergy and people of Rome. In 1059 election by cardinals was initiated. In 1417, no regular cardinals remaining, the Council itself elected Martin V. Never in the history of any civilized nation has the sovereign authority sunk to greater depth of infamy than did the occupants of the Papal throne from the beginning of the tenth century to the end of the fifteenth—thus: Pope Boniface VII., 894, having plundered the Basilica, and converted the booty into coin at Constantinople, returning, murdered Pope John XIV.

Pope Leo V., 903, was deposed and imprisoned by Pope Christopher. But this may be regarded as a mere prelude to the following:—In 904 began the ascendency of the two Theodoras and Marozia—three strongly depraved women—who for upwards of fifty years held the disposal of the Papacy, which they secured for their paramours, their children, and their grandchildren. Pope Sergius III., "a master of rapacity, lust, and cruelty," lived in acknowledged concubinage with Marozia. Pope John X., 914, lover of Theodora, who governed Rome as queen, through her influence secured the Papacy. After fourteen years he was starved or suffocated, his brother having been murdered in his very presence. Pope John XI., 931, is said to have been a bastard son of Pope Sergius and the infamous Marozia. Pope John XIII, 955, deposed Pope Leo VIII., in 964, and annulled all his ordinations. The absurdity of infallibility is here curiously manifest, for Leo VIII., after being reinstated, degraded Pope Benedict, reducing him to the rank of deacon. Pope Innocent XIII., 1484, is said to have had seven illegitimate children by as many mothers.

Baronius argues that when the Papacy was filled by a succession of "human monsters, most vile in life, most abandoned in morals, even to the utmost extent of infamy," its continuance—unlike other governments in which vice is followed by ruin—must be a token of special Divine patience.

Other most necessary depositions were those by King Henry and the Council of Lutri near Rome; "three devils," as Benzo terms them, being then deposed. The dissolute Pope Benedict IX., 1044, being twice driven from Rome, was succeeded by Sylvester III. After three months he found himself opposed by the exiled Benedict. The latter having sold his title to Gregory VI., finding himself disappointed, resumed his pretensions to the Papacy; so Rome found itself divided between them. But in 1046, all three were deposed, Sylvester being imprisoned for life. Pope John XXIII., 1415, who so treacherously violated the imperial safe-conduct in the case of John Huss; and who was told to his face by Hallam, Bishop of Salisbury, that a General Council was superior to the Pope; was commonly styled the "Devil Incarnate." Von der Hardt gives the fifty-four accusations preferred against him in the Council of Constance. As Pope he was charged with every conceivable crime, was thereupon deposed, May

29th, and was condemned to be kept in custody, the further disposal of him being left to the new Pope. In July following, this Council of Constance also deposed Pope Gregory XII. Two years later it deposed Pope Benedict XXIII. for perjury, schism, and heresy—this deposition being proclaimed with sound of trumpets throughout the streets of Constance. The Council of Pisa, 1409, had before this declared these two deposed and excommunicated. Another notable instance of the deposition of a Pope is that of Eugenius IV., by the Council of Basle, 1439, as incorrigible, schismatic, and obstinately heretical; its decrees being confirmed ten years later by Pope Nicholas V.

We may also note the charge of heresy against Pope John XXII., 1333, as to the "Beatific Vision," condemned by the doctors of the Sorbonne, and only retracted on his deathbed, this condemnation being formally decreed by his successor Benedict XII., January 29th, 1336.

As to this latter decision, Raynaldus and others say: "Some thought this decree heretical." So here are two Popes whose *ex-cathedrâ* pronouncements are in direct conflict, neither escaping the imputation of heresy. Here also may be mentioned the action of Boniface VIII., 1294, rescinding all the acts of Pope Celestine, and confining him in the Rock of Fumorn, where, after ten months, he died.

Pope Stephen VI., 891, caused the body of Pope Formosus to be dragged from its tomb, and placed for trial in the Papal chair, a deacon being assigned as advocate. A council having assembled, Formosus was accordingly condemned, the ordinations conferred by him were annulled; his corpse stripped of the pontifical robes; the fingers used in Benediction were cut off; and the body, after having been dragged about the streets, was cast "into the Tiber." Surely in all this there was nothing lacking of the *ex-cathedrâ* " or official procedure! And certainly the imprisonment, poisoning, and strangling which terminated the career of this Stephen were richly merited.

But still more of "*ex-cathedrâ*" action complicates this affair, for Pope John IX., 898, rescinded the condemnation of Pope Formosus, and stigmatized the proceedings of the council under Pope Stephen.

CHAPTER XVI.

ROMAN CATHOLIC LITERATURE AND ROMAN CATHOLIC HIGHER EDUCATION.

AGAIN we take the test of Roman Catholic statements of facts in regard to Roman Catholic literature and Roman Catholic education.

It is noteworthy that Roman Catholics who make the loudest complaints, when they dare, on these subjects, are the very first to denounce Protestants when they call attention to the absence of a Roman Catholic literature worthy of the name, or to the failure of Roman Catholic education.

Whenever a Protestant makes any observation on the subject of Roman Catholic literature, he finds a long list of names hurled at his head as specimens of the love which Rome has for intellectual progress. Just in the same way Protestants who complain of the evil lives of the Popes, are confronted with the names of the canonized saints. If only those who are thus deceived knew the facts in each case how different would be the verdict! But Rome possesses the immense advantage of not only being able to make dogma, but she can also make history and biography. And then she has the additional advantage over all other historians and biographers that she can compel her readers to accept what she says without doubt or inquiry.

With regard to the present state of Roman Catholic

literature, a glance at the serials and newspapers of the Roman Catholic Church should be quite sufficient to establish their character for utter inefficiency. The English Roman Catholic Press is certainly very superior to that of America, but the former has had the advantage of the editorship of men who did not owe their education to Rome. It is the same with regard to serial literature. Rome could not produce anything worth reading until the stream of perverts who came into her fold, and many of whom are leaving it of late, gave a literary and higher tone to her Press. It needs only to compare the Roman Catholic papers with those of other denominations to be at once convinced of the great inferiority of the former. I had at one time intended to take these papers one by one, or at least to take several of them to compare with the papers published by different denominations, but it would be simple waste of time; I will rather let Roman Catholics speak for themselves.

And it is easy to see why literature of the higher class can never flourish under Roman Catholic control. Any popular writer can be crushed easily and finally by a jealous inferior, and this is of frequent occurrence. And what man with a mind will be willing to occupy himself in intellectual research, when his sole reward may be to be silenced, as he cannot be burned! The Roman Catholic Press seems to exist only to applaud whatever the Pope or the local bishop says, to publish his many enactments, to find a reason to approve whatever he does, whether it is allowing incest, or permitting money given for Masses to be turned to other uses. The editor of a Roman Catholic paper, having expressed his regret that the Pope should have permitted the incestuous marriage of a royal uncle and niece, says that a recent editorial in the *Baltimore Mirror* defending such a marriage "has done more to injure Catholicism in this country than we wish to state. We have been guided by the Holy Father and the highest authorities in the Church in our defence of the truth. . . . Will not our Memphis brother smother his gloomy feelings in the matter, and obligingly state just how much Catholicity has been injured by our support of the act of the Sovereign Pontiff? Our esteemed contemporary, the *Baltimore Mirror*, unquestionably one of the ablest expounders of Catholicity among the papers published in America, stands on the basis of ecclesiastical law in defending the recent marriage, by special dispensation, of a titled European uncle and niece, and asks the *Memphis Catholic Journal* wherein it errs in so doing. We deem it almost unnecessary to inform the *Mirror* that there are some things that in sorrow the Church permits, but will not bless or approve. This is one of them; and the less frequently they occur, and the less said about them the better, for the laws of established society, under which Americans live. What might not have been considered unique in bygone ages is looked upon in a different light at the present time. What the Church does through the agency of the Holy Father, Catholics need not be afraid or ashamed to acknowledge at all times."

And it is to such puerile defence of what they know well is utterly indefensible, that thinking men are compelled by the terrible necessity of defending the unscriptural doctrine of the Pope's infallibility. Some swallow all infallible pronouncements with a grimace. What matter? They are not responsible for the doings of the Pope! He is infallible! their only duty is to insist on his infallibility and uphold it, no matter what he does. Some, whose consciences are not yet drugged to death by years of silent submission to evil, utter faint cries of pain and shame, but they are at once silenced by their bishops, who tremble lest it should be known at Rome that any publication under their control should have said one word other than of praise of the Pope, who has made them, and can unmake them in more ways than one.

One Roman Catholic writer, the editor of the *Milwaukee Catholic Citizen*, commenting on the *Freeman's Journal* editorial on burial abuses has dared to say: "What is a Catholic paper for? Is it to be a mere court journal, filling its columns with inane flattery, and monotonous laudations of everything to which the name of Catholic is attached? Must it play the cowardly parasite to its readers, picturing them as inchoate angels, shutting its eyes to evils that afflict them, and venturing to assail nobody nearer to them than the Mormons? There is such a thing as Catholic public opinion, whose influence must be brought into play in advancing the social, moral, and religious condition of the Catholic community. Unless Catholic public opinion is courageous enough to perceive and admit evils over which it has control and responsibility, no progress will ever be made. We shall go on electing saloon-keepers to office; filling the prisons and almshouses with an undue proportion of our race and creed; tolerating scandals which write us down among our fellow-citizens, and submitting to many other evils."

Another Roman Catholic paper declares that the test of a "good Catholic" is to take a Catholic paper, while yet other papers complain bitterly that Catholics will not purchase or support their own papers. The paper mentioned also says, in an article headed "A Good Catholic:"—

"The matter of Catholicity in good standing," says the *Western Chronicle*, "is determined by the test questions:—

"(1) Does he pay for a seat in the Church?

"(2) Does he send his children to the Catholic school?

"The cases are numerous, where these tests are inapplicable, but for general use they will do. We might further add—not as essential questions—but as standards which go far to determining the quality of a man's Catholicity:—

"(3) Does he belong to a Church society?

"(4) Does he take a Catholic paper?

"Certainly, if an affirmative answer is returned to all four questions, there can be little doubt of the sterling Catholicity of the man. He is a supporter of the Church. That is well, but we know that many merely nominal Catholics rent a pew for their families. These 'Catholics' also may send their children to the parochial school. But the further tests rule them out. They do not belong to a Catholic society, or they do not subscribe to a Catholic paper."

Complaints of the state of Catholic literature are far more outspoken in England than in America. Partly because the Englishman is given to speak out his mind plainly, Pope or no Pope; and partly because English Roman Catholics, who interest themselves in these matters, are generally educated perverts. A "martyr of history" is the name used by a recent writer in the London *Tablet*, to describe the Roman Catholic historian Mr. Burke. He says:—

"We can furnish a further instance of the indifference of Catholics for their literature. At this moment we are publishing a translation of Professor John Janssen's 'History of the German People from the End of the Middle Ages,' a work upon whose paramount importance you have already dwelt, and which is, indeed, a splendid apology for Catholicism. From amongst the hundreds of circulars and letters which have been sent to our co-religionists, we have not succeeded in securing one Catholic subscriber, and were it not for the help and support of our Protestant fellow-countrymen, we should never have been able to publish this work. Now we ask, Do Catholics read? Do they read history? What is the cause of their culpable indifference for historical works?

"Mr. Burke's works well deserve to have merited for their author a literary pension, but where is the Catholic who has sufficient patronage to get it? They should have brought him through their publisher a handsome remuneration for his pains, had Catholics the zest for, or did they take the trouble to read, history. Strange to say his writings, trenchant though they are against Protestantism, have been more sought after by Protestants themselves than by his co-religionists, and could merit an encomium from Mr. Gladstone, while by leading Catholics they have been simply ignored.

"Seldom have an historian's merits been recognised in his day, and Mr. Burke's, I fear, will prove no exception to the rule. If Dr. Lingard was slighted by his own, and his merits not acknowledged till pointed out by his opponents, so, too, must our present living historian suffer. Still, as he lives in my parish, I must in duty raise my voice in his behalf. In the last stage of poverty, his clothes in pawn, rent unpaid for months, and saved only from starvation by the little the priests can give, Mr. Burke's career must soon close, unless something be done to make his increasing years more comfortable, and stave off the end of a life which has already shed some considerable lustre on Catholic literature.

"Several valuable historical works still remain in manuscript, because the authors—men distinguished for their literary abilities and laborious research—are unable to encounter the ruinous cost of publication. As an instance in point, I may cite a fact which has just come to my knowledge. In the July of last year a work, combining both biography and history, was published by a well-known Catholic author, which has been most favourably noticed by the *Tablet*, and by its contemporary the *Weekly Register*, as well as by the *Month* and the *Dublin Review*. The book was published partly by subscription, yet at the present date only half the number of subscribers have paid for their copies, leaving the author burdened with a heavy deficit."

It should also be noticed that nearly all Cardinal Manning's works, and I think all of Cardinal Newman's, have been issued by Protestant publishers. My own experience in these matters, with an account of the injustices to which I was subjected by priests in connection with my literary work, will be found in my Autobiography.

A writer in the New York *Catholic Review* says:—

"The narrow views of some Catholics shock intelligent converts, and they provoke the thought that sometimes jealousy of the talents of certain converts has something to do with their harsh criticism. Did those persons know that the greater number of converts endure a martyrdom of the heart, their charity would induce them to spare and aid them, rather than disturb them."

Yet it is not for want of money that Roman Catholic literature has failed. The *Tablet*, of March 3rd, 1888, says:—

" We have seen a calculation, according to which the jubilee gifts of the Holy Father include no less than 800 episcopal rings, 9,000 chalices, 30,000 stoles, 100,000 pectoral crosses, 50,000 vestments for Mass, and 40,000 albs! And yet cases are daily arriving and being unpacked. With reference to the marvellous stole presented by the ladies of Bogotá, the capital of Colombia, it is affirmed to contain 14,800 pearls, 800 emeralds, and 340 diamonds."

The above list however does not include the enormous sums of money given to the Pope on this occasion, nor the gifts of other precious stones and valuables. Yet with all this wealth, the cry is still for more. Why, we may well ask, is not some of it used for the advancement of the Church? Why is it not used to teach the ignorant Italians of the Pope's own country, when even the editor of the Roman Catholic *Freeman's Journal*, says (sarcastically, it is true, but the admission is of value) that it would be better even to send out Methodist ministers to Italy to teach the people, than to have them in the state of ignorance of all religion, which Mr. Lynch describes in the leading and only Roman Catholic magazine of which America can boast. But whenever Rome is attacked for her saint-worship, and told that her religion is a religion of forms and ceremonies, her unvarying reply is, that she, and she alone, has the sacrament of the altar, and her strong point as she thinks, is her altar. And what of this? How does she show her respect and reverence for it? Is it not by lavish expenditure, whenever it will win the attention of the world at large, and by utter neglect whenever there are only the poor to consider.

The Tabernacle Society attached to the Convent of Notre Dame, Philadelphia, reports that it has exhausted its funds in supplying poor churches, and poor priests, with the things needful for the decorous worship of Our Lord. The Society needs material, silk, satin, velvet for the adornment of the Altar of God, and for the vestments of His priests. One priest writes from a lonely mission in Colorado: "I had to say Mass in vestments of old silk darned by my own hands, and always ready to fall to pieces until the Tabernacle Society sent me what I needed. If they know how bare the altars are in some of our poor missions, they would redouble their charity." Even in Ireland the condition of some country churches is wretched, though the collection for the Pope, in Archbishop Croke's diocese alone, exceeded by far the entire collection from the whole of England.

We might multiply such instances. We may add that "converts" who are charmed and fascinated by the exterior attractions of the Roman Church, know but little of its real state, or of the neglect and indifference of that Church where such neglect and indifference does not attract public attention. Even the wine used in the service of the altar, and sold by Roman Catholics, is sometimes of such a quality that a priest writes a protest on the subject to the *North-western Chronicle*. Pardon me, if I again call attention to the fact that this is a Roman Catholic paper, and the organ of the

Archbishop of St. Paul's, Minn., who has been so active in emigrating the Irish to a climate for which they were utterly unfitted. This priest says that he recently ordered some wine, warranted to be perfectly pure for altar use—and let it be remembered that not only is wine which is not pure forbidden for altar use, but that its use renders the sacrifice absolutely invalid.—The dealer, he says, was a Catholic; the wine bore all the usual episcopal recommendations; yet on testing it, he found that it was not only grossly adulterated, but that it was "not wine at all." Now it is quite certain that this Catholic dealer must have known perfectly well the quality of what he sold, and worse still, he must have known that he actually made every offering of the Mass with this wine invalid and sacrilegious. Truly it is only when one comes to know the terrible irreverence and habitual unbelief of many professing Catholics, that we can understand the state of countries where the Roman Catholic Church has substituted the teaching of the Church for the teaching of the Scriptures.

Nothing could be easier for a wine merchant than to secure the approbation of any number of bishops for his altar wine, by an easy assurance that it was all right, and a present of a supply for his lordship's use, at the altar or the table. Certainly some ecclesiastics were guilty of the greatest neglect in a matter which the Church professes to respect above life itself, when such a state of things could be. And we may be sure that the conscientious priest will suffer, sooner or later, for his interference with the episcopal recommendations of a favourite wine-seller. Probably he is yet young, and will be wiser in time. Indeed, when we consider all the requirements which Rome makes (on paper) in her regulations for the service of the altar, and all the omissions, or commissions, which will completely invalidate her sacraments, it is a wonder if she ever has a valid sacrament at all. A great deal, certainly, has to be taken on trust, even under the best auspices. And yet according to her theology how tremendous are the issues ! If one sacrament is invalid from even the carelessness of an official, a bishop may not have been consecrated, though he appears to be so. The faithful may be worshipping bread, where they think they are worshipping the truly consecrated host, and they may not have the benefit of Mass, though they have spent large sums of money in pious zeal for the repose of the faithful departed. Even in the matter of Masses, the Pope can dispense with the obligation of saying them at all, paid for or not paid for, as recent events have shown.

APPENDIX.

THE Rev. M. F. Foley, of De Land, California, writing on "The Progress of the Church in America," in the *Catholic Mirror*, remarks:—

"Catholics hear much on this subject. It is a favourite theme with some of our speakers and writers. It gives them a fair field for the exhibition of profound statistic knowledge, and for the display of lofty flights of eloquence. It is, too, a popular, a 'catching,' subject; it pleases all, and hurts nobody's feelings. It is not, then, to be wondered at that a Catholic mutual admiration society has come into being, the principal duty of whose members is to felicitate each other on 'our progress,' and to keep as far aloof as possible any rough men or rough things whose incoming might tend to mar the existing serenity.

"We are often told of the marvellous growth of the Church in this country; seldom are we put face to face with the truth that our gain has been to a great extent Europe's loss. Again, when we are told how immigration swells our numbers, seldom are we told that thousands of Catholic immigrants lose the faith here, who might under other circumstances have preserved it in the old world. Often is the great natural increase in our numbers pointed out, the fecundity of our healthy, virtuous matrons alluded to, yet rarely is it noted that tens of thousands of the children born in this country to Catholic parents are for one cause or other lost irrevocably lost to the Church. Much is said of converts, little of perverts. Our gains are often counted, our losses seldom reckoned. Some statisticians say that the Catholics in this country number eight millions. Are we eight millions? If we are, how many in this vast multitude are Catholics in little else than name? Our panegyrists are apt to measure the glory of the Church by her wealth in gold and silver, in buildings and lands, forgetting that her true glory lies not in these; forgetting that her Divine Founder had not whereon to rest His head, and that the Church was glorious even in the day when the prince of Apostles could say, 'Silver and gold I have none.'

"Our eulogists are fond too of measuring the glory of the Church by the honours showered upon her rulers; by procession, banquet, or reception; by those gatherings whither too often the time-servers flock, and where many times fulsome flattery is poured out as water.

"Why the silence of some pulpits on the temperance question? Why when drunkenness is denounced is the drunkard-maker so often left unscathed? Why in some great city parishes where drunkenness runs riot are there no temperance societies worthy of the name? I await the answer

"The liquor-seller may head subscription lists; he may have the first place at feasts, and the first chair in the synagogue; he may sit at the right hand of the mighty; but the angel of the Lord, who marches at the head of the Catholic total abstinence legions, has pointed at him the finger of contempt, and said to him in withering tones: 'Thou art the man.'

"Go into our prisons, our reformatories, our almshouses; go into our great asylums where numbers of children are being reared, in what must necessarily be a hot-house atmosphere, to face the storms of life. Go into the crowded tenements of our great cities, into their lowest dens and dives; see the misery, the squalor, reigning there; see the men and women low and besotted, see the little ones dying as flies in the fetid air—or, worse, living, to poison the nation's moral atmosphere: in a word see degradation in its most repulsive forms. In these abodes of crime, of poverty, of misery, you will find thousands of Catholics. Ask what has brought to prison and almshouse, to reformatory and orphanage, to dive and brothel, so many children of the Church. Trumpet-toned comes back the answer: 'Drink drink.'

"What is the attitude of Roman Catholic young men on the temperance question? This is important, as the future of America is in their hands—one of such grave importance that I give the following statement:—'The following resolution was twice voted down by the Catholic Young Men's National Union, which held a convention recently in Philadelphia: *Resolved*—That the Catholic Young Men's National Union, viewing the saloon as pre-eminently the source of evil to young men, use its utmost influence, and urge upon the societies connected with it to use their utmost efforts, to prevent Catholic young men from visiting saloons. And also to discountenance by all means possible the drinking customs of society.'

"The C.Y.M.N.U. refused to warn its members against frequenting saloons or to 'discountenance the drinking customs of society.' It did that deliberately and decisively. It twice had the report read, it twice had the vote taken on it. It twice voted down, decidedly and promptly, the recommendation.

"It is all very pretty to go on orating about our Catholic young men, their capacity for good, the value of their societies, their development; to ask the blessing of the Pope, to speak about our 'zealous and devoted clergy' and to load down official positions with them, to show how attached they are to our 'Holy Mother the Church.' But in this day of Catholic total abstinence extension and prosperity with the council adding to the odium of the saloon, no so-called Catholic Union can afford to wilfully, deliberately, positively, and decidedly vote down a resolution, *merely recommending Catholic young men not to frequent saloons*, and to discountenance the drinking customs of society.

"It is all very religious and devotional to urge attendance at Holy Communion on the annual day, and to boast of the thousands who answered the Union's call to be thus faithful; but how revolting to Catholic thought, and repulsive to Catholic instincts, is the action of the convention in sustaining the saloon. How it made Catholics shudder, to read in the daily report that such a resolution, offered in a Catholic convention, devoted professedly to the Catholic young men's interest, spiritual and temporal, met with 'considerable opposition.'

"Think, too, that not a word was spoken in favour of the resolution; though there were many there, of course, in favour of it. It was not through inattention. For attention was requested by the Rev. President to the second reading. The vote on being taken was largely in the negative; it was again put to a vote—again voted down.

"Had we not been there and especially interested in this question, and seen the thing done, it would not be thought probable. But our readers know it is a fact when the *Journal* declares it.

"The majority of the delegates to the last convention were no doubt exemplary Catholics, actuated with true Christian sentiments; but it was plain to any close observer that there were many also who lacked the first qualifications for such important work. For instance, the vote on the proposition 'Is the saloon dangerous to our Catholic young men?' was simply disgraceful. At least five-eighths of these Catholic delegates to a Catholic convention voted No—that is, they voted in favour of the saloon."

Yet the writer goes on to show by some curious manipulation, by no means uncommon when Roman Catholic priests have the management of affairs, that it was made to appear in the report as if the resolution *had been voted*. It is not possible to give here all that might be said on this, or indeed on any one of the subjects which are treated of in the present work; but I must refer to a place in my Autobiography where an account will be found of a priest, still an honoured member of Archbishop Ryan's diocese, who not only breaks his temperance pledge himself, but did his best to induce a young lawyer just rising in his profession in Philadelphia to break his also. I had the account from the very lips of the gentleman in question. If the priest had succeeded, what ruin would have followed! A career which was begun in honour and sobriety would have ended in misery, and perhaps in guilt, and a large family would have been sooner or later thrown on the public for support. Yet such is the hold which Romanism has on its votaries that this young lawyer is still, and is likely to remain, a "devoted son of the Church." This fact should explain to many Protestants why it is that so many remain in the Roman Church, who know but too well that it is a state of utter and hopeless corruption, while many will even deny the evil which they know exists. All this is possible, because the Church of Rome is a political system and not a religious system. It promises temporal as well as spiritual good for adhesion to its cause, and it has just enough Christianity to satisfy minds which do not look below the surface.

At a recent Roman Catholic Total Abstinence convention Father Hogan declared that it was "Protestant" to denounce men who went to the sacraments, even if they kept liquor-saloons; yet a preceding speaker (Father Eliot) said:

"It is from the door of the saloon that the bloodstained footsteps are tracked which lead down to the destruction of the family; it is the trail from the saloons to the low caucus, and from the low caucus back again to the saloons, that reeks with the deadliest venom that poisons our politics."

This just proves what we have been repeating so often: the Church does not consider the kind of lives her mem-

Justice Duffy in Essex Market Police Court to-day. The following are a few of the excuses given and their reception by the 'Little Judge :'—

"'Mary Shannon, you were intoxicated and sitting down on the sidewalk.' 'I had only taken a dose of bromide.' 'It was a dose of whisky, not bromide. I have seen you before, Mary; it is not the first case of bromide you have had. Ten days to ponder upon your offence.'

"'Daniel Shay, you were found drunk on the street.' 'I have been sick with pleurisy, and only took a couple of drinks.' 'I have seen you before. Five days.'

"'Daniel C. Flynn, what have you to say to the charge of drunkenness?' 'I am in the dry-goods business, and have never been drunk before.' 'Pay $2 for your load, and go on your way rejoicing.'

"'David Fitzgerald, you were unable to take care of yourself; you are disgracing an historical name.' 'I am a journeyman plasterer, and was working in a saloon. I took a little beer, and it went to my head.' 'Can you turn a cornice?' 'Yes, sir; and I have five children and a wife.' 'Instead of buying whisky you should buy bread; but I will let you go.'

"'Katie Brick, you were drunk and making a noise on the street; and collecting a crowd.' 'I was just going back to Brooklyn.' 'We have enough noisy women in New York without importing them from Brooklyn. Are you married or single?' 'I'm a widow.' 'Ever drunk before?' 'Only once.' 'Five days.'

"'Mary Hart, were you drunk?' 'It was the only time, your honour. I work for the Mutual Life Insurance Company in Nassau Street.' 'What do they pay you?' 'Ten dollars every two weeks.' 'Go home and don't drink any more.'

"Justice Hogan is the Tammany boss in the First Assembly District. John Cantlon, a liquor-dealer of No. 16, Morris Street, and 'Liverpool Jack's' friend, is on the

General Committee. Sunday last Cantlon called Policeman Tiernan of the Second Precinct into his place; and instead of arresting Cantlon for keeping his liquor-saloon open, the policeman at the Tammanyite's behest arrested his eleven-year-old nephew Edward. They hurried to the Tombs where Cantlon's countenance suddenly fell.

"'By Jupiter!' he exclaimed, 'Paterson's on the bench. I thought Hogan was to be here.'

"As is the custom the policeman reported the case to Agent Becker, of President Gerry's society, on his entrance to court.

"'Can't you lock up the boy until Paterson gets off the bench?' Cantlon inquired of the agent. 'I want the boy sent to the Catholic Protectory. Paterson will make me pay $2 a week and Hogan won't. I can't afford to pay.'

"As Cantlon is on the bond of 'Liverpool Jack' his claim of poverty was scarcely credited. The case was submitted, but Justice Paterson ordered Cantlon out of court, being convinced, as only the most trivial offences had been charged, that it was simply an attempt to get rid of the lad at the city's expense.

"But the friend of the mancatcher turned up at the Tombs yesterday with the boy. Justice Hogan was on the bench. Cantlon didn't take his turn in line. He went ahead of all and Justice Hogan promptly took up the case. Cantlon repeated the same story on which Justice Paterson had refused commitment. Justice Hogan nevertheless committed the lad to the Catholic Protectory, and in doing so disregarded a rule which is observed by every other Justice. It is to hold the lad for an examination pending an investigation made by Mr. Gerry's officers. The lad's parents are dead. Cantlon had promised to take care of him."

Some of the "Whyo" gang, recently hung for murder after a career of brutal crime and a life of drunkenness, certainly died in the odour of (Roman Catholic) sanctity, and were attended and comforted in their last moments by sisters and priests. But what of their unhappy offspring? Sentenced or sent to Roman Catholic institutions, where, to my personal knowledge, both their spiritual and temporal interests are utterly neglected, in consequence of the ignorance and indifference of the sisters. They are brought up to follow in the footsteps of their parents, with wrong ideas of virtue and vice. They are brought up according to the ideas of sisters and priests, and the future of these children proves plainly that neither sisters nor priests are fit to educate the young. Dirt, disease, and ignorance, are a poor help to health of body and mind.

Why should sisters or others, who receive money from the State, object to inspection by the State? I am well convinced that if Roman Catholic institutions were inspected by the State, unless indeed the inspectors were under the control of that Church, a great good would be gained for the poor children under their charge. I know an institution where, from gross ignorance, and that carelessness which is the natural outcome of uninspected independence, the children are constantly losing both their eyesight, and such poor health as they had when they entered the institution. But it is considered a crime even to suggest that a "sister" could fail in the least matter, either in the education of the young or in anything else. If Protestants could only know how this feeling prevails, and the unworthy motives from which it is kept up, they would be wiser than they are, and would look a little more sharply after the expenditure of public money in such institutions. Why should sisters be exempted more than others from giving an account of their stewardship, above all when the results of their system of education gives so much evidence of failure?

www.ingramcontent.com/pod-product-compliance
Lightning Source LLC
Chambersburg PA
CBHW020543300426
44111CB00008B/770